Other books in th   **S**

The Ten Golden Rules of preventing weight regain

1 Don't skip meals (or you will reduce your metabolic rate).

2 Eat a really good breakfast.

3 Eat at least three to four times a day.

4 Limit television to less than 12 hours per week.

5 Choose low GI carbs at every meal.

6 Eat lean protein sources at every meal.

7 Don't skimp on the fats—just choose healthy ones.

8 Eat seven serves of fruit and vegies every day.

9 Schedule moderate physical activity for 30–60 minutes on six days out of seven.

10 On the seventh day, relax and enjoy.

the Low GI Diet

12-Week Action Plan

The definitive GI based weight-loss program

Prof. Jennie Brand-Miller
Kaye Foster-Powell
Joanna McMillan-Price

HODDER

Paul's story

'I have tried every diet . . . and read every diet book. They never worked, and if I did lose weight I put it back on with interest when I resumed normal eating habits. At 168 kilograms I was desperate to find a way of eating that would work for me. My wife discovered *The New Glucose Revolution* . . . it was like someone had turned a light bulb on in my brain. Here was an eating plan that was a blueprint for life. Not a stunt diet, not a fad-eating plan, but a commonsense approach to eating . . . that I believed I could stick with. Twelve months later I had lost 64 kilograms, which was a direct consequence of eating the GI way and taking sensible exercise. My wife also lost 23 kilograms over the same period. The GI way of eating has revolutionised my life and I have maintained exactly the weight loss since. I have never felt healthier and, more importantly, I never feel I am denying myself my choice of food . . . the GI way of eating is the best way to lose weight and maintain that loss.'

Paul Jeffreys, *Diary of a Fat Man* (2003)

Contents

the Low GI Diet

introduction

the **low GI diet** delivers
long-term weight contro
and wellbeing

THE LOW GI DIET IS A REALISTIC DIET DELIVERING LONG-TERM WEIGHT control and wellbeing; its healthy eating and exercise program improves insulin sensitivity and reduces insulin resistance and food cravings. It's an eating plan that suits the whole family. It's safe for adults and children, and for people with pre-existing medical conditions such as diabetes, heart disease or polycystic ovarian syndrome (PCOS).

To ensure that you lose weight safely and sustainably we provide 10 energy levels—you can choose the one that's right for your current weight and activity level. This is where The Low GI Diet is unique. It is the definitive science-based diet that is designed to maximise your muscle mass (increase your engine size), minimise your body fat (decrease the cushioning) and keep you burning the optimal fuel mix (high octane energy with built-in engine 'protectants') for lifelong weight control. And by optimising your insulin sensitivity and decreasing your insulin levels over the whole day with its combination of healthy eating and exercise, it tackles the key factor that undermines all efforts of weight control.

The Low GI Diet '12-week Action Plan':

- Reduces weight at a faster rate than a low fat diet
- Decreases body fat, not muscle mass or body water
- Lowers day-long blood glucose and insulin levels
- Increases satiety and minimises hunger pangs
- Maximises the metabolic rate during weight loss
- Reduces the chance of weight regain

In *The Low GI Diet*, we explain how choosing low GI carbohydrates—the ones that produce only small fluctuations in your blood glucose and insulin levels—can help you feel fuller for longer and increase your energy levels, making weight loss achievable and sustainable.

LOWERING YOUR INSULIN LEVELS IS NOT ONLY A KEY INGREDIENT IN WEIGHT LOSS, IT IS ALSO THE SECRET TO LONG-TERM HEALTH—REDUCING YOUR RISK OF HEART DISEASE AND DIABETES.

The Low GI Diet works for another important reason: it deals not just with your energy intake (what goes in your mouth) but your energy output—energy expenditure and physical activity—getting the legs, not the fingers, to do the walking.

During the 12-week Action Plan you will lose at least 250 grams of body fat per week: not water, not muscle, but pure *body fat*, most of it from around the waist. And we promise that you will not be ravenously hungry between meals, you won't be weighing your food and you certainly won't be counting kilojoules. One of the reasons this diet is easy is its unique ability to keep you feeling fuller for longer. It helps control appetite by controlling blood glucose and stimulating the production of the body's own natural appetite suppressants. Metabolically, it reduces blood glucose and insulin levels and maximises the burning of fat.

> The aim when dieting is to eat less than your body needs so it has to dig into fat stores to make up the deficit. If you eat too little you will find it hard to stick to the diet long term and you risk losing a greater proportion of muscle—this in turn sets you on the yoyo dieter's cycle of regaining the weight and getting fatter in the process.

This is not a low carb diet, or a low fat diet, or a high protein diet: it is flexible and livable and, quite simply, it is a delicious way of eating that incorporates aspects of many ethnic cuisines. You will be eating sensible quantities of bread, pasta, breakfast cereal, rice and noodles—it is just a matter of choosing the low GI varieties. You will also eat plenty of lean meat, poultry, fish, shellfish and low fat dairy foods such as milk, cheese and yoghurt. Legumes play a starring role because they have the lowest GI of all, so this is an easy diet for vegetarians to follow. You will consume generous amounts of fruit and vegetables, *bar potatoes* (because they are high GI). Your salads will be dressed with vinaigrette made with healthy oils. You will have three balanced meals a day, including a dessert or an indulgence at dinner, and we encourage you to have both morning and afternoon tea. You can even have a glass of wine or beer with meals.

The Low GI Diet is family friendly too—your partner, your children, younger and older, will be sitting down to the same delicious food as you, only the quantities will vary. And, if you are planning a pregnancy, this is the safest diet for you and your baby right from the time of conception. If you have found it hard to become pregnant, this diet will increase your chances markedly. It does this by getting right to the root of the problem—insulin resistance—which affects about one in five women.

There are also many value-added benefits with The Low GI Diet: in addition to weight loss, you will reduce your risk of heart attack and diabetes, control blood glucose levels and improve your overall health and vitality.

Written by internationally recognised scientists who are qualified in nutrition, dietetics and fitness, *The Low GI Diet* is at the cutting edge of research on carbohydrates, the GI and weight loss. Our training and experience gives us the tools to help both men and women beat the battle of the bulge. The Low GI Diet is a lifestyle diet and exercise program aimed at reducing body fat and *keeping it off for life*. Easy to follow and based on making simple substitutions to the way you eat now, it will change the way you eat forever.

The Low GI Diet includes:

- The 12-week Action Plan based on smart carbs and smart moves to help you lose up to 10 per cent of your current body weight. Each week you will have a food goal, an exercise goal, an activity goal plus some food for thought
- The best way to balance protein and carbohydrate
- The tools and tips you need to maintain weight loss for life
- Delicious recipes, meal plans and a menu survival guide for eating out
- Simple, practical ways to build more activity into your day
- The GI tables, with the GI of your favourite foods

THE LOW GI DIET IS A BLUEPRINT FOR HEALTHY EATING FOR THE REST OF YOUR LIFE.

the Low GI Diet

PART ONE

understanding
the low GI diet

weight and today's diet dilemma

IT IS SAD BUT TRUE THAT NINETEEN OUT OF TWENTY people who lose weight by dieting will regain the lost weight. It's clear that a lifestyle solution to weight concerns, not another temporary fix, is needed. The Low GI Diet is about changing the way you eat for good.

Being slim or normal weight is no longer the norm. Between half and two-thirds of adults in Australia are classed as overweight or obese. Men are worse off than women, and our children are affected, too—approximately one in four weigh much more than they should for their age and height. Don't think this is just innocent 'puppy fat'—some overweight children are being diagnosed with a disease that used to be seen mainly in overweight adults, type 2 diabetes. Their lives may even be cut short or severely affected by blindness, kidney failure or heart disease.

Even our pets are suffering—over quarter of all cats and dogs are classed as overweight and many have diabetes as a result. And our pets don't drink soft drinks, eat fast food or watch television! Clearly, the origins of the obesity epidemic are complex.

Are you overweight, or just imagining it?

Women tend to see themselves as being larger than they actually are and aspire to an unattainable size. Men, on the other hand, are better judges of their size but often don't see excess weight as a health problem (real men don't diet!). Get the tape measure out and measure your waist circumference—the smallest circumference around your abdomen. This point will be close to your navel but perhaps not exactly on it. Here's what you need to know:

	Overweight and at increased risk of disease	Very overweight and at substantially increased risk of disease
Men	Over 94 cm	Over 102 cm
Women	Over 80 cm	Over 88 cm

Astoundingly, the proportion of people with excess body fat has doubled in the last two decades despite all our efforts to slim down. The food industry has met our demand for 'diet' and 'lite' foods, low fat foods, sugar substitutes, fat substitutes—you name it, they made it. But this has not stemmed the obesity epidemic. Indeed, some experts feel the food industry and its advertising are partly to blame.

Indigenous people, or those of Asian or African heritage, are at greater risk of disease even when they are only slightly overweight. For these groups, at any given weight and height, there is proportionately more body fat in the abdominal region. This fat causes much more harm than fat stored in other places. If this applies to you, and if your waist circumference is over 94 centimetres (men) or over 80 centimetres (women), count yourself as overweight and at substantially higher risk of medical complications.

We live in a push-button, 'let-your-fingers-do-the-walking' era and that means our food energy needs are very low, some would say pathologically low. Our current sedentary lifestyles require about 30 to 50 per cent less food energy than the daily demands experienced by our parents and grandparents. Fifty years ago, you were lucky if there was one car in the household—today there is likely to be two or more per family. Fifty years ago, television was in its infancy—now we watch an average of 21 hours per week. Surprisingly, eating only 400 extra kilojoules a day (about 100 calories—the equivalent of an apple) over and above what we really need is all it took to tip the balance. That simple difference between energy in and energy out gave rise to today's epidemic of being overweight. The good news, however, is that 100 calories is just 10 minutes of vigorous exercise or 20 minutes of brisk walking.

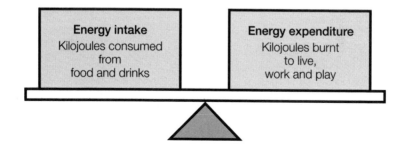

Energy intake and energy expenditure need to be in balance to maintain a healthy weight. You will find it easier to achieve weight balance if the energy expenditure side of the equation is high, permitting greater food intake, rather than the reverse. This is why diets that put the emphasis on low food intake are doomed to fail.

Being overweight puts you at an infinitely greater risk of a range of health problems, especially type 2 diabetes. You also have double or triple the risk of contracting heart disease, high blood pressure, cancer, gout, gallstones, reproductive abnormalities and arthritis. Being overweight even interferes with sleep because fat around the neck area induces a dangerous form of snoring called 'sleep apnoea'. So you become tired and cranky without knowing why. Along with this list of complications, there are emotional and psychological problems associated with being overweight. It can make you depressed, and depression can make you eat for comfort, forming a vicious cycle. Medical intervention may be needed. Lastly, obese people are often discriminated against in employment either consciously or unconsciously. And being jobless only compounds the problem.

Why traditional, restrictive diets fail

Chances are that you have already read several books and articles offering a solution to losing weight; miracle weight-loss solutions appear weekly. They are clearly good for selling magazines, but for the majority of people, the diets don't work—if they did, there wouldn't be so many! At best, while you stick to it, a restrictive diet will reduce your kilojoule (calorie) intake. At its worst, a restrictive diet will change your body composition for the fatter. The diagram opposite shows the yoyo pattern of weight gain and weight loss that may be all too familiar. The overall effect of this pattern is a weight increase of 2–3 kilograms per year. Why?

When you lose weight through severely restricting your food intake, you lose some of your body's muscle mass. Over the years this

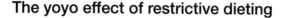

The yoyo effect of restrictive dieting

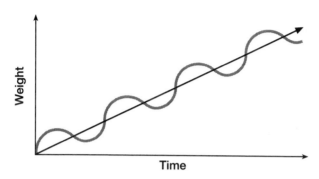

yoyo dieting will change your body composition to less muscle and proportionately more fat, making weight control increasingly difficult. Your body's engine requires less and less energy to keep it ticking over. This is nature's way of helping animals adapt to the environment in which they live—if food is scarce, then it is best to need less. The real goal in losing weight is to shed fat, not muscle mass or body water.

One of the loudest messages in this book—despite its title—is don't 'diet'

Don't severely restrict food intake, *don't* skip breakfast, *don't* skip meals, *don't* follow fad diets—you are just asking for trouble. Instead, we want you to adopt simple lifestyle 'manoeuvres', only some of which are specific to food. The aim is to maximise your muscle mass (increase your engine size), minimise your body fat (decrease the cushioning) and keep you burning the optimal fuel mix for lifelong weight control (high-octane energy with built-in engine 'protectants').

How much weight should you aim to lose?

Setting attainable goals is extremely important. You (and sometimes your doctor) may have completely unrealistic expectations of a weight-loss plan. You might be anticipating excessively rapid weight loss. A well-meaning doctor might encourage you to go back to your 'ideal weight', a body mass index (BMI) between 19 and 25—the so-called 'normal' range. Both of you need to think again and reconsider the rate of weight loss and the absolute amount.

To calculate your BMI, take your weight (in kilograms) and divide by your height (in metres) squared.

Example:

A woman who is 1.5 metres tall and weighs 70 kilograms would calculate her BMI like this $\left(\dfrac{70}{1.5 \times 1.5} \right) = 31$

A more realistic weight-loss goal that still brings about desirable benefits in health and psychological terms is aiming to lose between 5 and 10 per cent of your current weight over a period of 12 weeks. For example, if you currently weigh 100 kilograms, then a weight loss of 5 to 10 kilograms over 12 weeks is realistic, safe and enough to improve your health. If you achieve that and are able to *maintain* that weight loss long term, you are a success! Your risk of developing chronic disease would be substantially reduced.

If you would still like to lose more weight, then it is best that you only do that after a period of weight maintenance. Your body needs time to adjust to a lower weight, so aim to maintain the weight you have lost over the next three to six months before attempting further weight loss. Each 12-week period of weight loss using the Action Plan (see pages 70–201) should be followed by three to six months of weight maintenance as outlined in 'Doing It For Life' (see pages 203–70), before beginning another weight loss period. Using an alternating strategy like this takes the pressure off and improves your chances of success.

What about weight loss in children?

One in four children today are overweight. If one of your children is overweight, don't think in terms of a strict individual diet program just for them. Treatment of overweight children should involve the whole family. The Low GI Diet program is effective and safe for everyone.

In children and adolescents, the emphasis should be less about controlling food, and more about physical activity (the other side of the energy equation), particularly reducing sedentary activity such as watching television. We have given you some more tips on page 248. Because children are growing, they seldom actually have to lose weight—maintaining their current weight (avoiding weight gain) should be the first goal.

QUIZ: What is a healthy weight for you?

Assuming you're above a weight at which you feel healthy and comfortable, then it's reasonable to want to change. Let's begin by clarifying some details about why you might be overweight and what impact it's having on your life.

Place a tick next to the statements that apply to you.

A My weight (in kilograms) divided by my height squared (in metres) results in a number greater than 25. ☐

B I'm apple-shaped, rather than pear-shaped (i.e. bigger around my waist than I am around my hips). ☐

C Both my parents are overweight. ☐
I have been big most of my life. ☐

D My activity level has declined in the last 5 years. ☐
I think I eat more than I need. ☐

E I suffer from one or more of the following:
elevated blood glucose levels ☐
high blood pressure ☐
blocked arteries ☐
gout ☐
gallstones ☐
sleep apnoea or snoring ☐
osteoarthritis ☐
shortness of breath on exertion ☐
My body weight stops me from doing things I would like to do if I were thinner. ☐

A tick at A suggests you are carrying more weight than is normally considered healthy.

Waiting to hear something you didn't know? What you have calculated here is your body mass index (BMI). It is a measure of your weight in relation to your height and is a crude indicator of body fatness in a population. It has significant limitations when applied to an individual, however, and should be used in conjunction with other measures of body fat in clinical assessment. In Caucasian people, a BMI greater than 25 is classified as overweight, and above 30 classifies you as obese. Clinically, this implies an excess accumulation of body fat to the extent that your health may be impaired. Different cut-offs apply for other ethnicities (see box on page 4) and more muscular individuals should use a cut-off of 27 as suggestive of being overweight. Bear in mind that the cut-off points are arbitrary and the health risk does not start at the cut-off point.

A tick at B implies an unhealthy distribution of body fat.

It is a large mass of body fat that carries health risks, rather than simply weighing a lot on the scales. So how do you know if you are actually 'overfat'? Well, basically you can see it, you can pinch it and, if you are unsure, you can measure it. The simplest way is with a tape measure. Take it around your waist, approximately at the level of your belly button. As mentioned on page 4, a waist measurement greater than 80 centimetres for women and 94 centimetres for men indicates increased health risk due to intra-abdominal fat accumulation.

Ticks at C suggest you may have a genetic predisposition to being overweight.

Scientists recognise such people as 'easy gainers'—people who gain weight much more easily than others, thanks to their genetics. Weight and body shape are largely the result of genetic background as well as history of dieting and activity. Research suggests that those who have close relatives with a weight problem and more severe forms of obesity are more likely to have a genetic basis to their own weight problem.

Ticks at D suggest lifestyle factors that may be contributing to your weight.

What changes have caused a reduction in your daily activity? A change of occupation, moving closer to work, giving up smoking (which slows your metabolism), getting a car, an accident that immobilised you? Similarly, can you identify contributors to increasing energy intake such as changed shopping habits, greater wealth, retirement, more reliance on takeaway foods, etc.?

Ticks at E suggest that your weight is affecting your health and daily life.

It isn't true that to reach and maintain optimal health and personal happiness you have to be thin. Health and vitality come in all shapes and sizes. It is that deep, central body fat that we mentioned previously—what doctors know as visceral body fat (rather than fat just under the skin)—that seems to be linked with disease. Among these are heart disease, diabetes, high blood pressure, gout, gallstones, sleep apnoea and arthritis. Excess fat anywhere on the body can still affect your health by limiting your mobility, causing you to puff and pant with exertion. The good news is that when an overweight person loses just 5 to 10 per cent of their body weight and keeps it off, many of the adverse medical consequences of being overweight subside.

Unfortunately, most weight-loss programs, books and magazines are based on the premise that people can control their weight and redesign their bodies regardless of physiology or genetics. The Low GI Diet is not about reaching a goal weight. It is impossible for you, or anyone else, to predict a healthy, achievable, maintainable weight for you. Your chances of ill health are significantly lessened with loss of just 5 to 10 per cent of body weight, so long as you are active. A healthy, comfortable weight for you can only come about as a consequence of your behaviour change. By working through the 12-week Action Plan of The Low GI Diet you will gradually develop the good eating habits and daily exercise pattern that will carry you towards a healthy weight for life.

You and your genes

For a few blessed individuals, a constant weight is maintained year in year out without much conscious effort. Often, they are naturally active and their body instinctively gravitates to a healthy weight. For others who are overweight, regardless of their efforts—every fad diet, every exercise program, even operations and medications—body weight is regained over the years. Why?

Let's take a look at the role genetics play in weight control. There are many overweight people who tell us resignedly, 'Well, my mother's the same', 'I've always been overweight', or 'It must be in my genes'. In fact, these comments have some truth behind them.

There is plenty of evidence to back up the idea that our body weight and shape is at least partially determined by our genes. A child born to overweight parents is much more likely to be overweight than one whose parents are not overweight. Most of this knowledge comes from studies of twins. Identical twins tend to be similar in body weight even if they are raised apart. Twins adopted out as infants show the body-fat profile of their biological parents rather than that of their adoptive parents.

Are you an 'easy gainer'?

If you have been significantly overweight for a long time, have relatives with a weight problem and gain weight easily, scientists recognise you as an 'easy gainer' and suggest genetics as the basis of your weight problem.

We also know that when naturally lean people are fed 10 per cent more energy than they need, they increase their metabolic rate and their body *resists* the opportunity to gain weight. While overweight people, fed the same excess energy, pile on the kilos. The information stored in our genes governs our tendency to burn off or store excess kilojoules.

Our genetic make-up underlies our metabolic rate—how many kilojoules we burn per minute. Bodies, like cars, differ in this regard. An eight-cylinder car consumes more fuel than a small four-cylinder one. A bigger body requires more kilojoules than a smaller one. When a car is stationary, the engine idles—using just enough fuel to keep the motor running. When we are asleep, the 'revs' are even lower and we use a minimum number of kilojoules. Our resting metabolic rate (RMR)—the kilojoules we burn by just lying completely at rest—is fuelling our large brain, heart and other important organs. When we start exercising, or even just moving around, the number of kilojoules (the amount of fuel we use) increases. But the greatest proportion of the kilojoules used in a 24-hour period are those used to maintain our RMR.

Since our RMR is where most kilojoules are used, it is a significant determinant of body weight. The lower your RMR, the greater your risk of gaining weight, and vice versa. Whether you have a high or low RMR is genetically determined and runs in families. We all know someone who appears to eat like a horse but is positively thin. Almost in awe we comment on their fast metabolism, and we may not be far off the mark.

Men have a higher RMR than women because their bodies contain more muscle mass and are more expensive to run; body fat, on the other hand, gets a free ride. These days, too many men and women have undersized muscles that hardly ever get a workout. Increasing muscle mass with weight-bearing (resistance) exercise will raise your RMR and is one of the secrets to lifelong weight control.

Interestingly, we know that our genes dictate the fuel mix we burn in the fasting state (overnight). Some of us burn more carbohydrate and less fat even though the total energy used is the same. Scientists believe that subtle abnormalities in the ability to burn fat (as opposed to carbs) lie behind most states of being overweight and obese. This doesn't mean that if your parents are overweight you should resign yourself to being overweight too. But it may help you understand why you have to watch what you eat while other people don't. One way in which The Low GI Diet helps is that it facilitates greater use of fat as a source of fuel.

Now, here's the crunch: the current epidemic of overweight can't be blamed on our genes—our genes haven't mutated in a space of 20 years, but our environment has. So while genetics writes the code, environment presses the buttons. Our current sedentary lifestyles and food choices press all the wrong buttons!

Blaming mum

Can your weight problem be traced back to conditions in
the womb? Perhaps. Babies born with either a low (less than 2.5
kilogram) or high (more than 4 kilogram) birth weight are at increased risk
of health problems as adults. Known as 'foetal programming',
your metabolism might be insulin resistant right from the start.

So, if you were born with a tendency to be overweight, why does
it matter what you eat? Well, genes can be switched on or off. By being
choosy about carbohydrates and fats you maximise insulin sensitivity,
up-regulate the genes involved in burning fat and *down*-regulate those
involved in burning carbs. By moving your fuel 'currency exchange' from
a 'carbohydrate economy' to a 'fat economy', you increase the opportunity
of depleting fat stores over carbohydrate stores. This is exactly what
will happen when you begin to eat the foods we suggest in the 12-week
Action Plan.

Food choice affects your appetite

Foods affect your appetite; they dictate when and how much you eat.
If digestion takes time and involves lower parts of your intestine, you
stimulate natural appetite suppressants. Consequently, both quality and
quantity of food are important for weight control. These are some of
the mechanisms that lie behind the success of a healthy low GI diet for
weight control.

Among all four major sources of kilojoules in food (protein, fat,
carbohydrate and alcohol), fat has the highest energy content per unit

of weight, twice that of carbohydrate and protein. A high fat food is therefore said to be 'energy dense', meaning there are a lot of kilojoules in a standard weight of food. A typical croissant made with wafer-thin layers of buttery pastry contains about 2000 kilojoules—a whacking 20 per cent of total energy needs for most people for 24 hours! To eat the same amount of energy in the form of apples, you have to eat about six large apples. So, getting more energy—kilojoules—than your body needs is relatively easy when eating a high fat food. That's why there has been so much emphasis on low fat diets for weight control.

However, what really matters is not the fat content per se but a food's 'energy density' (kilojoules per gram). Some diets, such as traditional Mediterranean diets, contain quite a lot of fat (mainly from olive oil), but are not so energy dense because the oil comes with a large volume of fruits and vegetables. On the other hand, many new low fat foods on the market are energy dense. Indeed, some have much the same energy density as the original high fat food because 2 grams of carbohydrate have replaced every gram of fat. If a low fat food has the same kilojoules per serving as a high fat food, then it's just as easy to overeat. Nutritionists have therefore had to fine-tune the message about diets for weight control:

- Eating more fruit and vegetables is more important than simply eating low fat.
- The type of fat is more critical than the amount.
- The type of carbohydrate is important too.

THINK ENERGY DENSITY PER SERVING—

NOT HIGH FAT OR LOW FAT.

The insulin connection

You are probably familiar with the hormone insulin. It is the one that is missing in people with type 1 diabetes and needs to be injected daily for survival. Most of us have the opposite problem—we have far too much of it circulating at any one time. This is especially true of overweight people, those with type 2 diabetes or family history of it, and indeed any man or woman with a 'beer gut' or 'pot belly'. Excess fat around the waist causes a form of inertia or resistance to insulin's action, resulting in the need to secrete more and more insulin to overcome the hurdle (a bit like shouting to make a deaf person hear). These high circulating levels of insulin spell big trouble. The condition is known as 'insulin resistance' (also known as the metabolic syndrome or Syndrome X). Probably one in two adults has this condition but most of them are blissfully unaware. It is a silent epidemic, a ticking time bomb that sooner or later will erupt—most likely as sudden heart attack, stroke or a diagnosis of diabetes. By losing weight, you can substantially reduce your insulin levels, especially if you choose low GI carbs in place of your usual carbohydrate sources.

People with insulin resistance often have normal blood glucose and cholesterol levels, giving them and their doctors a false impression of their heart health. But insulin resistance is at the root of most common forms of heart disease and diabetes.

We are often asked why insulin resistance is so common. The answer is that both genes and environment play a role. People of Asian and African-American origins and the descendants of the original inhabitants of Australia and North and South America appear to be more insulin resistant than those of Caucasian extraction, even when they are still young and lean. But regardless of ethnic background, insulin resistance develops as we age. This has been attributed not to age per se, but to the fact that as we grow older, we gain excessive fat, become less physically active, and lose some of our muscle mass. Diet composition plays an important role, too. Specifically, diets with too much fat, especially saturated fat, and too little carbohydrate can make us more insulin resistant. If carbohydrate intake is high, high GI foods can worsen pre-existing insulin resistance.

The many guises of insulin resistance

If your doctor has told you that you have high blood pressure and 'a touch of sugar' (pre-diabetes or impaired glucose tolerance) then you probably have the insulin resistance syndrome. If you're female and have irregular periods, unwanted facial hair and/or acne, then your diagnosis could be a condition directly related to insulin resistance called polycystic ovarian syndrome (PCOS). If you're overweight, *not* a big drinker but have abnormal liver tests (indicative of fatty liver), then it's likely you, too, are severely insulin resistant.

Why insulin resistance is a big deal

Having persistently high insulin levels is likely to make you fatter and fatter, undermining all your efforts at weight control. It is the very reason why people with diabetes find it so hard to lose weight.

The higher your insulin levels, the more carbohydrate you burn at the expense of fat. This is because insulin has two powerful actions: one is to 'open the gates' so that glucose can flood into the cells and be used as the source of energy. The second role of insulin is to *inhibit* the release of fat from fat stores. Furthermore, the burning of glucose inhibits the burning of fat and vice versa.

These actions persist even in the face of insulin resistance because the body overcomes the extra hurdle by just pumping out more insulin into the blood. Unfortunately, the level that finally drives glucose into the cells is two to ten times more than is needed to switch off the use of fat as a source of fuel. If insulin is high all day long, as it is in insulin-resistant and overweight people, then the cells are constantly forced to use glucose as their fuel source, drawing it from either the blood or stored glycogen. Blood glucose therefore swings from low to high and back again, playing havoc with our appetite and triggering the release of stress hormones. Our meagre stores of carbohydrate in the liver and muscles also undergo major fluctuations over the course of the day. When you don't get much chance to use fat as a source of fuel, it is not surprising that fat stores accumulate wherever they can:

- Inside the muscle cells (a sign of insulin resistance)
- In the blood (this is called high triglycerides or TG and is often seen in people with diabetes or the metabolic syndrome)
- In the liver (non-alcoholic fatty liver, NAFL)
- Around the waist (the proverbial pot belly)

High insulin levels are closely associated with risk factors for heart disease and type 2 diabetes. When insulin and TG levels are high, this automatically reduces the good form of cholesterol (HDL-cholesterol), causing accelerated thickening and hardening of the arteries. High insulin levels also increase the factors responsible for blood clotting, thereby increasing the risk of blockage (thrombosis) in a narrow coronary artery and a heart attack. Just as importantly, continuously high insulin levels lead to greater and greater degrees of insulin resistance, and the need to secrete even more insulin. This escalating demand will eventually exhaust the insulin-making cells in predisposed individuals —just as shouting all the time eventually makes you hoarse! As insulin begins to fall, blood glucose levels begin to rise and the result is 'a touch of sugar' (pre-diabetes) and then type 2 diabetes.

A HEALTHY LOW GI DIET COMBINED WITH PHYSICAL ACTIVITY IS THE MOST POWERFUL WAY OF OPTIMISING INSULIN SENSITIVITY AND DECREASING INSULIN LEVELS OVER THE COURSE OF THE WHOLE DAY.

The real deal on carbohydrates

Carbs have had a lot of bad press lately and you might well be as confused as the next person. You may have been tempted to try a low carb diet. Well, let's start by telling you some facts about carbohydrate. Here are the advantages. Carbohydrate is the most widely consumed substance in the world after water. It is cheap, plentiful and often sweet. Sweetness was important in our evolutionary past—it flagged a safe and palatable source of energy—so much so that 'sweet' came to mean a lot of things: it was applied to love ('sweetheart') and everything that made us happy ('sweet success'). Our first food, human milk, contains more carbohydrate than any other animal milk, reflecting the huge demands of the human brain. Glucose, the simplest product of carbohydrate digestion, is the obligatory fuel of the brain, red blood cells and a growing foetus, and the main source of energy for the muscles during strenuous exercise.

For people in industrialised countries, avoiding carbs is a tricky business because the alternative sources of energy are often high in saturated fat, and by eating them we run the risk of doing long-term

---

Without carbs in our diet, we become heavily dependent on foods containing just fat and protein. That's not only unnecessarily restrictive, it is full of pitfalls.

Some human groups—the Inuit people of Alaska, for example—had few carbohydrates to choose from. Because of their climate, all their foods were animal foods apart from summer fruits and berries that supplied small amounts of carbohydrate. They depended on marine and land animals to supply protein and fat for over 90 per cent of their energy needs (there is little or no carbohydrate in animal food). We now know that there are limits on protein intake because the human liver has a finite ability to metabolise the building blocks of proteins—amino acids. This ceiling on human protein intake meant that the Inuit and similar groups had a habit of craving fat, lots of it, particularly the blubber of animals such as seals and whales. But, and this is a big but, they were eating highly *unsaturated* fat, not the sort that promotes heart disease.

If we eat excess protein in the absence of fat and carbohydrate, ammonia builds up in the blood stream, we feel nauseous and we can eventually die. Indeed, that actually happened to explorers of America's west who, when times were tough, shot and ate skinny rabbits as their sole source of food for weeks on end. Within weeks they suffered from a condition known as 'rabbit starvation' because, paradoxically, they were starving to death on rabbits.

damage to blood vessels and the heart. Indeed, there is more evidence against saturated fat than any other single component of food. When people with diabetes were treated with low carb diets in the first half of the last century, it helped control their high blood glucose levels, but they often died prematurely from heart disease.

Nutritionists are also concerned that a low carb diet will mean you miss out on all the valuable micronutrients that are found in wholegrains, fruits and vegetables. The vitamin and mineral supplements that are strongly advocated by the proponents of low carb diets represent an admission that their diets are not balanced. What's more, supplements are not a satisfactory answer because you still miss out on the protective substances that occur naturally in plant foods but not in pills.

Low fat or low carb?

There is much debate today about the optimal diet for weight loss. And not just among frustrated consumers, but nutritionists and dietitians, too. On one side of the ring you have experts who consider a low fat diet to be the best diet for weight loss. It is true that liberal consumption of a low fat diet leads to a small weight loss. But, on the other side of the ring, Professor Walter Willett, head of the Harvard School of Public Health, and other notable experts believe that a low fat diet based on any old carbohydrate is decidedly unhealthy. We agree. The reasoning behind this alternative thinking is as follows:

• Today's low fat diet can be as energy dense as a high fat diet.
• Carbs that are quickly digested and absorbed can stimulate appetite.
• Fast-release carbs will produce a marked increase in insulin levels.
• High insulin levels will compromise the body's ability to burn fat.

Proponents of low carb diets claim that the best way to reduce insulin and body weight is to cut out the carbs altogether. They are right in some respects—you will lose weight much faster on a low carb diet than on a conventional low fat diet. But there is a catch: some of that weight is muscle mass and body water, not body fat. And while a low carb diet might make you slimmer, you are not necessarily healthier. Indeed, you may be a step closer to a heart attack because you have substituted saturated and trans fat (partially hydrogenated vegetable oil found in some margarines, biscuits, crackers and snack food) for carbohydrate.

The burning question is *why* people lose weight faster on a low carb diet. There are varying opinions among the experts. It could be just sheer boredom with such a small range of foods to choose from—you can't eat *any* cereal products, most fruits are off the menu and sooner or later you can't bear the thought of yet another egg or piece of steak. It could also be related to the known appetite-suppressing effects of protein and high ketones in the blood (see page 44). It might be something to do with the ability of protein to increase our metabolic rate, even though this effect is fairly small.

Our belief is that it has more to do with the drawbacks of a conventional low fat diet than any special benefit of low carb eating. Most foods that are 97 or 99 per cent fat free are invariably high in carbohydrate and increase blood glucose and insulin levels. Furthermore, most people who are overweight are highly insulin resistant. Consequently, their insulin response to carbohydrates will be five or even ten times greater than that of a slim individual. High insulin levels inhibit fat burning and experts agree that bringing insulin down by any mechanism is one of the keys to weight loss. However, cutting out carbs is *not* the best solution. When you cut out carbs, there is a big gaping hole to fill with just protein and fat. It makes food choices unnecessarily restrictive and besides, protein stimulates insulin secretion too. Recommending low carb diets to reduce insulin reflects ignorance of all the facts. It is overkill and you don't need to go to such an extreme.

If we look at the science objectively, it is clear that Dr Atkins (the low carb diet guru) was *half* right. High carb diets that produce high insulin levels make it hard to lose weight, forcing our bodies to burn glucose instead of fat. But as we have learnt, carbs are not a homogeneous lot—there are high GI carbs and low GI carbs. Low GI carbs produce much less insulin because they are slowly digested and absorbed, and improve the body's insulin sensitivity. Indeed, in our lab at the University of Sydney, we showed that acute insulin secretion after meals is no higher after low GI carbs than after high protein foods—the ones Atkins recommends in large quantity. See the graph below.

Low GI foods have the same insulin scores as low carb foods

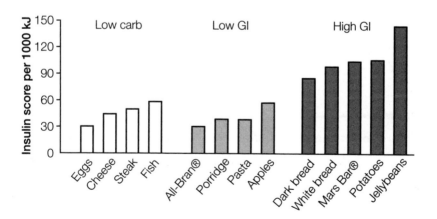

The benefits of The Low GI Diet

You will be pleased to hear that there is a happy, healthy medium between a low fat diet and a low carb diet; a diet that reduces insulin levels and increases the rate of weight loss without any potential to do harm in the long term.

The Low GI Diet gives you the best of both worlds, the optimal balance between a conventional low fat diet and a low carb diet. Its emphasis on slowly digested carbs rather than no carbs means it is delicious, safe and satiating, and reduces day-long insulin levels just as effectively as any low carb diet.

The Low GI Diet allows:

- food patterns that are familiar to you
- all food groups in normal proportions
- distinctive ethnic and regional cuisines
- vegetarianism
- inexpensive food choices
- sensible, practical, flexible food choices
- delicious food choices

. . . that won't leave you bored and hungry.

the glycemic index: the dietary power tool

TRADITIONALLY, THE NATURE OF CARBOHYDRATES WAS described by their chemical structure: simple or complex. Sugars were simple and starches were complex, only because sugars were small molecules and starches were big. By virtue of their size, complex carbohydrates were assumed to be slowly digested and absorbed, causing only a small and gradual rise in blood glucose levels. Simple sugars, on the other hand, were assumed to be the villains—digested and absorbed quickly, producing a rapid rise in blood glucose. We now know that the whole chemical concept of 'simple' versus 'complex' carbohydrates tells us nothing about how they really behave in our bodies. Another system of describing the nature of carbohydrates and classifying them according to their true effects on blood glucose was needed: enter the glycemic index. It took 25 years of scientific research—much of it controversial in the beginning—to prove that the glycemic index was not only a useful tool but had enormous implications for everybody.

Low GI foods have two important advantages for people trying to lose weight:

- They fill you up and keep you satisfied for longer than their high GI counterparts.

- They reduce insulin levels and help you burn more body fat and less muscle, so that your metabolic rate is higher.

It may seem surprising today, but scientists did not study the actual blood glucose responses to common foods until the early 1980s. Since 1981, hundreds and hundreds of different foods have been tested as single foods and in mixed meals with both healthy people and those with diabetes. Professors David Jenkins and Tom Wolever at the University of Toronto were the first to introduce the term 'glycemic index' to compare the blood glucose-raising (*glycemic*) potential of different carbohydrates.

The glycemic index, or GI, is simply a numerical way of describing how much the carbohydrates in individual foods affect blood glucose levels (glycemia). Foods with a high GI value contain carbohydrates that cause a dramatic rise in blood glucose levels, while foods with a low GI value contain carbohydrates with much less impact.

THE GI IS A MEASURE OF HOW FAST CARBOHYDRATES

HIT THE BLOOD STREAM.

IT COMPARES CARBOHYDRATES WEIGHT FOR WEIGHT,

GRAM FOR GRAM.

This research has turned some widely held beliefs upside down. The first surprise was that the starch in foods such as white bread, potatoes and many types of rice is digested and absorbed very quickly—not slowly, as had always been assumed.

Second, scientists found that the sugar in foods (such as fruit, chocolate and ice-cream) did not produce more rapid or prolonged rises in blood glucose, as had always been thought. The truth was that most of the sugars in foods, regardless of the source, actually produced quite moderate blood glucose responses, lower than most starches.

So we can discard the old distinctions that have been made between starchy foods and sugary foods, or simple versus complex carbohydrates. They have no relevance at all when it comes to blood glucose levels. Even an experienced scientist with a detailed knowledge of a food's preparation and chemical composition finds it difficult to predict its GI value.

FORGET ABOUT SIMPLE AND COMPLEX CARBOHYDRATES.
THINK IN TERMS OF LOW AND HIGH GI.

The key to understanding GI is the rate of digestion

Foods containing carbohydrates that break down quickly during digestion have the highest GI values. The blood glucose response is fast and high. In other words, the glucose (or sugar) in the blood stream increases rapidly. Conversely, foods that contain carbohydrates that break down slowly, releasing glucose gradually into the blood stream, have a low GI value. An analogy we like to use is the popular fable of the tortoise and the hare. The hare, just like high GI foods, speeds away but loses the race to the tortoise with his slow and steady pace. Similarly, the slow and steady low GI foods produce a smooth blood glucose curve without wild fluctuations. To show you the difference we have drawn a graph. The diagram below shows the different effects of slow and fast carbohydrates on blood glucose levels.

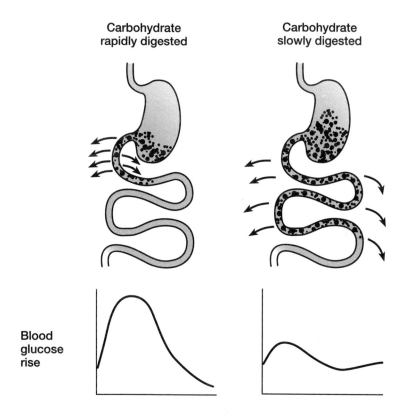

For most people, the foods with low GI values have advantages over those with high GI values. However, in elite sport, there are times when a high GI carbohydrate will be the best choice.

The substance that produces one of the greatest effects on blood glucose levels is pure glucose (sold as powder and in energy drinks).

GI testing has shown that most foods have less effect on blood glucose levels than glucose itself. The GI value of pure glucose is set at 100, and every other food is ranked on a scale from 0 to 100 according to the actual effect on blood glucose levels. There are a few foods that have GI values of more than 100, for example, jasmine rice. While this seems extraordinary, there is a simple explanation. In testing, glucose is given as a highly concentrated solution that tends to be held up briefly in the stomach. On the other hand, jasmine rice contains starch that leaves the stomach without delay and is then digested at lightning speed.

Because low GI foods have a slow rate of digestion and absorption, foods reach lower parts of the small intestine, stimulating the secretion of powerful 'satiety factors' that help people feel satiated. The Low GI Diet therefore harnesses nature's own appetite suppressants so that weight loss is easier to achieve than ever before.

THE GLYCEMIC INDEX IS A CLINICALLY PROVEN TOOL FOR APPETITE CONTROL, DIABETES MANAGEMENT AND CORONARY HEALTH.

Low GI smart carbs help you lose weight

In our previous books we discussed the benefits of low GI diets mainly in terms of appetite and blood glucose control. Now we can argue confidently, on the basis of good scientific evidence that the GI helps people lose weight, specifically that dangerous fat around the belly we mentioned earlier. There is concrete evidence that a low GI diet increases the rate of weight loss compared to a conventional low fat diet.

The confirmation comes from both our own weight loss studies at the University of Sydney, as well as research from Harvard University and Hotel Dieu Hospital, Paris, France. We have summarised the evidence in the table on pages 362–63.

What's more, some small but extremely well designed studies have confirmed that the fat loss is maintained long term. That is a critically important point because it is where the other diets fail. Let's take a close look at all the facts supporting our healthy low GI diet.

Overcoming hunger

One of the biggest challenges to losing weight is ignoring that gnawing feeling in your gut: hunger. Indeed, it is impossible to deny extreme hunger—food-seeking behaviour is wired into our brains to ensure we survive when energy intake is too low. Extreme hunger followed by binge eating can develop into a vicious cycle—and that is one reason we discourage rapid weight loss.

The Low GI Diet is based on an important scientifically proven fact—that foods with low GI values are more filling than their high GI counterparts. They not only give you a greater feeling of fullness instantly, but delay hunger pangs for longer and reduce food intake during the remainder of the day. In contrast, foods with a high GI can actually stimulate appetite sooner, increasing consumption at the next meal (as shown in the table overleaf).

When it comes to filling power, foods were not created equal. Some foods and nutrients are simply more satiating than others, kilojoule for kilojoule. In general, protein packs the greatest punch, followed by carbohydrate and fat. Most of us can relate to the fact that a good

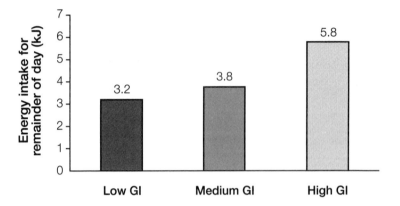

Low GI meals are more satiating

Voluntary food intake in 12 obese teenage boys
following test breakfast and lunch of varying GI

steak has greater filling power than a croissant, despite the fact that they
provide an equal number of kilojoules.

There are also foods that are 'more-ish'—corn chips and potato
crisps, for example—we can't stop at one, just as the advertisement says.
Fatty foods, in particular, have only a weak effect on satisfying appetite
relative to the number of kilojoules they provide. This has been demonstrated clearly in experiments where volunteers were asked to eat until
their appetite was satisfied. They ate far more kilojoules if the foods were
high in fat than when they were starchy or sugary foods. Even when the fat
and carbohydrate were disguised in yoghurts and milk puddings, people
consumed more energy from the high fat option. This may surprise you
but remember, a gram of fat contains twice as many kilojoules as a gram
of protein, starch or sugar.

In our laboratory at the University of Sydney, Dr Susanna Holt
developed the world's first satiety index of foods. Volunteers were given
a range of individual foods that contained equal numbers of kilojoules,
and then their satiety responses and subsequent food intake were

compared. She found that the most important determinant of satiety was the actual weight or volume of the food—the higher the weight per 1000 kilojoules, the higher the filling power. So foods that were high in water (and therefore the least energy dense), such as porridge, apples and broccoli, were the most satiating. When water contents were equal, however, protein and carbohydrate were the next best predictors of satiating power.

Then, if carbohydrate contents were similar, the GI became the most important determinant—low GI foods being more satiating than high GI foods. (It is true that potatoes, despite their high GI, are high on the satiety index scale, but if we could 'invent' a low GI potato, it would be even more satiating!)

Invariably, foods that provided a lot of kilojoules per gram (energy-dense foods such as croissants, chocolate and peanuts) were the least satisfying. These foods are more likely to leave us wanting more and to lead to what scientists call 'passive overeating' without realising it. In developing The Low GI Diet, we made good use of these findings, encouraging food choices that will keep you feeling fuller for longer.

In addition to our own research, at least 20 other studies from around the world have confirmed the remarkable fact that low GI foods, in comparison to their nutrient-matched high GI counterparts, are more filling, delay hunger pangs for longer and/or reduce energy intake during the remainder of the day. There are several explanations: low GI foods remain longer in the gut and reach much lower parts of the small intestine, triggering receptors that produce natural appetite suppressants. Many of these receptors are present only in the lower gut. It doesn't take a genius to appreciate that a food that empties rapidly from the stomach and gets digested and absorbed in minutes won't satisfy for hours on end.

In summary:

- High GI foods may stimulate hunger because the rapid rise and then fall in blood glucose level appears to stimulate counter-regulatory responses to reverse the decline.
- Stress hormones such as adrenalin and cortisol are released when glucose levels rebound after a high GI food. Both hormones stimulate appetite.
- Low GI foods may be more satiating simply because they are often less energy dense than their high GI counterparts. The naturally high water and fibre content of many low GI foods increases their bulk without increasing their energy content.

Fat loss is faster with low GI foods

There are now at least ten studies showing that individuals eating low GI foods lose more body fat than those eating normal high GI foods (a summary of these studies can be found on pages 362–63).

In one study conducted at Boston Children's Hospital, adolescents were instructed to follow either a conventional high fibre, low fat diet or a low GI diet containing a little more protein and less carbohydrate. The low GI group's diet emphasised foods such as oatmeal, eggs, low fat dairy produce and pasta. In contrast, the low fat diet emphasised grainy high fibre cereal products, potatoes and rice. Both diets contained the same number of kilojoules and were followed for 12 months. At the end of the first six months, the people in the group eating low GI foods had lost 3 kilograms of body fat while the low fat group lost none. Furthermore, at the end of that year, the low GI group had maintained their fat loss, while the other group gained.

Diets based on low GI foods prevent fat regain

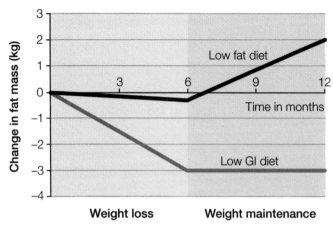

In our own research unit, we have made similar findings in a group of young overweight adults. To ensure dietary compliance, we gave them most of the food they needed for the whole 12-week period. At the end, we found that weight and body fat loss were 50 per cent greater in those following the low GI regime than those following the conventional low fat approach, as you can see below.

Comparison of conventional low fat and low GI diets

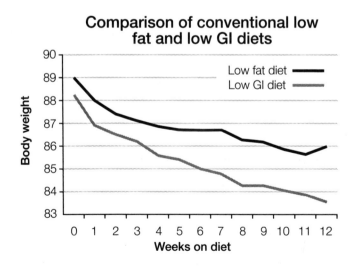

How did the low GI diet work? The most significant finding was the different effects of the two diets on the day-long insulin level. Low GI foods resulted in lower levels of insulin over the course of the day, as shown in the figure below.

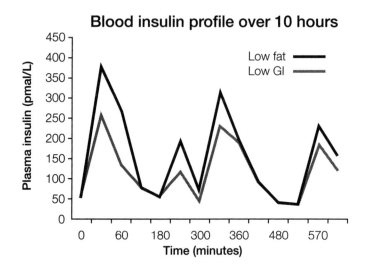

Blood insulin profile over 10 hours

The hormone insulin is not only involved in regulating blood glucose levels, but also plays a key part in fat storage. High levels of insulin mean the body is forced to burn carbohydrate rather than fat. Thus, over the day, even if the total energy burnt is the same, the proportions of fat and carbohydrate are different. Oxidising carbohydrate won't help you lose weight, but burning fat will.

People who are obese appear to have high glycogen (carbohydrate) stores that undergo major fluctuations during the day. This suggests that glycogen is a more important source of fuel for them. If glycogen is being depleted and replenished on a regular basis (before and after each meal, for example), it is displacing fat from the engine. Each meal restores glycogen to its former high level (especially if the food has a high GI value) and the cycle repeats itself.

There are even more good reasons to choose The Low GI Diet for weight loss:

- When you first begin a diet, your metabolic rate drops in response to the reduction in food intake, which makes weight loss hard to sustain. Your metabolic rate drops much less, however, on The Low GI Diet than a conventional low fat diet. So your engine revs are higher.

- The Low GI Diet brings about a reduction in the dangerous fat— around the abdomen—with minimal loss of muscle.

- Large-scale studies in people with diabetes have found that diets including low GI carbs are linked not only to lower waist circumference, but also to better diabetes control.

The Low GI Diet for lifelong health

One of the best reasons to adopt The Low GI Diet for weight loss and weight control is the value-added benefits you get for your long-term health. People who *naturally* eat a diet with a low GI or lower glycemic load (that is the overall GI multiplied by the carbohydrate content) have been found to be at much lower risk of developing chronic and crippling disease; not just one disease, but the whole gamut of afflictions that adversely affects adults in the industrialised world. These include: type 2 diabetes, cardiovascular heart disease and cancer of the large bowel, breast, upper gastrointestinal tract, pancreas and uterus. The evidence for this comes from epidemiological studies based on large cohorts of people (10 000 to 100 000 or more), including the famous Nurses' Health Study being carried out by the Harvard School of Public Health in the USA.

What is the glycemic load?

Glycemic load (GL) provides a measure of the degree of glycemia and insulin demand produced by a normal serving of a particular food.

Glycemic load is calculated simply by multiplying the GI of a food by the amount of carbohydrate per serving and dividing by 100.

$$GL = (GI \times carbohydrate\ per\ serving) \div 100$$

The glycemic load is greatest for high GI foods which provide the most carbohydrate, particularly those we tend to eat in large quantities. Some nutritionists have argued that the glycemic load is an improvement on the GI because it provides an estimate of both quantity and quality of carbohydrate (the GI gives us just the quality). In large-scale studies at Harvard University, however, the risk of disease was predicted by the GI of the overall diet as well as the glycemic load. The use of the glycemic load strengthened the relationship, suggesting that the more frequent the consumption of high carbohydrate, high GI foods, the more adverse the health outcome.

Don't make the mistake of using GL alone. If you do, you might find yourself eating a diet with very little carbohydrate but a lot of fat, especially saturated fat, and excessive amounts of protein. Use the GI to compare foods of similar nature (e.g. bread with bread). Ignore the GI of foods such as watermelon, rockmelon and pumpkin—they contain so little carbohydrate, it doesn't matter.

You will find both the GI and GL of many foods in the *The New Glucose Revolution Shopper's Guide to GI Values 2006*.

This type of study controls or adjusts for all the known confounding factors associated with disease risk: age, body weight, family history, physical activity, alcohol intake, fibre intake, etc. Hence it is highly unlikely that a low GI diet is just a coincidental marker of a group of people at low risk of disease. The remarkable fact is that GI and GL are often showing strong relationships with disease risk while total carbo-hydrate, sugar and total fat are not.

Furthermore, the GI of self-selected diets has correlated in a reciprocal fashion with the strongest risk factor for coronary heart disease—your HDL-cholesterol (good cholesterol). So if your diet has a low GI, chances are you have a high good cholesterol value. That is an important finding because nutritionists have struggled in the past to find appropriate nutritional advice for people whose HDL levels are low. Low HDL levels are also a feature of the metabolic or insulin resistance syndrome, which puts you not only at higher risk of heart attack and type 2 diabetes, but also polycystic ovarian syndrome (in women) and non-alcoholic fatty liver (more often seen in men).

Epidemiological studies also prove to us that many people are already eating a diet that has a low GI. In other words, it is practical and feasible to select low GI foods from the vast array of foods currently on supermarket shelves. You don't have to jump through a hoop or turn yourself inside out to adopt a diet that gives you the benefits of lifelong health and weight control. *The Low GI Diet* gives you all the information you need to make it happen for you and your family.

The Low GI Diet is the long-term answer

Any diet or exercise program can help you lose weight. But *maintaining* weight loss—preventing weight regain—is the real aim of the game. Why go to all that effort if you put the weight back on again three months later? Weight maintenance sorts the good diets from the bad ones.

Low carb diets won't suit most of us or work in the longer term because they represent such a huge departure from our normal eating habits. Most of us would find it simply too demanding to live in a modern world without our carbs and starchy staples, be they bread, pasta, noodles or plain old rice. Avoiding sugars is twice as hard because enjoying sweetness is programmed into our brains.

Fruit, yoghurt and even ice-cream are part and parcel of our healthy low GI eating plan but are either off limits or highly constrained on a low carb diet. Eating such a restricted diet is not only hard on you long term, it's also awkward for your family and friends, even antisocial. You might end up alienating them if they see you rejecting the food habits you 'inherited' from your childhood. Unless they want to join you, your family won't be the sources of support that are essential to long-term weight control. What's more, if you are constantly besieged by advice on how harmful it is, then you are likely to be stressed out, too.

In contrast, The Low GI Diet is a diet you can live with, taking you as close as possible to your normal 'comfort' zone while still keeping your weight under control. You will be eating the same delicious diet during weight loss (the 12-week Action Plan) and weight maintenance (Doing It For Life)—only the quantities differ—and it will be enjoyed, rather than suffered, by the whole family.

Carbs boost mood and brain power

The benefits of eating carbs on mental performance are well documented. Glucose (from digested carbohydrate or made in the liver) is the only source of fuel that our brains can use (except during starvation). The brain is the most energy-demanding organ in the body; it is responsible for over half our obligatory energy requirements. Unlike muscle cells, which can burn either fat or carbohydrate, the brain does not have the capacity to burn fat. If you fast for 24 hours or decide to avoid carbohydrate, the brain initially relies on small stores of carbohydrate in the liver, but within hours these stores become depleted and the liver begins synthesising glucose from non-carbohydrate sources—but it only has a limited ability to do this. We know now that any shortfall in glucose availability has negative consequences for brain function.

Recent medical literature shows that intellectual performance improves following the consumption of a carbohydrate-rich food (or a glucose load). The tests carried out included various measures of 'intelligence', including word recall, maze learning, arithmetic, short-term memory, rapid information processing and reasoning. An improved mental ability following a carbohydrate meal was demonstrated in all types of people—young people, university students, people with diabetes, healthy elderly people, and those with Alzheimer's disease. Interestingly, it appears that low GI carbohydrates enhance learning and memory better than high GI carbohydrates, probably because there is no rebound fall in blood glucose. All this evidence supports our belief that smart carbs (of the healthy, low GI type) should play an important role in your diet.

EATING TO LOSE WEIGHT WITH LOW GI SMART CARBS GIVES YOU FREEDOM, FLEXIBILITY AND SECURITY.

What you should know about low carb diets and ketosis

At all times, our bodies need to maintain a minimum threshold level of glucose in the blood to serve the brain and central nervous system. If, for some reason, glucose levels fall below this threshold (a very rare state called hypoglycemia), the consequences are severe including trembling, dizziness, nausea, incoherent rambling speech, and lack of coordination. When necessary, the brain will make use of ketones, a byproduct of the breakdown of fat. In people losing weight on a low carb diet, the level of ketones in the blood rises markedly, a state called ketosis, which is taken as a sign of 'success'. The brain, however, is definitely not at its best using ketones, and mental judgement is impaired.

Ketosis is a serious concern in pregnant women. The foetus can be harmed and brain development impaired by high levels of ketones crossing from the mother's blood via the placenta. Because being overweight is often a cause of infertility, women who are losing weight may fall pregnant unexpectedly. Thus one of the very good reasons we advocate a healthy low GI diet in this context is that there are absolutely no safety concerns for mother or baby. Indeed, there is some evidence that a low GI diet will help mothers control excessive weight gain during pregnancy.

We've summarised all the benefits of The Low GI Diet over a low carb diet in the table opposite.

The Low GI Diet	Low carb diet
You feel good, you can think straight	You may feel headachy and light-headed
You lose fat, *not* water and muscle	You lose fat, water and muscle
Insulin sensitivity is enhanced	Glucose tolerance worsens
You have energy for exercise	You feel lethargic, exercise is tough
Low in saturated and trans fats	*Unavoidably* high in the bad fats
No concerns about safety in children	Immense concerns about long-term safety in children
No concerns about safety in pregnancy	Immense concerns about safety in pregnant women
Benefits for mental function	Decline in mental performance
Fits in easily with family and friends	Antisocial, often alienates friends/family
Value-added benefits for long-term health	Serious doubts about long-term safety

**QUITE SIMPLY, THE LOW GI DIET IS NOT A FAD,
BUT A BLUEPRINT FOR HEALTHY EATING
FOR THE REST OF YOUR LIFE.**

How much carb?

When pushed, humans can scrape by with no carbohydrate in the diet at all—your liver can synthesise most of the glucose your brain needs, and use ketones to make up the shortfall. But you won't be operating at your peak either physically or mentally.

A low carb diet is definitely not a good idea if you are trying to be more active—something we strongly encourage because activity is the *key* to lifelong weight control. The more strenuously you exercise, the more carbs you need and no serious athlete follows a low carb diet long term (though they may use it for a few days to deplete all carbohydrate stores as part of a process called 'glycogen loading').

What then is the optimal level of carbohydrate in the diet? Not so long ago, everyone was told a high carbohydrate diet (more than 50 per cent of energy intake as carbs) was the *only* diet for optimum health and weight control. Thankfully, nutrition science has progressed since then and we are now given much more flexibility.

In 2002, the National Institute of Health (NIH) in the USA advised that a *range* of carbohydrate intakes could adequately meet the body's needs while minimising the risk of disease. Specifically, they advised the following ranges:

CARBOHYDRATES: 45 TO 65 PER CENT OF ENERGY

FAT: 25 TO 35 PER CENT OF ENERGY

PROTEIN: 15 TO 35 PER CENT OF ENERGY

We like these figures because they allow for individual tailoring. The American Heart Association even ruled that as little as 40 per cent of energy as carbs could be eaten and still be good for the heart.

Chances are your diet already falls within these flexible ranges and, if so we encourage you to stick with what you have. If your preference is for more protein and more fat than you are currently eating, then go ahead—just be choosy about quality. We believe that you are the best judge of what you can live with for the rest of your life and, anyway, there is plenty of room for flexibility.

If you have been making a concerted effort to follow a low carb diet, your carbohydrate intake may be as low as 20 per cent of energy. We believe that is unnecessarily restrictive and possibly harmful in the long term, and encourage you to increase your carb intake. Because we want you to incorporate daily exercise as part of your weight control strategy, you need your carbs!

We recommend you consume at least 130 grams of carbohydrate a day, even during active weight loss. Whatever the number, the type of carbohydrate is important. And that's where the GI comes to the fore.

The seven guidelines of The Low GI Diet

Choosing low GI foods is one of *the* most important dietary choices you can make. As well as identifying your best low GI smart carb choices, our seven dietary guidelines below give you a blueprint for eating for life.

1   Eat seven or more servings of fruit and vegetables every day.

2   Eat low GI breads and cereals.

3   Eat more legumes, including soybeans, chickpeas and lentils.

4   Eat nuts more regularly.

5   Eat more fish and seafood.

6   Eat lean red meats, poultry and eggs.

7   Eat low fat dairy products.

LOW GI: 55 OR LESS

MEDIUM/MODERATE GI: 56–69

HIGH GI: 70 OR MORE

1 EAT SEVEN OR MORE SERVINGS OF FRUIT AND VEGETABLES EVERY DAY

Why?

Being high in fibre and therefore filling, and low in fat (apart from olives and avocado, which contain some 'good' fats), fruit and vegetables play a central role in The Low GI Diet. In addition to protecting you against diseases (ranging from high blood pressure through to cancer), they are bursting with nutrients that will give you a glow of good health, such as:

- Beta-carotene—the plant precursor of vitamin A, used to maintain healthy skin and eyes. A diet rich in beta-carotene may even lessen skin damage caused by UV rays. Apricots, peaches, mangoes, carrots, broccoli and sweet potato are particularly rich in beta-carotene.

- Vitamin C—nature's water soluble anti-oxidant. Anti-oxidants are a bit like your personal bodyguard, protecting your body cells from the damage that can be caused by pollutants in our environment and which also occurs as a natural part of ageing. Guava, capsicum, orange, kiwi fruit and rockmelon are especially rich in vitamin C.

- Anthocyanins—the purple and red pigments in blueberries, capsicum, beetroot and eggplant which also function as anti-oxidants, minimising the damage to cell membranes that occurs with ageing.

How much?

Aim to eat at least two serves of fruit and five serves of vegetables every day, preferably of three of more different colours. A serve is about one medium-sized piece of fruit, half a cup of cooked vegies or 1 cup raw.

Which vegetables are low GI?

Most vegetables contain so little carbohydrate that they don't have a GI value. Potato is a notable exception, however—it has a high GI. If you are a big potato eater, try to replace some of the potato in your diet with these low GI alternatives.

SWEET CORN (GI 46–48)

Sweet corn contains folic acid, potassium, the anti-oxidant vitamins A and C, and dietary fibre. Add canned or frozen kernels to soups, stews, relishes, salsas and salads, or simply enjoy it on the cob. For the best flavour, buy fresh corn with the husk intact, because the sugar in the kernels transforms into starch the moment the husk is removed.

Corn is often used as a base for gluten-free products. However, many products manufactured from corn such as cornflakes, cornmeal and corn pasta do not have a low GI. Check the GI table first (see pages 332–360).

SWEET POTATO (GI 46)

Sweet potatoes are an excellent source of beta-carotene, vitamin C and dietary fibre. They make a great substitute for potatoes. Peel them or simply scrub the skins and steam, boil, bake or microwave. Try mashing them with a little mustard seed oil or wrapping them in foil and cooking on the barbecue. They also make a tasty addition to casseroles, stir-fries and soups and (roasted first) to salads.

TARO (GI 54)

Taro is a traditional slowly digested food eaten widely throughout the Pacific Islands. It has a dry texture, a flavour similar to sweet potato and can be used the same way. Before cooking, peel off the thick skin wearing rubber gloves (as the juice has been known to cause skin irritation), then cut into wedges and steam, boil or bake.

YAM (GI 37)

Yam, with its thick brownish skin and creamy flesh, is high in fibre and nutrient dense. It's a good source of vitamin C and potassium. Similar to sweet potato and taro but with an earthier flavour, yam can be steamed, microwaved, boiled or baked in wedges or roasted and added to salads.

Fruit

Most fruits have a low GI thanks to the presence of the low GI sugar fructose, soluble and insoluble fibres and acids (which may slow down stomach emptying).

The lowest GI fruits—apples, pears, all citrus (oranges, grapefruit, mandarins) and stone fruits (peaches, nectarines, plums, apricots)—are those grown in temperate climates. Generally, the more acidic a fruit the lower the GI. Tropical fruits such as pineapple, paw paw, rockmelon and watermelon tend to have intermediate GI values but they are excellent sources of anti-oxidants and in average servings their glycemic load is low.

Most berries have so little carbohydrate that their GI is impossible to test. Strawberries have been tested, however, and they are low GI. Enjoy them by the bowl.

2   EAT LOW GI BREADS AND CEREALS

Why?

What affects the GI of your diet the most? The type of bread and cereals you eat. Mixed grain breads, sourdough, traditional rolled oats, cracked wheat, pearl barley, pasta, noodles and certain types of rice are just some examples of low GI cereal foods. The slow digestion and absorption of these foods will fill you up more, trickle fuel into your engine at a more useable rate and keep you satisfied for longer.

How much?

Most people need at least four serves of grains each day (very active people need much more), where a serve is two slices of bread or half a cup of rice or small grains.

BREAD

For most people, bread forms an important part of their diet. One of the most important changes you can make to lower the GI of your diet is to choose a low GI bread. Choose a really grainy bread, granary bread, stoneground wholemeal bread, sourdough bread, or bread made from chickpea or other legume-based flours. Small, specialty bakers are the most likely places you will find them. Some healthy low GI choices are listed below.

Grainy or multigrain breads—These breads contain *lots* of 'grainy bits', tend to be chewy and are nutritionally superior, containing high levels of fibre, vitamins, minerals and phytoestrogens.

Choose breads made with whole cereal grains such as barley, rye, triticale (a wheat and rye hybrid), oats, soy and cracked wheat, and have seeds such as sunflower seeds and linseeds added.

Pumpernickel—Also known as rye kernel bread, pumpernickel contains 80–90 per cent whole and cracked rye kernels. It is dense and compact and is usually sold thinly sliced. The main reason for its low GI value is its content of whole cereal grains.

Sourdough—Sourdough results from the deliberately slow fermentation of flour by yeasts which produces a build-up of organic acids. These acids give sourdough its characteristic taste. This flavourful low GI bread is a popular choice for sandwiches (its compact structure keeps the sandwich intact), makes great toast and is generally considered acceptable by those family members who absolutely insist on white bread. The flavour blends well with all kinds of fillings and toppings, making it ideal for lunch boxes, snacks and to serve with soups, salads and main meals.

Stoneground wholemeal or whole-wheat breads—This means that the flour has been milled from the entire wheat berry (the germ, endosperm or starch compartment and the bran) and that the milling process uses a method of slowly grinding the grain with a burrstone instead of high-speed metal rollers to distribute the germ oil more evenly. Virtually none of the ingredients packaged in the wheat berry get lost in this processing method and that is why this bread is such a rich source of several B vitamins, iron, zinc and dietary fibre.

Fruit loaf—The GI of fruit loaf is relatively low because of the part substitution of wheat flour (high GI) with dried fruits (lower GI). The presence of sugar in the dough also limits gelatinisation of the starch.

Chapatti-baisen—Chapatti is unleavened or slightly leavened bread that looks rather like pita bread. It is widely eaten throughout the Indian subcontinent and is available in Indian restaurants worldwide. While it is often made with wheat flour, it is also made from baisen or chickpea flour, giving it a significantly lower GI (63) than that made from wheat flour, due to the nature of the starch. All legumes, including chickpeas, have a higher proportion of amylose starch than that found in cereal grains. So, before you order, ask what flour was used.

BREAKFAST CEREALS

Traditional rolled oats cooked into porridge is about the closest most of us come to a true grainy cereal. Although many commercial cereals are labelled 'grainy', the processing they have undergone has destroyed the original physical form of the grain. Some commercial breakfast cereals, however, still do have a low GI thanks to a less extreme degree of processing and the presence of other factors (such as protein or soluble fibre) which slow down digestion—see the GI Table (pages 332–360) for the best low GI commercially available cereal choices. Or try making your own muesli using rolled oats and a mixture of dried fruit, nuts and seeds.

OTHER LOW GI CEREAL GRAINS

BARLEY (GI 25)

One of the oldest cultivated cereals, barley is very nutritious and high in soluble fibre, which helps to reduce the post-meal rise in blood glucose and lowers its GI. Look for products such as pearl barley to use in soups, stews and pilafs, and barley flakes or rolled barley, which have a light, nutty flavour and can be cooked as a cereal and used in baked goods and stuffing.

BULGUR (GI 48)

Also known as cracked wheat, bulgur is made from wheat grains that have been hulled and steamed before grinding to crack the grain. The whole-wheat grain in bulgur remains virtually intact—it is simply cracked—and the wheat germ and bran are retained, which preserves nutrients and lowers the GI. Bulgur is used as the base of the Middle Eastern salad tabbouli, but can also be used in pilafs, vegie burgers, stuffing, stews, salads and soups or as a cereal.

NOODLES

Many Asian noodles such as Hokkien, udon and rice vermicelli have low to intermediate GI values because of their dense texture, whether they are made from wheat or rice flour. Lungkow bean thread noodles (GI 33), also called cellophane noodles or green bean vermicelli, are a smart carb choice. These shiny fine white noodles are usually sold in bundles wrapped in cellophane in the Asian food aisle of your supermarket or in an Asian food market. Soak them in hot water for 10 minutes then add to stir-fries and salads as they tend to absorb the flavours of other foods they are cooked with. The reason for their low GI includes their legume origin (they are made from mung beans) and their noodle shape and dense texture.

OATS (rolled oats GI 59)

Rolled oats are grainy oats that have been hulled, steamed and flattened; this popular cereal grain lowers the GI of oatmeal, muesli, biscuits, bread and meatloaf. Oat bran also has a low GI.

PASTA

Pastas of any shape or size have a fairly low GI and are a great stand-by for quick meals. Served with vegetables or tomato sauce and/or accompaniments such as olive oil, fish and lean meat, plenty of vegetables and small amounts of cheese, a pasta meal gives you a healthy balance of carbs, fats and proteins. Pasta should be slightly firm (al dente) and offer some resistance when you are chewing it. Not only does it taste better this way but it has a lower GI as overcooking boosts the GI. While pasta is a good low GI choice, a huge amount will have a marked effect on your blood glucose. Remember, a standard serve of cooked pasta is one cup, which may be less than you are used to eating.

Most pasta is made from semolina (finely cracked wheat) which is milled from very hard wheat (durum) with a high protein content. There is some evidence that thicker types of pasta have a lower GI than thinner types because of the dense consistency and perhaps because they cook more slowly and are less likely to be overcooked. Adding egg to fresh pasta lowers the GI by increasing the protein content.

Note: Canned spaghetti has a higher GI value.

RICE

Rice can have a high GI value (80–109) or a low GI value (48–58) depending on the variety and, in particular, its amylose content.

Basmati rice (GI 58) and Doongara or CleverRice™ (GI 56) contain higher proportions of amylose (a type of starch that we digest more slowly), which produces a lower glycemic response, is more compact in structure and more slowly digested. Koshihikari rice, eaten all over Japan, is a short-grain variety with a low GI value (48).

Waxy or glutinous rice, often used for rice desserts as it becomes sticky when cooked, has a high GI. Arborio rice, which is especially good for making Italian risotto, releases its starch during cooking and has a high GI as a result. Eat less of these kinds of rice.

Sushi (GI 48)—These bite-size parcels of raw or smoked fish, chicken, tofu and/ or pickled, raw or cooked vegetables wrapped in seaweed with rice that has been seasoned with vinegar, salt and sugar, make ideal snacks and light meals. Even though the rice used to make sushi in Australia and New Zealand is short grain and somewhat sticky, sushi still has a low GI value (in Japan they use koshihikari, GI 48). In addition, sushi made with salmon and tuna boosts your intake of the healthy omega-3 fats.

RYE (GI 34)

Whole kernel rye is used to make certain breads, including pumper-nickel and some crispbreads. Rye flakes can be used in a similar way to rolled oats: you can eat them as a cooked cereal or sprinkle them over bread before you bake it.

WHOLE-WHEAT KERNELS (GI 41)

Wheat provides a staple food to half the world's population. Soak whole-wheat overnight and simmer for about an hour to use as a base for pilaf. Some people enjoy wheat bran as a cooked breakfast cereal. Cream of wheat is made from very fine semolina; you can use it as a breakfast cereal or in puddings, custards, soufflés and soups.

3 EAT MORE LEGUMES INCLUDING SOYBEANS, CHICKPEAS AND LENTILS

Why?

You need to look no further than legumes for a low GI food that is easy on the budget, versatile, filling, nutritious and low in kilojoules. Legumes are high in fibre, too—both soluble and insoluble—and are packed with nutrients, providing a valuable source of protein, carbohydrate, B vitamins, folate, iron, zinc and magnesium. Whether you buy dried beans, lentils and chickpeas and cook them yourself at home, or opt for the very convenient, time-saving canned varieties, you are choosing one of nature's lowest GI foods.

Legumes have two particularly special properties among their armour of health benefits. The first is their content of phytochemicals—natural plant chemicals that possess antiviral, antifungal, antibacterial and anti-cancer properties. Plus, legumes are prebiotics. This means that they provide food for our gut bacteria or 'intestinal flora', keeping our digestive system healthy.

A bean meal doesn't always have to be strictly vegetarian—try using beans in place of grains or potatoes. You could try serving a bean salsa with fish or cannellini bean purée with grilled meat. Butter beans can also make a delicious potato substitute. Although they will keep indefinitely, it is best to use dried legumes within one year of purchase.

How much?

At least twice a week as a main meal such as bean soup, chickpea curry or lentil patties, or as a light meal such as beans on toast, mixed bean salad, or pea and ham soup.

BEANS

When you add beans to meals and snacks, you reduce the overall GI of your diet and gain important health benefits. Beans are available dried or in cans. Young beans cook faster than old ones and will also be more vividly coloured. Substitute one 400-gram can of beans for three-quarters of a cup of dried beans. Dried beans usually have a lower GI than canned, but using cans is more convenient and the GI remains low.

Baked beans—GI 49

Black-eyed beans—GI 42

Butter beans—GI 31

Cannellini beans—GI 31

Haricot beans—GI 33

Lima beans—GI 32

Mung beans—GI 39

Red kidney beans—GI 36

CHICKPEAS (GI 28)

These large, caramel-coloured legumes are popular in Middle Eastern and Mediterranean dishes. You can buy them in cans or dried. To cook chickpeas, place them in a bowl, cover them with plenty of cold water and soak overnight. Drain the water, then put the chickpeas in a saucepan and cover them with clean water. Bring the beans to the boil for 10 minutes then simmer for 1½ hours until they're tender.

You can also roast and salt whole chickpeas for a delicious snack food. Ground chickpea flour (also called gram flour or baisen) is used to make unleavened Indian bread.

LENTILS (GI 26)

Lentils are rich in protein, fibre and B vitamins. All colours and types have a similar low GI value, which is increased slightly if you opt to buy them canned and add them at the end of cooking time.

Lentils are one food that people with diabetes should learn to love—they can eat them until the cows come home. In fact we have found that no matter how much of them people eat they have only a small effect on blood glucose levels. Lentils have a fairly bland, earthy flavour and are best prepared with onions, garlic and spices. Use them as a 'bed' for grilled fish or meat. They are great for thickening any kind of soup or extending meat casseroles.

Channa dhal (also called Bengal gram dhal) are husked, split, polished Bengal gram (GI 11), the most common type of gram lentil in India. They are often cooked with a pinch of asafoetida (an Indian spice) to make them easier to digest.

SOYBEANS (GI 14)

Soybeans and soy products have been a staple part of Asian diets for thousands of years and are an excellent source of protein. They are also rich in fibre, iron, zinc and vitamin B. They are lower in carbohydrate and higher in fat than other legumes but the majority of the fat is polyunsaturated.

Soy is also a rich source of phytochemicals, phytoestrogens in particular, which are plant oestrogens with a structure similar to the female hormone oestrogen. Some studies link phytoestrogens with improvements in blood cholesterol levels, relief from menopausal symptoms and lower rates of cancer.

SPLIT PEAS (GI 32)

Split peas are prepared from a variety of the common garden pea with the husk removed. They may be yellow or green. They take about an hour to cook after soaking and are traditionally used in pea and ham soups or for making an Indian dhal.

4   EAT NUTS MORE REGULARLY

Why?

Although nuts are high in fat, it is mainly polyunsaturated and mono-unsaturated so they make a healthy substitute for less nutritious high saturated fat snacks such as potato chips, chocolate and cookies.

Nuts are one of the richest sources of vitamin E, which, with the selenium they contain, works as an anti-oxidant. Selenium helps guard against harmful UV rays to reduce damage caused by the sun and premature ageing of your skin.

How much?

Aim for a small handful of nuts (30 grams) most days.

Here are some easy ways to eat more nuts:

- Use nuts and seeds in food preparation. For example, use toasted cashews or sesame seeds in a chicken stir-fry; sprinkle walnuts or pine nuts over a salad; top fruity desserts or granola with almonds.
- Use hazelnut spread on bread or try peanut, almond or cashew butter rather than butter or margarine.
- Sprinkle a mixture of ground nuts and linseeds over cereal or salads, or add to baked goods such as muffins.

5 EAT MORE FISH AND SEAFOOD

Why?

Fish does not have a GI as it is a source of protein, not carbohydrate. Increased fish consumption is linked to a reduced risk of coronary heart disease, improvements in mood, lower rates of depression, better blood fat levels and enhanced immunity. Just one serving of fish a week may reduce the risk of a fatal heart attack by 40 per cent. The likely protective components of fish are the very long chain omega-3 fatty acids. Our bodies only make small amounts of these fatty acids and so we rely on dietary sources, especially fish and seafood, for them.

How much?

One to three meals of fish each week.

Which fish is best?

- Oily fish, which tend to have darker-coloured flesh and a stronger flavour, are the richest source of omega-3 fats.
- Canned salmon, sardines, mackerel and, to a lesser extent, tuna are all very rich sources of omega-3s; look for canned fish packed in water, canola oil, olive oil, tomato sauce or brine, and drain well.
- Fresh fish with higher levels of omega-3s are: Atlantic salmon and smoked salmon; Atlantic, Pacific and Spanish mackerel; sea mullet; southern bluefin tuna; and swordfish. Eastern and Pacific oysters and squid (calamari) are also rich sources.

Mercury in fish

Due to the risk of high levels of mercury in certain species of fish, Food Standards Australia and New Zealand (FSANZ) advises limiting them in your diet to one serve per week, eating no other fish in that week. They are billfish (swordfish, broadbill and marlin), shark (flake), orange roughy (also sold as sea perch) and catfish.

Pregnant women, women planning pregnancy and young children should limit their intake of shark (flake), broadbill, marlin and swordfish to no more than one serve per fortnight with no other fish to be consumed during that fortnight. For orange roughy and catfish, the advice is as for the general population—one serve per week, with no other fish being consumed during that week.

6   EAT LEAN RED MEATS, POULTRY AND EGGS

Why?

Again, these foods do not have a GI because they are protein food, not a carbohydrate. Red meat is the best source of iron (the nutrient used for carrying oxygen in our blood) you can get.

Good iron status can increase energy levels and improve our exercise tolerance. While adequate iron can be obtained from a vegetarian diet, women particularly must select foods carefully to prevent iron deficiency. A chronic shortage of iron leads to anaemia with symptoms including pale skin, excessive tiredness, breathlessness, irritability and decreased attention span.

How much?

We suggest eating lean meat two or three times a week, and accompanying it with a salad or vegetables. One hundred grams of lean edible meat as part of a balanced diet will meet the daily nutrient needs of an adult, but larger amounts can also be part of a healthy diet. A couple of eggs or 120 grams of skinless chicken provide options for variety once or twice a week.

7 EAT LOW FAT DAIRY PRODUCTS

Why?

Milk, cheese, ice-cream, yoghurt, buttermilk and custard are the richest sources of calcium in our diet. Calcium is vital in many body functions so if we don't get enough in our diet, the body will draw it out of our bones. This bone loss over a number of years may lead to osteoporosis and loss of height, curvature of the spine and peridontal disease (deterioration of bones supporting the teeth). By replacing full fat dairy foods with reduced fat, low fat or fat-free versions you will reduce your saturated fat intake and actually boost your calcium intake. Plus, new research shows that calcium and other components in dairy play a vital role in fat burning.

How much?

To meet calcium requirements, experts recommend that adults eat two to three servings of dairy products every day. Good low fat dairy choices include skim, no fat or low fat milk and no fat or low fat yoghurts. A serve is a cup of milk, 40 grams of cheese or 200 grams of yoghurt.

If you're lactose intolerant, you can still eat yoghurt and cheese. You can also try lactose-reduced milk, high calcium soy milk, salmon (canned, with bones), high calcium tofu, calcium-fortified breakfast cereal and dried figs—all great tasting non-dairy sources of calcium.

MILK (GI 27)

Milk is a rich source of protein and vitamin B2 (riboflavin). As whole milk is also a rich source of saturated fat, choose low fat and no fat milk and milk products. The surprisingly low GI of milk is a combination of the moderate GI effect of the lactose (milk sugar) plus the effect of the milk protein, which forms a soft curd in the stomach and slows down the rate of stomach emptying.

YOGHURT (GI 19–50)

Yoghurt is rich in calcium, riboflavin and protein. Low fat natural yoghurt provides the most calcium for the fewest kilojoules. The combination of yoghurt's acidity and high protein contributes to its low GI. Fruit yoghurts made with a sugar-sweetened fruit syrup have a GI of around 33, whereas artificially sweetened yoghurts have a GI of around 14.

LOW FAT ICE-CREAM (GI 37–49)

Low fat ice-cream is a delicious source of all the goodies found in milk. It is important that you choose a low fat (less than 3 grams of fat per 100 grams) variety for regular consumption so that you don't overdo your saturated fat intake. Save the gourmet varieties for an occasional indulgence. Ice-cream has a slightly higher GI than milk because of the presence of sucrose and glucose in addition to lactose.

the
other side
of the energy
equation

LET'S BE BLUNT. IF YOU DON'T BUILD PHYSICAL ACTIVITY into your life, you have very little chance of changing your body shape for life. You can certainly lose weight through dieting alone, but chances are you will regain any weight lost (and probably gain more) over the weeks and months after you stop actively 'dieting'.

THE PEOPLE MOST LIKELY TO KEEP THE WEIGHT OFF ARE THOSE WHO RAISE THEIR ACTIVITY LEVELS AND MAKE EXERCISE A NATURAL PART OF LIFE.

How can exercise help break the dieting cycle?

Exercising while you lose weight will help you to maximise fat loss and minimise lean muscle loss. This means you get *leaner faster*. Since you maintain or even build muscle you can help to prevent the drop in your metabolic rate caused by your decreasing body weight. This, in turn, means that you burn more energy each and every minute of every day. All good news!

But the benefits don't stop there. Fit people *burn more fat.* So once you have lost weight, continuing to exercise makes your body a fat-burning machine which is much more effective at resisting weight regain. Furthermore, exercise and the amount of muscle you have affects your body's ability to respond to insulin—fit people need less insulin to do the job of maintaining blood glucose levels because their muscles are primed and trained to respond quickly and effectively to incoming fuel. Alongside a healthy low GI diet, these changes maximise your chances of maintaining a lean, fit body for life.

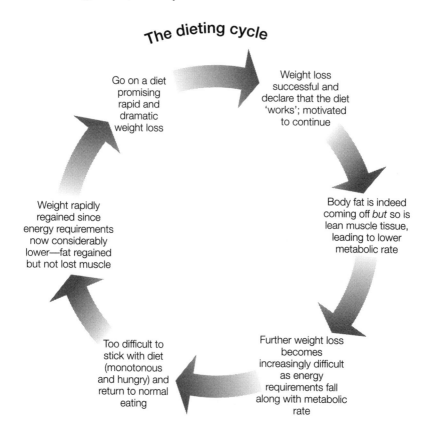

The dieting cycle

Go on a diet promising rapid and dramatic weight loss

Weight loss successful and declare that the diet 'works'; motivated to continue

Body fat is indeed coming off *but* so is lean muscle tissue, leading to lower metabolic rate

Further weight loss becomes increasingly difficult as energy requirements fall along with metabolic rate

Too difficult to stick with diet (monotonous and hungry) and return to normal eating

Weight rapidly regained since energy requirements now considerably lower—fat regained but not lost muscle

Before you start the Action Plan

Remember, The Low GI Diet is not a fad diet. It is a serious diet and exercise program aimed at reducing body fat and *keeping it off for life*. Completing the Action Plan is the first step to better health and weight loss. It is followed by step two, 'Doing It For Life', which gives you the whole weight loss *tool kit*—an assortment of strategies and tips to make lifestyle change easier, incorporating food, exercise and behavioural change. The GI is just one of these tools but, nonetheless, an important one that makes a world of difference to your chances of successful long-term weight control.

The magic pill

'In the bottle before you is a pill, a marvel of modern medicine that will regulate gene transcription throughout your body, help prevent heart disease, stroke, diabetes, obesity, and 12 kinds of cancer—plus gallstones and diverticulitis (inflammation of the intestines). Expect the pill to improve your strength and balance as well as your blood lipid profile. Your bones will become stronger. You'll grow new capillaries in your heart, your skeletal muscles and your brain, improving blood flow and the delivery of oxygen and nutrients. Your attention span will increase. If you have arthritis, your symptoms will improve. The pill will help you regulate your appetite and you'll probably find you prefer healthier foods. You'll feel better, younger even, and you will test younger according to a variety of physiologic measures. Your blood volume will increase and you will burn fats better. Even your immune system will be stimulated. There is just one catch.

'There's no such pill. The prescription is exercise.'

Jonathan Shaw, *Harvard Magazine* (March–April 2004)

the Low GI Diet

PART TWO

the 12-week action plan

about the 12-week action plan

DURING THE '12-WEEK ACTION PLAN' YOU WILL LOSE
at least 250 grams of fat per week, most of it from around the waist. You
won't lose water or muscle, you will lose *pure body fat*. Week by week,
step by step, we advise you what to eat and do to get those kilos moving
and help you make good eating habits and physical activity a natural part
of your life. Each week's plan combines energy intake (the menus) with
energy output (a specific exercise and activity program) to help you use
exercise as a weight loss tool—to decrease your body fat and maximise
your metabolic rate during weight loss. To help you achieve this, we ask
you to focus on three goals each week:

- *The food goal* will make you aware of your current eating patterns
  and behaviour and help you identify areas where you can make
  changes for the better. It includes tips for putting our seven dietary
  guidelines into practice so that healthy eating simply becomes a way
  of life.

- *The exercise goal* includes a combination of aerobic and resistance
  exercises to increase fat-burning muscle and tone your body.

• *The activity goal* will show you ways to build more physical activity into your daily life. The single most important difference between long-term weight losers and weight gainers is the amount of activity they build into their day.

About the menu plans

Each week's sample menu is designed to illustrate appropriate food and meal choices to help you achieve a balanced low GI diet. You can follow the menus strictly if you wish, or vary them according to your tastes using the simple guidelines for creating balanced low GI meals on pages 213–16.

How much food is right for you?

We don't give you specific quantities of food in the menus. This is because we are all different. One restricted energy diet can't fit all because each one of us has different energy requirements that are affected by things such as how active we are, our size, how much muscle we have, whether we have a sedentary job or a physically demanding one, etc.

In The Low GI Diet we provide you with a choice of 10 different weight-based energy levels (5 for men and 5 for women). All you do is select the right energy level based on your current weight. This will give you the number of daily serves you need of carb-rich foods, protein-rich foods and the good fats to make sure you lose weight at a rate appropriate for you—and maximise your engine revs during weight loss. Whatever your energy level, everyone needs to eat five serves of vegetables and two serves of fruit every day. Here's how you do it:

Step 1: Identify the energy level that corresponds to your current weight.

Women		Men	
Weight (kg)	**Energy level**	**Weight (kg)**	**Energy level**
<70	1	<90	6
71–80	2	91–100	7
81–90	3	101–110	8
91–100	4	111–120	9
>100	5	>120	10

Step 2: Highlight the row that corresponds to your energy level—this gives you the recommended number of daily serves of each food type.

	Recommended number of daily serves		
Energy level	**Carb-rich foods**	**Protein-rich foods**	**Fat-rich foods**
1	3	3	2
2	4	4	2
3	5	5	3
4	6	6	3
5	7	7	3
6	8	8	4
7	9	9	4
8	10	10	4
9	11	11	5
10	12	12	5

Step 3: Plus five serves of vegetables and two serves of fruit every day.

Serving sizes

1 serve of vegetables

½ cup (75 g) cooked vegetables (other than potato, sweet potato
    and corn)

1 cup raw/salad vegetables

1 cup vegetable soup or juice

1 serve of fruit

1 medium piece or 2 small pieces (150 g) fresh fruit

1½ tablespoons sultanas, 4–5 dried apricots/figs/prunes (30 g dried fruit)

½ cup (125 ml) fruit juice

1 cup diced or canned fruit

Carb-rich foods: 1 serve provides 20–30 g carbohydrate

2 slices bread

1 cup breakfast cereal

½ cup oats or muesli

½ cup cooked rice or other small grains such as cracked wheat (bulgur)
    or couscous

1 cup cooked pasta or noodles

2 small potatoes or half a medium sweet potato (180 g)

½ cup corn, beans or chickpeas (can also count as a
    protein-rich food)

1 corn cob

Protein-rich foods: 1 serve provides 10–15 g protein

50 g raw lean meat, poultry, fish or seafood

3 slices (60 g) ham/pastrami/deli-sliced meat

50 g canned fish

1 cup skim milk

200 g carton low fat yoghurt

1 cup beans or chickpeas (can also count as a carb-rich food)

100 g tofu

2 eggs

Fat-rich foods: 1 serve provides 10 g fat

2 teaspoons (10 ml) oils

1 tablespoon oil and vinegar dressing

2 teaspoons (10 g) margarine/butter

3 teaspoons (15 g) reduced fat spread

3 teaspoons peanut butter*

30 g raw nuts or seeds*

2 tablespoons (40 g) reduced fat cream cheese*

40 g (2 pre-packed slices) reduced fat hard cheese*

30 g regular cheese*

*These foods are also good sources of protein, but have a particularly high fat content.

Do you prefer to let your appetite be your guide?

While we suggest that most people start off by measuring their serving sizes according to the previous tables, some prefer a less structured approach. If this sounds like you, you may be able to use your appetite as the best indicator of how much food you need. To ensure your meals are correctly balanced, follow these three simple steps when planning meals:

1 *Start* with your low GI carbohydrate.

2 *Add* a generous serve of vegetables or fruit.

3 *Plus* some protein for good measure with a little healthy fat if you wish.

Now all you need to do is adjust your proportions to match our 'plate'.

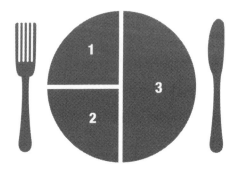

The plate model is adaptable to any serving sizes.

- Keep your daily serves of carb-rich, protein-rich and fat-rich foods to your appropriate energy level.
- Keep food to the proportions shown here on the plate, and your meals will be balanced.
- Choose foods that fit within the seven guidelines of The Low GI Diet (pages 47–64) and you should have a healthy diet overall.

How to apply your energy level to a daily menu

Following are two examples of dieters to illustrate how the menu plans work. Fiona and Dave both need to lose some weight. Fiona currently weighs 76 kilograms and is looking to lose 6 kilograms over the 12-week Action Plan. Dave weighs in at 115 kilograms and would like to lose about the same amount for starters—and keep it off. They want to be able to enjoy their meals together and on the Action Plan they can. Here's how.

According to the tables on page 73, Fiona is on level 2 and should be aiming to include four serves of carb-rich foods, four serves of protein-rich foods and two serves of fat-rich foods in addition to her five serves of vegetables and two of fruit each day.

If Dave ate the same amount as Fiona, he would be ravenously hungry and unlikely to stick with the Action Plan for long. All he needs to do is change the quantities of foods, sometimes adding extra foods for his size and energy requirements. Using the tables Dave sees that he is on energy level 9 and should be aiming to include 11 serves of carb-rich foods, 11 serves of protein-rich foods and five serves of fat-rich foods a day plus his five servings of vegetables and two of fruit.

A typical day for Fiona	Vegeta-bles	Fruit	Carb-rich foods	Protein-rich foods	Fat-rich foods
Breakfast: ½ cup muesli with ½ cup skim milk and a handful of sliced strawberries		1	1	½	
Lunch: 1 cup of tomato soup with a sandwich of 1 slice grainy bread with 3 slices ham, 1 cup salad vegies, flavoured with mustard	2		1	1	
Dinner: 100 g grilled salmon served with a cob of corn, 1 cup mixed bean salsa, 2 cups green salad and 1 tablespoon olive oil and vinegar dressing	2		2	2	1
Snacks: 1 cup fruit salad topped with ½ carton low fat yoghurt		1		½	
30 g almonds and 1 cup of vegetable juice	1				1
TOTALS	5	2	4	4	2

Fiona's day at a glance

Fiona's four serves of carbohydrate come from:

- ½ cup muesli (1 serve) at breakfast
- 1 slice bread (1) at lunchtime
- 1 corn cob (1) and 1 cup mixed bean salsa (1) at dinner

Her four serves of protein come from:

- ½ cup skim milk (½) at breakfast
- 3 slices ham (1) at lunchtime
- 100 grams salmon (2) at dinner
- Half a carton yoghurt (½) as a snack

Her two serves of fat come from:

- 1 tablespoon oil and vinegar dressing (1) at dinner
- 1 serve of nuts (1) as a snack

This day provides 5800 kilojoules, 85 grams of protein, 166 grams of carbohydrate, 40 grams of fat and 35 grams of fibre.

A typical day for Dave	Vegeta-bles	Fruit	Carb-rich foods	Protein-rich foods	Fat-rich foods
Breakfast: 1 cup muesli with 1 cup skim milk and a handful of sliced strawberries		1	2	1	
2 boiled eggs with 2 slices grainy toast spread with 2 teaspoons butter/margarine			1	1	1
Lunch: 1 cup tomato soup with 1 sandwiches of 2 slices grainy bread with 6 slices of ham, 2 cups salad vegies, flavoured with mustard	3		2	2	
Dinner: 200 g salmon grilled served with 2 cobs of corn, 1 cup mixed bean salsa, 3 cups green salad and 2 tablespoons olive oil and vinegar dressing plus 1 cup mashed sweet potato	3		4	4	2
Snacks: 1 cup fruit salad topped with 1 carton low fat yoghurt		1		1	
Grainy muffin topped with baked beans			2	1	
60 g almonds and a fruit smoothie made with 1 cup skim milk		1		1	2
TOTALS	**6**	**3**	**11**	**11**	**5**

Dave's day at a glance

Dave's 11 serves of carbohydrate come from:

- 1 cup muesli (2) and 2 slices toast (1) at breakfast
- 4 slices of bread (2) at lunchtime
- 2 corn cobs (2) and 1 cup bean salsa (2) at dinner
- 1 grainy muffin (1) with baked beans (1) as a snack

His 11 serves of protein come from:

- 1 cup skim milk (1) and 2 boiled eggs (1) for breakfast
- 6 slices lean ham (2) for lunch
- 200 grams grilled salmon (2) and 1 cup bean salsa (2) for dinner
- 1 carton low fat yoghurt (1), baked beans (1) and a smoothie made with 1 cup skim milk (1) as snacks

His four serves of fat come from:

- 2 teaspoons of margarine on his toast for breakfast (1)
- 2 tablespoons of olive oil and vinegar dressing on his salad at dinner (2)
- 60 grams almonds as a snack (2)

Dave's typical day has similar proportions of energy from protein, fat and carbohydrate, but larger quantities of each, providing 12 800 kilojoules, 190 grams of protein, 100 grams of fat, 348 grams of carbohydrate and 69 grams of fibre.

Re-evaluating your energy level

Of course, as you lose weight you may find that you move down an energy level—this is because with less weight to move around, your energy requirements also fall. Re-evaluate how much you should be eating every month to ensure the best success in reaching your goals.

Keeping your food intake in line with your needs

1. Listen to your body's cues for food intake.
2. Make sure you are eating foods in the correct proportions whether you are eating at home, out or away on business:
   - Start with a low GI carbohydrate.
   - Add a generous serve of vegetables or fruit.
   - Plus add some protein with a little healthy fat for good measure.
3. Make breakfast a priority—it really is the most important meal of the day.
4. Prepare the same meal for the whole family.
5. Eat well on weekends and holidays—think of it as an extension of your new healthier lifestyle.
6. When you know you will be eating and drinking more than usual, do some extra exercise beforehand.
7. When eating out, ask for water as soon as you arrive and send the bread basket away (unless it is exceptional or low GI).

About the exercise plans

To gain the most benefit from the exercises outlined in the Action Plan you need to work at an appropriate intensity—if the exercise feels too easy, you are not maximising your energy expenditure or the amount of fat burnt to fuel the exercise; if you try too hard you will struggle to keep going for the allocated time, you will find it uncomfortable and unenjoyable, and you are unlikely to keep it up on a regular basis.

You don't need fancy equipment such as heart rate monitors to measure your exercise intensity—all you need is a simple scale of how you feel. The Perceived Rate of Exertion (PRE) scale has been used for years by fitness instructors to guide their clients in their workouts. We will use a modified version of this scale to help you to maximise your fat loss and energy expenditure at each workout session. As you are exercising, ask yourself, on a scale of 1 to 10, how you are feeling, using the following table as a guide.

The good news is that during the 12-week Action Plan you will never be working above level 5. This means you will never need to experience intense or uncomfortable exercise. Levels of intensity above 5 are useful for people such as athletes who need to stretch their fitness levels to the extreme in order to improve their performance in their sport. Thankfully, if you are seeking the health benefits of exercise and aiming to lose body fat, working at the lower, more comfortable levels will better help you to reach your goals. In fact, in the early days of the program, you are going to be sticking to a PRE level of 3–4, the perfect level to improve your health and get you burning fat. As you progress and become fitter, we incorporate short sessions at level 5. This will help you to keep your weight under control for a lifetime as your body becomes a far more efficient fat-burning machine.

The exercise involved in the Action Plan incorporates both aerobic and resistance training:

- **Aerobic training** is any movement that gets you breathing a little harder—by definition, aerobic means 'using oxygen'. This sort of exercise works your heart and lungs and burns energy, helping you to increase your daily energy expenditure and burn body fat. We have opted to use walking as our aerobic exercise but cycling, running, swimming, aerobics, rowing and stepping are all good forms of aerobic exercise.

The PRE Scale

FOR HEALTH

1 At rest

2 Minimal exertion

3 Comfortable and could easily continue for some time

4 Starting to get a little breathless but relatively comfortable

FOR FITNESS

5 A little breathless and can feel heart rate elevated

6 Breathing harder, heart rate elevated but can still talk comfortably

7 Breathing hard, exercise much more difficult and cannot maintain for more than a few minutes

FOR PERFORMANCE

8 Much more intense and difficult to maintain, can only keep going at this intensity for a short time

9 Extremely intense exercise, cannot talk comfortably and breathing hard

10 Maximum intensity which can only be maintained for a few seconds

- **Resistance training** is any exercise that makes your muscles work against a resistance. This includes lifting weights, using resistance bands or simply using your own body weight as resistance. This sort of exercise is crucial to strengthen muscles, achieve and maintain good posture and tone your body. In addition, by building a little more lean muscle mass you increase your metabolic rate. As muscle is far more metabolically active than fat, the more muscle mass you have, the more energy you burn all of the time. To achieve fat loss and maintain that fat loss, resistance training offers great advantages and is an invaluable part of the Action Plan.

AT THE START OF EACH WEEK, GET OUT YOUR DIARY AND SCHEDULE IN AN EXACT TIME FOR ALL YOUR WALKS AND WORKOUTS. IF YOU LEAVE IT TO HAPPEN SPONTANEOUSLY, THE WEEK WILL BE OVER BEFORE YOU KNOW IT AND YOU WON'T HAVE STARTED.

Treat each exercise session as any other appointment and stick to it—if you have to postpone a session, make sure you reschedule it for another time. With the walking sessions, you have the option of breaking the walk into two shorter walks if you don't have enough time all at once. You could try doing ten minutes of walking first thing in the morning and the rest in the evening.

You won't need any specialist equipment. Simply wear comfortable, loose clothing and supportive walking shoes—trainers are perfect, or use any comfortable, supportive shoe you have.

While it is commonly thought that moving more quickly makes exercise harder, the opposite is in fact true for resistance exercise. To gain the best results from the resistance exercises, move slowly and focus on getting your technique spot-on. Try counting in seconds, taking two seconds to get to the end position and two seconds to get back to the start.

REMEMBER THAT *ANYTHING* YOU DO MORE THAN YOU ARE CURRENTLY DOING IS A STEP IN THE RIGHT DIRECTION.

Use the exercise plan as a guide and do as much as you can. If the weeks are progressing too quickly for you, simply stick with the same plan for a few more weeks, moving on to the next week's plan once you feel ready.

The resistance exercises may not be suitable for those with limiting injuries or conditions such as arthritis. If you feel pain at any time, you should stop the exercise. Consult a qualified personal trainer for an individualised program.

Week 1

Are you ready to begin? For this first week, focus on the following goals:

FOOD GOAL

Increase your awareness of what you eat and why.

EXERCISE GOAL

Aim to walk at a steady, comfortable pace for a total of 20 minutes on four days. *Plus* complete the two resistance exercises outlined on three days.

ACTIVITY GOAL

Rather than standing still on escalators and moving walkways, keep moving and walk to the end.

FOOD FOR THOUGHT

What is the GI of your diet?

> ### FOOD GOAL
>
> Increase your awareness of what you eat and why.

Your first dietary goal with the Action Plan is to keep a food diary (see page 361) to identify exactly what you usually eat and why you make the choices you do. You may think you already know what you eat, but there is nothing like writing it down to increase your awareness of all that you eat and drink.

Looking back over the record at the end of the week will enable you to compare your eating habits with The Low GI Diet recommended food choices (see pages 47–64) and serving sizes (see pages 74–76), and help you identify foods that you could substitute or minimise. A food diary can also reveal links between what you eat and the mood, environment or situations you find yourself in—we look at alleviating problem areas next week.

- Try to keep a diary, just for one week. You can keep it for longer if you wish, but it can become tedious and ends up being incomplete. One complete week is better than three sketchy weeks.
- Choose a normal week in your life—one that is representative of most weeks (not one where you are away on holidays, for example).
- Use a small notebook that you can take everywhere and write down everything you eat and drink as soon as possible after you have eaten it (or while you are eating it). Note where you are, what you are doing and how you feel.

You can also use the diary to write down your physical activity. We have included a template for your diary on page 361.

> ### EXERCISE GOAL
>
> Aim to walk at a steady, comfortable pace for a total of 20 minutes on four days. *Plus* complete the two resistance exercises outlined on three days.

Walking

Using the PRE scale on page 84, aim to walk at about level 3—this means you should feel comfortable at all times and be able to carry out a conversation while walking. You should feel warmer as the blood flow around the body increases, taking fuel to your working muscles—this means you are burning more fat and increasing your daily energy expenditure.

Resistance exercises

Lower body exercises	Upper body exercises	'Core' strength abdominals and back
Squats 2 sets of 10		Leg extensions 10 each leg

NEW EXERCISES

Squats

The squat is arguably the best lower body exercise you can do. The muscles of your thighs and bottom are the biggest muscle group in the body and this means exercises involving these muscles use the most energy—exactly what you want to help you lose body fat.

Strengthens and tones: thighs and bottom

How to do it:

1 Stand with your feet parallel and just wider than hip-distance apart. Extend your arms directly in front of you at chest height, with hands clasped.

2 Lengthen your spine by standing tall and pulling in your belly below the navel to support the lower back.

3 Imagine you have a chair behind you and sit back until you 'touch' the imaginary chair. As you sit back, make sure you keep your arms parallel to the floor and your chest 'proud'.

4 Squeeze your bottom muscles and push your heels into the floor to get back to the standing position.

Remember: Throughout the exercise, keep your weight on the back two-thirds of your feet: you should be able to wiggle your toes. One last thing—don't forget to breathe normally.

How many: 2 sets of 10 with a short rest in between

Single leg extensions

One of the most important groups of muscles for you to exercise are those involved in posture and back support. (These are the deep abdominal muscles that lie below the sixpack of stomach muscles you can see on the very lean men seen advertising unnecessary abdominal trainer machines.) They lie across your body and act like a belt, holding in your waist to provide support, particularly for the lower back. By working this group of muscles you develop core strength that will immediately improve your posture (making you look slimmer), reduce the risk of back pain and strengthen you from the inside out.

Strengthens and tones: the 'core' (deep abdominals)

How to do it:

1 Lie flat on your back on the floor with your knees bent in towards your chest, and arms by your sides with hands flat to the floor.
2 Pull in your belly as if trying to shorten the distance between your navel and spine—it should feel as if you are bracing the abdominal wall. Extend one leg out parallel to the floor while keeping the abdominals braced.
3 Bring the leg back in and repeat on the other side.

Remember: Breathe normally (it's easy to hold your breath subconsciously during this exercise).

How many: 20 (10 on each leg)

Sample diary

Monday	Tuesday	Wednesday	Thursday	Friday	Saturday	Sunday
	20 min walk		20 min walk		20 min walk	20 min walk
	+ resistance exercises		+ resistance exercises		+ resistance exercises	
	25 mins		25 mins		25 mins	20 mins

FOOD FOR THOUGHT

What is the GI of your diet?

Using the information from your food diary, answer the quiz below to gain a clearer idea of where you need to make changes to lower the GI of your diet.

QUIZ: What is the GI of your diet?

Simply circle the option that most closely matches your usual diet.

1 The type of bread I most often eat is

   a a grainy low GI variety (see page 51 for examples)

   b sourdough or 'health' loaf

   c regular white or wholemeal sandwich bread

2 The type of breakfast cereal I usually eat is

   a traditional rolled oats, muesli, or a commercial low GI type

   b a higher fibre commercial cereal such as wheat biscuits or flakes

   c A low fibre puffed or flaked cereal

3 I eat 2 or more different pieces of fruit

   a most days

   b 3–4 days a week

   c 1–2 days a week

4 I eat legumes (including baked beans, lentils, chickpeas, kidney beans, salad beans, etc.) or barley

   a 2 or more times a week

   b once a week

   c rarely or never

5 I eat pasta or noodles

   a 2 or more times a week

   b once a week

   c rarely or never

6 I eat sweet potato and/or sweet corn as whole or partial substitutes for potato

   a 2 or more times a week

   b once a week

   c rarely or never

7 Of the following serves of food:

- 1 cup milk (any type)
- 1 cup yoghurt (any type)
- ½ cup custard
- 2 scoops low fat ice-cream

I would eat at least 2 serves

a most days
b 3–4 days a week
c 1–2 days a week or less

Your score card:

Score 1 point for each time you answered (**a**)

Score 2 points for each time you answered (**b**)

Score 3 points for each time you answered (**c**)

If your total was:

7–10   Well done—your diet is likely to have a low GI. The carbohydrate foods you have indicated you eat most frequently are low GI choices. You may still need to consider serving sizes to facilitate weight loss. Keep reading because there is lots more to a healthy low GI diet than low GI foods alone.

11–17   Your diet is likely to have an intermediate GI. This is the same as the average diet of most people in Western countries. You have indicated that you eat a mixture of low, medium and possibly high GI carbohydrate choices, and, while variety is good, high GI foods may be hindering your efforts at weight loss. Choosing more foods that fit option (a) will reduce the GI of your diet.

18–21   Your diet is likely to have a high GI. Many of your carbohydrate choices have high GI values, increasing your insulin demand and keeping your body in a state that favours fat storage. In order to lose weight it will be beneficial to swap at least half of your high GI carb foods for those with a low GI. Choosing more foods that fit option (a) will reduce the GI of your diet.

Week 1 Menu Plan

	BREAKFAST	SNACK
MONDAY	Grainy toast with peanut butter (no butter) and a glass of fruit or vegetable juice	Canned fruit snack pack
TUESDAY	Grainy toast with low fat cheese	A banana
WEDNESDAY	Low fat milk coffee or hot chocolate with raisin toast	Dried fruit and nut mix
THURSDAY	Natural muesli with low fat milk, topped with fruit and no fat yoghurt	A banana
FRIDAY	High fibre cereal with low fat milk and fruit	An apple
SATURDAY	Sautéed mushrooms with parsley and shallots, low GI toast and a poached egg	A mandarin
SUNDAY	A boiled egg, lean bacon, tomato, mushrooms and baked beans, and a glass of vegetable juice	Small fruit smoothie

LUNCH	SNACK	DINNER
Sourdough rye with roast beef, horseradish, sliced tomato and snowpea sprouts	Reduced fat cheddar cheese with an apple and grainy crackers	Baked white fish fillets with chopped parsley. Serve with chopped spinach and lemon, yellow squash, carrots and a couple of baby new potatoes. Low fat yoghurt
Tuna, celery, onion, tomato and olives tossed in balsamic vinaigrette with lettuce and grainy crackers	Low fat yoghurt	Vegetable Frittata (see page 278) and tossed salad. Baked apple and low fat custard
Avocado, chicken and lettuce wrap	Frooh fruit	Lean steak with mushrooms, sweet potato mash, green beans and zucchini
Salad with lettuce, celery, apple, walnuts, mayonnaise and tuna	Low fat ice-cream in a cone	Tuna with canned tomatoes, artichoke quarters, kalamata olives, garlic, sliced zucchini and tomato paste tossed through spiral pasta
Chinese combination long soup	Low fat yoghurt	Pork and vegetable (broccoli, carrot, capsicum and onion) stir-fry with cashew nuts and Doongara rice
Toasted soy and linseed English muffins bread with creamed corn, sliced fresh mushrooms and a sprinkle of grated cheese, heated under the grill	Oatmeal biscuits	Lamb roast with mint sauce, baked sweet potato, pumpkin, onion and steamed peas, beans and cauliflower. Fresh fruit salad
Thai beef salad made with lean beef strips, mixed salad greens and a dressing of chilli, garlic, lime juice, brown sugar and Thai fish sauce, sprinkled with cellophane noodles	A small handful of almonds	Minestrone soup. A low fat yoghurt and fruit

Week 2

Being overweight is *not* about lacking willpower, and if you have ever been on a diet you will know that to be the case. Changing habits that are ingrained in our daily lives is extremely difficult and takes time (about a year to be exact!). Through Week 1 the focus was on becoming more aware of what you eat and starting to incorporate more low GI foods in your diet. This week we help you pinpoint your bad habits and set goals that will lead you towards healthier habits. Your goals to work on this week are:

FOOD GOAL

Pinpoint your bad habits and set three SMART food goals.

EXERCISE GOAL

Aim to walk at a steady, comfortable pace for 20 minutes on four days. *Plus* complete the three resistance exercises outlined on three days.

ACTIVITY GOAL

For all short journeys that would take less than five minutes in the car, walk instead.

FOOD FOR THOUGHT

Time for a change.

FOOD GOAL

Pinpoint your bad habits and set three SMART food goals.

Having put in the effort and recorded your eating patterns last week, you now have the opportunity to identify the eating habits that you're going to change. Making changes begins with setting goals. Ideally your goals should be Specific, Measurable, Achievable, Realistic and Time-specific.

For example, it is unrealistic to set the goal 'I'll stop eating chocolate' and may be unachievable to say 'I will take my lunch from home every day'. These all-or-nothing goals tend to set us up for failure and are not helpful in achieving long-term changes.

Examples of SMART goals in these instances:

- I will allow myself a chocolate bar once a month.
- I will start preparing my own lunch to take to work on Mondays and Tuesdays.

Habits that you want to change may also relate to your eating behaviour. The following checklist is to help you identify problem eating behaviours. Referring back to your food diary if you need to, tick off any of the following that are regular events for you.

❏   Too many snacks

❏   Irregular meals

❏   Nibbling all day

❏   Eat while watching television

❏   Eat when preparing food

❏   Serve or am served more than I need, but eat it anyway

❏   Impulse-buy unplanned foods

☐　Eat when not hungry, but because I'm either bored, tired, depressed or angry

☐　Eat out too often

☐　Eat when driving or travelling

☐　Eat too fast

☐　Linger at the table, eating more even though I'm satisfied

☐　Go back for seconds

☐　Overeat night snacks

☐　Always finish plate even if I feel full

☐　Drink too much alcohol

☐　Buy foods for the family that I don't intend eating, but can't resist

Now, given your checklist of problem eating behaviours and your food diary, select two or three of your eating habits or food choices that you would like to change and brainstorm possible solutions.

Set yourself three goals relating to what or how you eat. Remember, your goals must be relevant to you and your situation, and should be specific, measurable, achievable, realistic and time-specific. Commit to these goals, trying to adhere to them as much as you can. At the end of the week, think about how successful you were in sticking to your goal. Did it work for you? Are you willing to keep it going? If the answer is no, then try setting another goal, based on a different solution to your habits and keep experimenting until you find the change that works for you.

YOUR GOALS SHOULD BE:

- **specific**
- **measurable**
- **achievable**
- **realistic**
- **time-specific**

EXERCISE GOAL

Aim to walk at a steady, comfortable pace for 20 minutes on four days. *Plus* complete the three resistance exercises outlined on three days.

Resistance exercises

Lower body exercises	Upper body exercises	'Core' strength abdominals and back
Squats 2 sets of 10	Assisted push-ups 2 sets of 10	Leg extensions 10 each leg

NEW EXERCISE
Assisted push-ups

The push-up is undeniably one of the best upper body exercises you can do. The push-up involves the muscles of the chest, shoulders and arms and is therefore an efficient means of toning the upper body all at once.

Why do most people hate push-ups? The answer is easy—because they are hard! In fact, they are even harder if you are carrying too much body weight since you are effectively lifting your own body weight against gravity. Here is a modified version of the traditional push-up, which enables you to gain the benefits of the exercise but makes it easier for you to perform it correctly. You will need a low coffee table—alternatively, use the second or third bottom step of your stairs.

Strengthens and tones: chest, shoulders and arms

How to do it:

1 Start in a kneeling position with your hands wider than your shoulders on the edge of the table/stair. Move your knees back until your body is a straight diagonal line from head to knee.

2 Slowly lower your chest towards the edge of the table/stair while keeping your back flat and without letting your bottom stick up.

3 At the bottom of the move, your elbows should be directly above your hands—adjust your hand position as appropriate before returning slowly to the starting position.

How many: 2 sets of 10 repetitions with a short rest in between

Sample diary

Monday	Tuesday	Wednesday	Thursday	Friday	Saturday	Sunday
	20 min walk		20 min walk		20 min walk	20 min walk
	+ resistance exercises		+ resistance exercises		+ resistance exercises	
	25 mins		25 mins		25 mins	20 mins

FOOD FOR THOUGHT

Time for a change.

The fact that you are reading this very page suggests that you are at least *contemplating* making some changes to the way you eat. People don't make changes instantaneously; they work their way up to it gradually, often going through definable stages. A description of the stages of change in relation to our eating habits looks like this:

Pre-contemplation

At this stage you're not thinking about changing your eating habits; what you're doing is appropriate for *you* at this time in your life. You could read this book and then put it away for later reference.

Contemplation

Now you're beginning to think about change but just haven't got around to it. Weigh up the benefits and costs of making a change. If the benefits outweigh the costs, then you're ready to move on to preparation.

Preparation

Now you have decided to change and are preparing to do so. Attempting change without prior planning makes relapse more likely. So, ask yourself, what do you think you can change?

↓

Action

You are now actually in the throes of making changes to the way you eat. Your goals ought to be SMART—Specific, Measurable, Achievable, Realistic and Time-specific, for example:

- Every two days buy four nice pieces of fresh fruit to eat.
- Buy and use only fat-reduced milk for the next month as a trial.

Your goals must be relevant to you and your situation, so checking back through your food diary could be a good place from which to plan your behaviour changes.

↓

Maintenance

At this point you're committed to maintaining your changes and have no desire to return to your old ways. You face relapses every so often but getting through them will lead to your changes becoming your new healthy habits.

Identifying at which stage you are currently should help you move forward to the next stage.

At what stage of change are you?

Circle the answer that best fits you and identify the stage you are at using the key below.

Have you been trying to lose weight?

a Yes, I have been working on losing weight for more than 3 months.

b Yes, I have been trying to lose weight within the last 3 months.

c No, but I intend to make a start.

d No, and I do not intend to at the moment.

Key:

Answer (**a**) = maintenance stage

Answer (**b**) = action stage

Answer (**c**) = contemplation/preparation stage

Answer (**d**) = pre-contemplation stage

A word of warning: change can be difficult and changing the way you eat is no exception. Even with all the good will in the world, celebrations, cheesecakes, cravings, nights out or chocolate will always be lurking around the corner just waiting to test your resolve. It might help to bear in mind that normal, healthy eating includes all foods, and 'lapses' are just a normal part of change.

Our tips for approaching dietary change

1 Aim to make changes gradually. Acknowledge your stage of change.

2 Attempt the easiest changes first. Nothing inspires like success!

3 Break big changes into a number of smaller changes.

4 Accept lapses in your habits as a characteristic of being human.

If you feel like you need some extra help in changing the way you eat, seek out professional assistance from an accredited practising dietitian (APD). (For details on finding an APD near you, see page 263.)

Week 2 Menu Plan

	BREAKFAST	SNACK
MONDAY	Fruit loaf lightly spread with ricotta cheese and jam	An apple and a few almond
TUESDAY	Multigrain English muffin with scrambled egg and a tomato juice	2 kiwi fruit
WEDNESDAY	Grainy toast with hazelnut spread and an apple	Small handful of unsalted n
THURSDAY	Low fat vanilla yoghurt with sliced fresh nectarine and strawberries, topped with muesli	An Apricot and Almond Co (see page 315)
FRIDAY	Low GI cereal topped with sliced pears, low fat milk and a freshly squeezed orange juice	2 ginger nut biscuits
SATURDAY	Lean grilled bacon with sliced tomato on grainy toast	A low fat fruit yoghurt
SUNDAY	Porridge with a garnish of frozen or fresh berries, low fat natural yoghurt and a sprinkle of brown sugar	A slice of raisin toast

UNCH	SNACK	DINNER
am and salad grainy roll, skim milk te	Wedge of melon	Moroccan-style Lentil and Vegetable Stew with Couscous (see page 308)
reek salad with low fat feta and olives d a small grainy roll	Some low fat ice-cream	Tandoori chicken with Basmati rice, lentil dhal and cucumber raita plus a mango lassi
asted sourdough with avocado, ced tomato and grilled lean bacon or uble smoked ham	Fresh orange quarters	Lamb shish kebabs with garlic and tahini sauce served with tabbouli and pieces of flatbread
arden salad with sliced chicken breast	Fresh pear	Spinach and ricotta cannelloni with pine nuts and tomato sauce. Serve with a mixed green salad with vinaigrette
holemeal Lebanese bread with aved ham, grated carrot, shredded tuce, sliced tomato, low fat grated eese and mayonnaise	Fruit salad	Cook a whole fish, such as snapper, by wrapping in two layers of foil and cook on the barbecue for 25–30 minutes. Serve with roasted sweet potato wedges
na, onion, lettuce and cheese on a ainy roll	Fruit and nut mix	Prawn and Mango Salad with Chilli Lime Dressing (see page 306). A wedge of melon with a scoop of low fat ice-cream
cos topped with Mexican beans, ced tomato, shredded lettuce, ocado and grated reduced fat eese	An apple	Barbecued steak with roast vegetable salad and green salad

Week 3

Unless you have diabetes and are diligent about testing your blood glucose levels, you are probably completely unaware of your own glucose fluctuations over the course of a day. Yet this can have a major effect on what, how much and when you eat, as well as whether you store or burn body fat. This week, focus on these goals:

FOOD GOAL
Minimise your blood glucose fluctuations by getting the smart carbs going.

EXERCISE GOAL
Aim to walk at a steady, comfortable pace (level 3 on the PRE scale) for a total of 20 minutes on five days. *Plus* complete the four resistance exercises on three days.

ACTIVITY GOAL
Arrange a social activity for the weekend that does not involve food or drink, but something active instead. Why not try going to the golf driving range, cycling in the park or ten-pin bowling with a bunch of friends.

FOOD FOR THOUGHT
Why your blood glucose level is so important.

FOOD GOAL

Minimise your blood glucose fluctuations by getting the smart carbs going.

Want to keep your engine running smoothly all day? Then *slow release* low GI smart carbs are the ones for you. The slow digestion of low GI carbs trickles fuel into your system at a steady rate, reducing insulin levels and minimising blood glucose fluctuations. This small change can potentially make a huge difference to your waistline in the long term. It's the starchy carb staples in your diet that have the greatest impact—so check you are eating the right carbs using the following table.

Starchy staples	Minimise these high GI choices	Use these low GI varieties instead
The bread you eat	Soft white breads	Sourdough
	Light and airy, smooth-textured white and wholemeal bread	Dense, grainy breads
	Scones, pikelets, dampers	Fruit bread
The cereals in your pantry	Refined, commercial processed cereals	Traditional rolled oats and barley-based cereals
Main meal carbs	Potatoes: mashed, chips and French fries	Sweet potato, sweet corn, pasta, noodles, butter beans, lentils, chickpeas
	Jasmine, brown and Arborio rice	Basmati, Doongara, koshihikari (sushi) rice
The foods you snack on	Light and crispy crackers, doughnuts, pretzels	Fresh or dried fruit, low fat yoghurt and nuts

Base your food goals this week around making your starchy staples the smart low GI types.

EXERCISE GOAL

Aim to walk at a steady, comfortable pace (level 3 on the PRE scale)

for a total of 20 minutes on five days. *Plus* complete

the four resistance exercises on three days.

Resistance exercises

Lower body exercises	Upper body exercises	'Core' strength abdominals and back
Squats 2 sets of 10	Assisted push-ups 2 sets of 10	Leg extensions 10 each leg
Lunges 10 each leg		

NEW EXERCISE
Lunges

This week we add one more exercise for the lower body. Lunges are a little more difficult than squats because one leg has to work harder. Again, they are very effective at working the thighs and bottom, with the lower leg also doing some work for a complete lower body workout. The most common mistake is to have your feet too close together, which makes it difficult to lunge without bringing your weight forward over the front foot—aim for a long stride and work on keeping the upper body upright with your chest proud. Use a broom handle or the back of a chair to help with balance when you first do this exercise; as you become stronger you will be able to complete the exercise without assistance.

Strengthens: bottom and legs

How to do it:

1 Stand with your feet hip-width apart and then step one foot back in a long stride behind you. Your feet should still be parallel—you should not feel like you are tightrope walking, but in a strong, tall stance.

2 Centre your body weight between your feet and tuck your hips under to maintain a long, strong spine. Slowly drop your body weight down until your front thigh is parallel to the floor and the back knee is under your hip.

3 Push your front heel into the floor to push you back to the top.

Remember: Your back heel should not touch the floor during the exercise—you should be up on the ball of your foot throughout the motion.

How many: 10 lunges on each leg

Sample diary

Monday	Tuesday	Wednesday	Thursday	Friday	Saturday	Sunday
20 min walk	20 min walk		20 min walk		20 min walk	20 min walk
	+ resistance exercises		+ resistance exercises		+ resistance exercises	
20 mins	30 mins		30 mins		30 mins	20 mins

FOOD FOR THOUGHT

Why your blood glucose level is so important.

A normal blood glucose level is the difference between life and death—literally. A low blood glucose level can result in coma and death within minutes. A high blood glucose level will kill you too but the process takes years. If a high blood glucose condition is not treated, it will result in blindness, heart disease and kidney failure. Unless you have diabetes or its predecessor (pre-diabetes), such morbid thoughts won't trouble you.

In healthy individuals blood glucose levels are held automatically within a fairly narrow range (between 3 and 10 millimoles per litre). They go up and down when we eat; if we skip a meal (or exclude carbs), the liver draws on its reserves of carbohydrates. When those run out, the liver will make glucose using building blocks from the breakdown of protein and fat stores. The reason for such fine control is that glucose is virtually the sole fuel of our metabolically expensive brain. Without glucose, it shuts down and everything else grinds to a halt, too.

How and why high blood glucose spells trouble

One in four adults (especially those with excess fat around the middle) has undesirably high blood glucose levels. Every time they eat, their blood glucose increases rapidly and stays high for the following two to three hours. During that time, excess glucose circulates to all the tissues and organs around the body. The cells lining the blood vessels and those in the eyes and kidneys are extremely vulnerable because they can't control the amount of glucose that enters them. The end result is oxidative stress caused by highly reactive oxygen molecules. These 'free radicals' inflame cells, eventually causing swelling, scarring, thickening, hardening and the inability to dilate and contract as needed. In time, the chances of a small blood clot lodging and blocking a narrow artery increases. If it happens in a major vessel of the heart, you have a heart attack on your hands. If it's a minor vessel in the heart, it causes chest pain (angina). If it happens in the brain, it's called a stroke.

But that's not all: high blood glucose levels affect the function of many proteins and enzymes, such that the chances of dying prematurely from any cause are higher. You don't need to be in the diabetic range to be at risk. High glucose and insulin levels fuel the growth of abnormal cells that cause various types of cancer—breast, colon, endometrial and pancreatic—which have all been associated with high blood glucose.

High glucose levels also spell trouble for weight control because insulin will be secreted in an effort to bring glucose down. High insulin in turn causes insulin resistance, causing even higher insulin levels— a vicious cycle. Insulin drives glucose into the 'engines' in each cell, forcing them to burn glucose and pushing fat to the side. In time, fat accumulates all around the body—in the blood (causing high triglycerides), in the liver (causing fatty liver) and in the abdomen (causing the most dangerous form of excess body fat).

Rapid rises and falls in blood glucose are also blamed for increasing appetite. The suddenly low glucose level stimulates the release of stress hormones such as cortisol which stimulate hunger, causing you to think about the next meal. Studies show that slowly digested and absorbed low GI smart carbs induce greater satiety, delaying the time to the next meal and/or reducing energy intake in comparison to their quickly digested counterparts.

HIGH GLUCOSE LEVELS SPELL TROUBLE FOR WEIGHT CONTROL

Week 3 Menu Plan

	BREAKFAST	SNACK
MONDAY	Natural muesli with low fat yoghurt and peach slices	Whole-wheat crackers and low fat sliced cheese
TUESDAY	Multigrain English muffin melts: top with creamed corn, sliced mushrooms and low fat mozzarella	2 kiwi fruit or mandarins
WEDNESDAY	Grainy toast spread with your favourite nut butter, plus a bowl of fresh chopped melon	Fresh carrot and pineapple juice
THURSDAY	Fruit and nut bar and a skim milk cappuccino	A handful of cherries or oth small fruit
FRIDAY	Egg flip made with low fat milk, whole egg, vanilla and sugar	An apple
SATURDAY	Sweet corn fritters with fried tomato and onion	A bunch of grapes
SUNDAY	Sautéed mushrooms with parsley and shallots on low GI toast with a poached egg	A small banana

LUNCH	SNACK	DINNER
Pasta salad with canned corn, peas, diced red capsicum, grated carrot, chopped tomato and mayonnaise	Small handful of almonds	Pan-fry a lean steak then deglaze pan by adding a little red wine, beef stock and 1 teaspoon Dijon mustard. Simmer for a minute then pour over steaks. Serve with steamed or microwaved new potatoes and broccoli
Flat bread with hommous, tabbouli salad and felafel	Low fat banana smoothie	Dust boneless fish fillets (e.g. ocean peach) in cornflour. Melt 1 teaspoon margarine in a frypan and add the juice of an orange and a lemon. Add the fish, cover and poach until starting to flake, turning once. Serve with steamed vegetables
Canned tuna with lettuce, tomato, cucumber, feta, olives and balsamic dressing with a grainy roll	A bunch of grapes	Eggplant and Zucchini Pilaf with Lamb (see pages 297–98), plus a low fat fruit yoghurt
Sweet potato salad: grilled red capsicum with steamed sweet potato and salad greens in balsamic dressing	Grainy toast and chocolate hazelnut spread	Tomato and onion omelette with green salad, plus sliced pineapple and low fat ice-cream
Cheese, tomato, lettuce, beetroot and grated carrot on a grainy sandwich	Low fat yoghurt	Chicken and Rice Salad (see page 293)
Stir-fry Asian mixed vegetables with cubed firm tofu and garlic, ginger, soy sauce and honey, stirred through hokkien noodles	A handful of popcorn and a small orange juice	Rosemary-studded rack of lamb with sweet potato mash, green beans and slow-roasted tomatoes, plus a low fat chocolate mousse
Salmon frittata with tomato onion salsa, salad greens and a slice of sourdough bread	Fruit with a scoop of low fat ice-cream	Vegetarian (bean) nachos made with salt-reduced oven-baked corn chips, served with avocado salsa

Week 4

You are four weeks into the Action Plan now, so it is a good time to re-evaluate your food quantities based on your current weight, using the tables on page 73.

Focus on the following goals this week:

FOOD GOAL

Lowering the GI of your diet with less processed foods.

EXERCISE GOAL

Aim to walk at a slightly more brisk, but still comfortable pace (level 4 of the PRE scale), for a total of 20 minutes on five days. *Plus* try to complete each of the two resistance workouts, focusing on the upper and lower body respectively, twice during the week.

ACTIVITY GOAL

Whenever you are talking on the telephone, stand up, pace the floor and have a stretch.

FOOD FOR THOUGHT

How and why foods vary in their GI.

FOOD GOAL

Lowering the GI of your diet with less processed foods.

Porridge, barley, split peas and lentils are remnants from our grandparents' generation that once served us so well. Today we recognise these as some of the lowest GI foods—high in fibre, rich in nutrients, bulky and filling—it is a shame they dwindled in popularity. Once, a hearty bowl of porridge was enough to sustain a person through their morning; now, many people rely on a quick bowl of crispy light flakes. This highly processed alternative is digested so quickly that it spikes blood glucose and insulin levels and leaves you hungry by mid-morning.

This week, consider how many processed foods you rely on and come up with alternatives. Wise ways to lower the GI of your diet include:

- Choose less processed starchy foods—use rolled oats, pearl barley, lentils, split peas and chickpeas. Limit commercial crackers, biscuits and cakes.
- Look for low GI snacks such as low fat yoghurts, fresh fruit, dried fruit and nut mix, and low fat milk.
- Combine high GI with low GI foods to produce an intermediate overall GI—lentils plus rice, tabbouli plus bread and potato mixed with sweet potato.
- Add a little acid to your meal—vinaigrette with salad, yoghurt with cereal, lemon juice on vegetables, sourdough bread. All of these contain acids, which slows stomach emptying and lowers your blood glucose response to the carbohydrate with which they are eaten.

AIM FOR AT LEAST ONE SMART LOW GI CARB PER MEAL.

EXERCISE GOAL

Aim to walk at a slightly more brisk, but still comfortable pace (level 4 of the PRE scale), for a total of 20 minutes on five days. *Plus* try to complete each of the two resistance workouts, focusing on the upper and lower body respectively, twice during the week.

Resistance exercises

We have now split the resistance training into two workouts. The first focuses on the lower body and the second on the upper body. The 'core' abdominals and back are worked in each one as these areas are so important for your posture and strength.

Workout 1	Lower body exercises	'Core' strength abdominals and back
	Squats 2 sets of 10	Three-quarter hover 2 x 20 seconds
	Lunges 10 each leg	
Workout 2	Upper body exercises	
	Assisted push-ups 2 sets of 10	Leg extensions 10 each leg
	Standing tricep extensions 2 sets of 10	

NEW EXERCISES

Three-quarter hover

This exercise is fantastic for developing core strength and narrowing your waist. It may feel quite challenging to start with, but you will be amazed at how quickly you improve and reap the rewards of your efforts.

Strengthens and tones: waist

How to do it:

1 Lie face-down on the floor with your toes turned under and prop yourself up on your elbows.

2 Now lift your hips until they are in line with your shoulders and feet—it's important to make sure you don't stick your bottom out but maintain a straight line through the body from shoulder to knee.

3 As you hold the position think of narrowing your waist and breathe normally throughout.

How long: Hold the hover position for 20 seconds, rest for a few moments and then repeat for a further 20 seconds.

Standing tricep extensions

The back of the upper arms is a common problem area for women in particular—we tend to store body fat here and lack muscle tone. You will need a weight to provide resistance in this exercise. You can buy small hand-held weights at any good sports shop or department store. Alternatively, improvise from your kitchen cupboard: a bag of rice or an unopened can can be used as a good starting weight—anything around the 400-gram mark.

Strengthens and tones: the back of the upper arm

How to do it:

1 Stand tall and hold the weight overhead with both hands, with your arms straight. Make sure you are standing with good posture and eyes straight ahead, rather than looking up at the weight.

2 Keeping your arms close to your ears, lower the weight behind your head.

3 Keeping the upper arm still, lift the weight back to the top.

How many: 2 sets of 10 with a short rest between sets

Sample diary

Monday	Tuesday	Wednesday	Thursday	Friday	Saturday	Sunday
20 min walk	20 min walk		20 min walk		20 min walk	20 min walk
+ workout 1	+ workout 2		+ workout 1		+ workout 2	
25 mins	25 mins		25 mins		25 mins	20 mins

FOOD FOR THOUGHT

How and why foods vary in their GI.

From a weight loss point of view, the longer the process of digestion takes and the more gradual the rise and fall in blood glucose, the better. You don't have to eat all your carbs in low GI forms. Studies have shown that when a low and a high GI food are combined in one meal (such as lentils and rice), the overall blood glucose response is intermediate between the two. You can keep both glucose and insulin levels lower over the course of the whole day if you choose at least one low GI food at each meal.

What determines a food's GI value?

The speed with which carbs reach the blood stream has little to do with sugar or fibre content. In fact, many sugary foods produce lower blood glucose responses—gram for gram of carbohydrate—than many wholemeal products. By far the most important factor is the physical state of the starch in a food. If the starch granules have swollen and burst, that food will be digested in a flash. On the other hand, if they are still present in their 'native' state as found in the raw food, then the process of digestion will take much longer. Advances in food processing over the past 100 years have had a profound effect on the overall GI values of the carbohydrates we eat.

How do we know if a food is low GI?

The only sure way of knowing the GI value of a food is by measuring it. This means having a group of volunteers eat the food in a controlled setting and comparing their blood glucose levels after the food with their levels after the same carbohydrate load of a standard food, such as glucose. It is a lengthy and labour-intensive procedure, but at least 1500 foods have already been tested and more are being tested all the time in laboratories around the world.

Watch out for this symbol on foods! It is your guarantee that the GI value on the label is correct (it has been tested by an accredited laboratory). This will also assure you that the food makes a nutritious contribution to your diet. Visit the website for more details: **www.gisymbol.com.au**.

Factors that influence the GI of a food

Carbohydrate

Remember, only carbohydrate foods have GI values. So any food that is high in carbohydrate has a measurable GI value, but you can't guess what it is without testing it by the standard procedure. If the carbohydrate is predominantly in the form of starch, particularly cooked starch, the food is likely to have a high GI.

Example: cooked flour products such as bread, pancakes and doughnuts

Fat

Fat tends to slow down stomach emptying so high fat foods often have lower GI values. This doesn't necessarily make high fat foods good for you.

Example: potato chips, french fries

Protein

If your carbohydrate food is also high in protein, its GI may be lower thanks to slower digestion or a higher insulin response.

Example: Kellogg's® Special K®

Acidity

Just like fat, acid tends to slow down stomach emptying and lowers the GI of carbohydrate foods with which it is eaten. Sometimes the food itself is acidic by nature.

Example: vinaigrette on salad with bread

Soluble fibre

Although you can't see soluble fibre in food, the way it increases the viscosity of your intestinal contents will slow down carbohydrate digestion and lower the GI.

Example: rolled oats

Is it as nature intended?

The less processed the food, the more likely it is to have a low GI. The intact seed coat around wholegrains contributes to their low GI.

Example: legumes such as beans, chickpeas and lentils

Sugar

Just because a food is sweet, it doesn't make it high GI. The GI depends on the type of sugar and the other sources of carbohydrate in the food. Table sugar or sucrose has an intermediate GI.

Week 4 Menu Plan

	BREAKFAST	SNACK
MONDAY	Traditional rolled oat porridge	A handful of peanuts in the shell
TUESDAY	Half a grapefruit followed by boiled eggs with sourdough toast	An orange
WEDNESDAY	Natural muesli with sliced apple, low fat milk and natural yoghurt	A handful of dried apricots
THURSDAY	Fruit salad with low fat natural yoghurt and a sprinkle of mixed nuts and seeds	Low fat flavoured milk
FRIDAY	Traditional rolled oats topped with fresh or frozen raspberries and low fat natural yoghurt	Low fat fruit yoghurt
SATURDAY	Poached eggs with wilted spinach, grilled tomato and dry-fried mushrooms with a slice of grainy bread	A cup of vegetable soup
SUNDAY	Heavy fruit toast with low fat cream cheese and finely sliced apple or pear	A handful of cherries

LUNCH	SNACK	DINNER
Bowl of minestrone soup with grainy bread dipped in a teaspoon of olive oil	A pear	Grilled lean lamb fillets sliced and served on a sweet potato salad and topped with a spoonful of tzatziki
Mixed box of sushi with miso soup	Small handful of dried fruit and nut mix	Grilled salmon fillet with mashed sweet potato and steamed broccoli, green beans and carrots
Toasted grainy bread topped with a small can of baked beans and served with a raw tomato	Slice of multigrain toast with a teaspoon of peanut butter	Cover a skinless chicken breast with a basic tomato sauce (ready-made pasta sauce is fine) and bake for 30 minutes. Serve with a steamed ear of corn, wilted spinach and dry-fried mushrooms
Fill a wholemeal pita bread with hommous, tabbouli, lettuce and sliced tomato	Fresh fruit	Chilli con carne made with premium beef mince and kidney beans, served with steamed Doongara or Basmati rice and a large green salad
Steak sandwich—grilled minute steak in multigrain bread with lettuce, beetroot, grated carrot, tomato and mustard	Carrot sticks with hommous dip	Bake a firm white fish fillet in white wine, lemon juice, chopped ginger, garlic and coriander for 20 minutes. Serve with steamed koshihikari rice and stir-fried Asian greens in oyster sauce
Lentil soup with grainy bread and low fat cheese	Strawberries topped with natural yoghurt and some flaked toasted almonds	Grill a chicken breast, slice and serve over a small bowl of pasta in tomato sauce accompanied by a large green salad
Tuna salad with rocket, shallots, baby beets, olives, cherry tomatoes, cucumber, blanched green beans and capsicum, drizzled with a little olive oil and balsamic vinegar dressing	Muesli and Honey Slice (see page 316)	Grilled or barbecued pork skewers marinated in spicy sauce. Serve with a large mixed salad and a few baby new potatoes

Week 5

We have already learnt that low GI foods keep us full for longer and this week we focus on how protein-rich foods can also help. Focus on the following goals this week:

FOOD GOAL

Incorporate a lean protein source in every meal.

EXERCISE GOAL

Aim to walk at the same pace as last week (level 4 of
the PRE scale) for a total of 20 minutes on six days. *Plus* try to complete
each of the two resistance workouts, focusing on the upper and
lower body respectively, three times during the week.

ACTIVITY GOAL

Whenever there is the option of taking the stairs, the lift or an escalator,
choose to take the stairs for at least one flight. If you are heading for the 12th
floor of a building, for example, take the stairs to the first floor before taking
the lift the rest of the way.

FOOD FOR THOUGHT

The real deal on protein and health.

FOOD GOAL

Incorporate a lean protein source in every meal.

Clearly the best foods for weight control would be those that filled you up and stopped you from getting hungry again too quickly. Protein-rich foods tend to be the most satiating, followed by carbohydrate-rich and, in last place, fat-rich foods. In practical terms, this means that by including a protein-rich food in each meal, you can help to satisfy your appetite and delay the return of hunger, seeing you through to the next meal or snack.

While it is unlikely that you have been eating insufficient protein to meet your body's needs, if you have been focusing on reducing your fat intake, you may have inadvertently made it difficult for yourself by omitting the power of protein-rich foods to fill you up. Typical dieters' lunches of a salad sandwich or bowl of vegetable soup may sound like a healthy choice, but on their own these meals are likely to leave you ravenous within a couple of hours of eating them, particularly if the meal included high GI carbs such as white bread. Add a protein-rich food to the meal, along with a moderate portion of a low GI carb, and you have a more balanced and filling meal.

For example:
- At breakfast include low fat milk, yoghurt, eggs, baked beans, lean bacon, smoked salmon, sardines, cottage cheese, ricotta cheese, herrings, nuts or nut butters.
- At light and main meals include lean meat, poultry, fish, reduced fat cheese, eggs, tofu or legumes (beans, chickpeas or lentils).

EXERCISE GOAL

Aim to walk at the same pace as last week (level 4 of the PRE scale) for a total of 20 minutes on six days. *Plus* try to complete each of the two resistance workouts, focusing on the upper and lower body respectively, three times during the week.

Resistance exercises

Workout 1	Lower body exercises	'Core' strength abdominals and back
	Squats 2 sets of 10	Three-quarter hover 2 x 20 seconds
	Lunges 10 each leg	Pointer 10 each side
Workout 2	Upper body exercises	
	Assisted push-ups 2 sets of 10	Leg extensions 10 each leg
	Standing tricep extensions 2 sets of 10	

NEW EXERCISE

Pointer

This is a simple but effective exercise for strengthening the back and bottom muscles, as well as continuing to work on your core abdominal strength.

Strengthens and tones: back, bottom and core abdominals

How to do it:

1 Start on all fours and align your spine by keeping your eyes on the floor just in front of your hands and pulling your navel up towards your spine, without allowing your back to arch. Both your hands and knees should be hip- and shoulder-width apart.

2 Lift your right hand and left leg and extend slowly over a count of four until they are straight and in line with your torso—you are aiming for length rather than height. Hold for 4 seconds before slowly pulling the arm and leg back in close to the torso, then repeat the movement.

3 Repeat with the left arm and right leg.

How many: Repeat 10 extensions on each side.

Sample diary

Monday	Tuesday	Wednesday	Thursday	Friday	Saturday	Sunday
20 min walk	20 min walk	20 min walk	20 min walk		20 min walk	20 min walk
+ workout 1	+ workout 2	+ workout 1	+ workout 2		+ workout 1	+ workout 2
30 mins	30 mins	30 mins	30 mins		30 mins	30 mins

FOOD FOR THOUGHT

The real deal on protein and health.

Adding more protein to your diet makes good sense for weight control. In comparison with carbohydrate and fat, protein makes us feel more satisfied immediately after eating and reduces hunger between meals. In addition, protein increases our metabolic rate for one to three hours after eating. This means we burn more energy by the minute compared with the increase that occurs after eating carbs or fats. Protein foods are also excellent sources of micronutrients, such as iron, zinc, vitamin B12 and omega-3 fats.

Which foods are high in protein?

The highest sources of protein are meats (beef, pork, lamb, chicken), fish and shellfish. As long as these are trimmed of fat and not overlaid with creamy sauces, you can basically eat to suit your appetite. You will find there are natural limits on your appetite for lean protein. Go for the leanest cuts in the supermarket, cut off all the visible (selvage) fat and panfry, grill, bake, stir-fry or barbecue.

Dairy products are not only good sources of protein—the combination of protein and calcium that is unique to dairy foods can aid weight control. The more calcium or dairy foods (it's hard to separate the two) people eat, the lower their weight and fat mass. Calcium is intimately involved in the burning of fat—and that is something we want to encourage! Choose low fat dairy products including milk, yoghurt and cottage cheese. Go easy on high fat cheeses such as cheddar, feta, camembert and brie. You don't have to cut them out completely though.

It is preferable to have a small serve of these than a giant serve of some reduced fat version that doesn't taste anywhere near as good.

Nuts are excellent sources of protein and micronutrients but we have to be careful not to overdo them, as they are energy dense—they pack a lot of kilojoules into a small weight. While it is easy to overeat nuts, you don't necessarily have to avoid them. They are high in the good fats. People who eat a small serve of nuts each day have significantly less risk of heart disease. We suggest you have about 30 grams most days. Put a small handful in a small bowl—don't eat straight from the pack.

It is a great shame that eggs have an undeserved bad reputation because of their cholesterol content—in fact they are great sources of protein and several essential vitamins and minerals. We now know that high blood cholesterol results from eating large amounts of saturated fat (rather than cholesterol) in foods. If you select the 'omega-3 enriched' eggs on the market, you are boosting the good fats along with your protein intake.

Can you eat too much protein?

The American Institute of Medicine recommends that no more than 35 per cent of energy in our diets comes from protein. That is 175 grams of pure protein for a person consuming 8500 kilojoules a day. In practice, most people will have no desire to eat beyond that amount.

A high protein intake has been criticised because it might also mean a high intake of saturated fat. That is not true if you stick to lean meat and low fat dairy products. Concerns about the effect of high protein intake on kidney function are limited to people who already have compromised kidney function: people with diabetes, the very elderly and young infants.

Week 5 Menu Plan

	BREAKFAST	SNACK
MONDAY	Muesli with fruit and low fat yoghurt	Wholegrain cracker and Vegemite®
TUESDAY	Grainy toast spread with avocado and topped with lean grilled bacon and sliced fresh tomato	An apple
WEDNESDAY	Commercial breakfast drink and a nut bar	Snack pack of peaches
THURSDAY	Grainy toast with peanut butter, Yellowbox honey and sliced banana	Low fat yoghurt
FRIDAY	Fresh or canned fruit salad with low fat natural yoghurt and a sprinkle of mixed nuts and seeds	Raisin toast with a light spread of canola marga
SATURDAY	Baked beans and scrambled egg with low GI toast	A handful of dried aprico
SUNDAY	Grilled tomato, egg and grainy toast	A banana

LUNCH	SNACK	DINNER
Toasted cheese and apple sandwich	Low fat chocolate mousse	Tuna pasta with tomato and cucumber salad
Plain hamburger with lettuce, tomato, beetroot, onion and sauce	Low fat yoghurt and fresh fruit	Chicken Stuffed with Spinach and Cheese (see page 292) served with sweet potato mash
Vegetarian doner kebab with falafel and tabbouli	Snack-size (25–30 g) chocolate bar	Home-made fried rice using Doongara rice
Grainy sandwich with ham and salad	A fresh pear	Spaghetti bolognaise: make your favourite bolognaise sauce with lean minced beef, allowing about 120 g mince per person. Serve with spaghetti (1 cup cooked per person) and a big green side salad tossed in vinaigrette or balsamic dressing
Chickpea salad: mix canned chickpeas, button mushrooms, diced red onion, capsicum, parsley and mint with vinaigrette dressing	An apple	Panfry boneless fish fillets for 2–3 minutes on each side with a spray of olive oil. Serve with a squeeze of lemon, black pepper and baby new potatoes, steamed broccoli florets, carrot and asparagus spears
Bruschetta with tomato topping and a frozen yoghurt ice-cream cone	An apple	Quick Thai noodle curry: stir-fry some diced trim tofu, sliced onion, red capsicum strips, baby corn, and snowpeas (or any stir-fry vegetable mix) in a large pan or wok. Add 1 tablespoon red curry paste. Prepare Asian noodles according to directions on the packet. Add the noodles to the vegetables with enough stock to make a sauce. Stir in 1 tablespoon light coconut milk, heat through, and it's ready to serve
Minestrone soup and a small grainy roll	Dried fruit and nut mix	Barbecued steak with corn, tomato, mushrooms and salad

Week 6

This week is all about changing your thinking on fats and seeing the good as well as the bad. Focus on the following goals this week:

FOOD GOAL

Break out of the 'low fat' dieting mentality.

EXERCISE GOAL

Aim to walk at the same pace as last week (level 4 of the PRE scale) for a total of 20 minutes on six days. *Plus* try to complete each of the two resistance workouts, focusing on the upper and lower body respectively, three times during the week.

ACTIVITY GOAL

For every hour that you spend sitting down, get up and do something more active for five minutes—have a quick stretch, walk to the printer, hang out the washing or complete some other household or office chore.

FOOD FOR THOUGHT

The fats of the matter.

> ## FOOD GOAL
> Break out of the 'low fat' dieting mentality.

Your food goal this week involves looking at the fats in your diet—not to discard them, but to ensure that you are eating the right balance of good and bad fats. By allowing yourself to incorporate healthy fats you will enjoy your meals more (fat tastes good) and gain the long-term benefits of fat-soluble vitamins and anti-oxidants. The following are the guidelines we recommend.

Eat Less Saturated Fat

Reducing your total fat intake will lower the energy density of your diet and help you lose weight, but it is important to focus on specifically reducing the saturated fats as your highest priority. Saturated fats should constitute less than 10 per cent of total kilojoules for the day. For a person eating 6400 kilojoules this means eating less than 16 grams of saturated fat per day. (See table on page 135.)

Boost your omega 3 intake

These unique fats found in seafood can reduce inflammation in the body, iron out irregularities in heart beat, reduce blood fat levels and might play a valuable role in treating depression and Alzheimer's disease. Modern Western diets almost certainly do not provide enough of the polyunsaturated omega-3 fats. Around 650 milligrams of omega-3 fats are considered an adequate daily intake for adults. The following foods contain approximately 650 milligrams of omega-3 fats:

- 40 g canned sardines
- 30 g canned mackerel

- 40 g smoked salmon
- 30 g canned red salmon
- 50 g canned pink salmon
- 110 g fresh Atlantic salmon
- 180 g canned tuna
- 4 omega-3 eggs

Replace bad fats with good fats

Replacing saturated fats with monounsaturated fats will lower your bad cholesterol and increase your good cholesterol.

- Substitute butter with canola margarines and spreads.
- Use liquid oils (or oil-based sprays) for frying, including canola and olive oils.
- Cold-pressed olive oil contains anti-oxidants that are not found in refined oils.
- Check for the presence of these oils (such as canola or olive) in commercially fried and 'oven-bake' products (if you use them), in preference to animal fats and unspecified vegetable oils.
- Use low fat milk (or soy substitute) in place of full cream milk.
- Eat a handful of nuts as an alternative to potato chips and other commercial packet snacks.

Grams of saturated fat found in everyday servings of

common foods

Chicken drumstick, 1 including skin	4 g
Cream cheese, 1 tablespoon	4 g
Sausage, 1 thin	4 g
Lamb loin chop (not trimmed), 1 grilled	4 g
Milk chocolate, 4 squares, 30 g	5 g
Sour cream, 1 tablespoon	5 g
Cream, 1 tablespoon	6 g
Milk, full fat, 1 cup	6 g
Rich chocolate cake, iced and filled, 1 piece, 100 g	6 g
Salami, 2 thin slices	6 g
Pizza, supreme, 2 slices	6 g
Cheddar cheese, 40 g	7 g
Chips, 50 g packet	7 g
Hamburger, 1 average	7 g
Shortbread, 3 biscuits	7 g
Butter, 1 tablespoon	10 g
Croissant, 1	10 g
Doughnut, 1 cinnamon and sugar	10 g
Meat pie, 1	10 g
Cheesecake, 1 large slice, 120 g	12 g
Sausage roll, 1 small	17 g
Coconut cream, 140 g can	25 g
Fried chicken takeaway meal, average	25 g

EXERCISE GOAL

Aim to walk at the same pace as last week (level 4 of the PRE scale) for a total of 20 minutes on six days. *Plus* try to complete each of the two resistance workouts, focusing on the upper and lower body respectively, three times during the week.

Resistance exercises

This week we make the resistance exercises you have already learnt a little harder by omitting the rest between sets.

Workout 1	Lower body exercises	'Core' strength abdominals and back
	Squats 1 set of 20	Three-quarter hover 2 x 30 seconds
	Lunges 10 each leg	Pointer 10 each side
Workout 2	**Upper body exercises**	
	Assisted push-ups 1 set of 20	Leg extensions 10 each leg
	Standing tricep extensions 1 set of 20	Ab curl 1 set of 20

NEW EXERCISE

Ab curl

Now that we have started to strengthen the deep abdominal muscles involved in posture and support of the lower back, we can add an exercise for the outer muscles. A basic ab curl works the sixpack—these are the ab muscles that you use to sit up from lying down or to curl the torso forward. It is crucial to continue working the core muscles as well so that you strengthen and tone from the inside out. The old-fashioned ab curl you may remember from school days (where you hooked your feet under a bar and sat up all the way) is not a good idea—this simply pulls into play your hip flexor muscles instead of making the abs do all the work.

Note: Without great care this exercise can strain the back and neck.

Strengthens and tones: the sixpack abs

How to do it:
1 Lie on the floor with your knees bent and your feet flat on the floor.
2 Lightly place your fingertips behind your ears and keep your elbows pointing to the side to avoid pulling on your head and neck.
3 Pull in your navel and curl your torso up about 45 degrees, then return to the floor.

Remember:
• Keep the small of the back in contact with the floor.
• Imagine you are holding an orange under your chin to maintain a space between your chin and chest.
• Keep your eyes focused diagonally over your knees rather than looking straight up at the ceiling—a good place to look is where the ceiling meets the wall.

How many: 20 curls

Sample diary

Monday	Tuesday	Wednesday	Thursday	Friday	Saturday	Sunday
20 min walk	20 min walk	20 min walk	20 min walk		20 min walk	20 min walk
+ workout 1	+ workout 2	+ workout 1	+ workout 2		+ workout 1	+ workout 2
30 mins	30 mins	30 mins	30 mins		30 mins	30 mins

Dancing in some form has always been important for humans around the world. Find a class close to you—salsa, folk, ballroom, jazz, funk, ballet (or whatever takes your fancy) and hit the floor. Or simply throw on your favourite CD at home and get moving.

FOOD FOR THOUGHT

The fats of the matter.

To most people, 'low fat' is still synonymous with 'healthy' and 'weight loss'. Unfortunately, it is not that simple. Once upon a time, when fruit, vegetables and wholegrains were the staples of a low fat diet this might have been true. But it is no longer so—indeed, the typical low fat diet may be distinctly unhealthy and one of the reasons behind our expanding waistlines.

In the 1990s, the experts told us to eat low fat diets because they were concerned about two things. First, they believed saturated fat increased the risk of heart disease, and second, that fatty foods were too easily overeaten because they were energy dense. Those concerns are still valid today—the experts haven't changed their minds again. But the solution to the problem—eating a low fat diet—has not been a successful strategy. While we have cut down on total fat, we haven't cut down on saturated fat, and the food industry (with the best of intentions) gave us a myriad of low fat foods that were just as energy dense as their full fat counterparts. So during the 1990s, the era of '99 per cent fat free', the prevalence of obesity soared and with it heart disease and diabetes.

As a result of these unexpected events, the heart foundations and health organisations around the world went back to the drawing board and remodelled their dietary advice, as follows:

1 The *type* of fat is more important for health than the total amount.
2 The energy density of a food (kilojoules per 100 grams) is more important to weight control than the fat content.

Furthermore, most of us need to eat more of certain kinds of fat for optimal health (yes, you read it right). These include the omega-3 fats found in fish and seafood, walnuts and canola-based products. Eating these and more monounsaturated fats such as those in olive oil and canola oil has been shown to reduce the risk of heart attack significantly. Indeed, one of the most important diet studies ever carried out, the Lyon Heart Study, showed that a diet with more fish, fruit, vegetables and good fats was twice as effective in reducing cardiovascular 'events' as the low fat diet recommended by the American Heart Association. In fact, it is a whole lot better than most of the expensive drugs used to reduce the risk of heart attack.

There is another excellent reason why you should aim to increase these monounsaturated fats at the expense of the saturated ones. While all fats have the same number of kilojoules per gram, they may not all have the same effect on your weight. For reasons that are not yet clear, a high fat diet based on fish oil or olive oil is much less likely to expand the waistline. Research is also showing that people who eat diets rich in the omega-3 fats are less likely to suffer rheumatoid arthritis, psoriasis, ulcerative colitis, depression (and other mental illness), and possibly some cancers. We recommend that you eat the food fats in the form of food rather than pills or just oils. In the whole food, you get the whole package that nature provided.

Where do you find the good oils?

- Fish such as salmon, tuna, herrings and sardines—canned or fresh
- Shellfish
- Walnuts, almonds and cashews—best unsalted
- Avocado—spread it on as an alternative to margarine or butter

- Spinach, bok choy, leafy green salads
- Olives—spread as a tapenade or add whole to almost anything—pasta sauces, couscous or salads
- Muesli—mix sunflower seeds and pumpkin seeds with ground almonds or hazelnuts
- Linseed (flaxseed) is a great source of omega-3 fats; a good way to eat it is in soy and linseed bread.

A LOW FAT DIET IS NOT NECESSARILY THE BEST DIET FOR WEIGHT LOSS OR OVERALL HEALTH.

'FAT FREE' AND 'REDUCED FAT' ON THE LABEL IS NOT A LICENCE TO EAT MORE.

EATING LESS SATURATED FAT AND MORE MONOUNSATURATED AND OMEGA-3 FATS IS THE BEST OPTION FOR LONG-TERM HEALTH.

Week 6 Menu Plan

	BREAKFAST	SNACK
MONDAY	Orange and grapefruit segments with prunes and a low fat honey-flavoured yoghurt, sprinkled with toasted flaked almonds	Raisin toast
TUESDAY	Soy and linseed toast with margarine and a boiled egg, plus a low fat milky coffee	A banana
WEDNESDAY	Muesli with sliced pear and low fat milk, sprinkled with chopped almonds or hazelnuts	Small vegetable juice, grai crackers
THURSDAY	Banana smoothie made with an omega-3 egg	Hot chocolate with low fat
FRIDAY	Toasted cheese and tomato sandwich and an apple	Low fat yoghurt
SATURDAY	High fibre, low GI cereal with low fat milk and canned peach slices	Dried fruit biscuits
SUNDAY	Egg, lean bacon, tomato, mushrooms and grainy toast with grapefruit juice	An apple

LUNCH	SNACK	DINNER
Miso soup with sushi rolls	An apple	Stir-fried beef with garlic, onion, capsicum, carrot, zucchini and snowpeas dressed with sweet chilli sauce and served with Doongara rice
Chicken and coleslaw on a mixed grain roll with fresh or canned fruit salad	Low fat milk with Milo®	Spread a round of pita bread with pesto or tomato paste. Top with sliced tomato, mushrooms, roasted capsicum, black olives, chopped spring onions and a sprinkle of grated Parmesan cheese. Heat through in a hot oven
Salmon and lettuce sandwich on grainy bread	2 kiwi fruit	Beef stroganoff with mushrooms (substitute light sour cream for sour cream) with fettuccine pasta, steamed broccoli and cauliflower
Lean ham, pineapple and grated light cheese on a toasted, mixed grain muffin	An orange	Commercial oven-bake fish and potato wedges with carrot and zucchini julienne alongside
Steak sandwich made on grainy bread with salad	A banana	Thai-style Tofu and Noodle Soup (see page 289)
Minestrone soup and a crusty white roll	An apple	Thinly slice and pan-fry pork loin steak. Toss with baby spinach, sliced red onion and steamed new potatoes (halved or quartered)
Macaroni cheese made with light milk and reduced fat cheese. Throw in a bag of frozen mixed vegetables with the macaroni	Snack-size chocolate bar (25–30 g)	Roast leg of lamb with a small roast potato, roast sweet potato, pumpkin, steamed beans and peas, served with mint sauce

Week 7

This week, focus on these goals:

FOOD GOAL

Think about what you are drinking.

EXERCISE GOAL

Aim to walk at the same pace as last week (level 4 of our PRE scale), but for a total of 25 minutes on six days. *Plus* try to complete each of the two resistance workouts, focusing on the upper and lower body respectively, three times during the week.

ACTIVITY GOAL

Watch no more than two hours of television on any day and choose one day where you will not watch television at all.

FOOD FOR THOUGHT

Wholegrains—the whole story.

FOOD GOAL

Think about what you are drinking.

Did you realise that it is a good idea to drink more when you are losing weight? One reason is that a large part of our fluid intake comes from food, so if we are eating less food, we are also taking in less fluid. Additional fluid is also helpful for removing extra toxins which can be released during weight loss. What you choose to drink, however, can have a major impact on your success with weight loss.

Many things we drink would be better thought of as food due to the kilojoules they contain. Fruit juice might sound like a healthy option but ordering a glass of orange juice in a cafe can be the equivalent of the energy (kilojoules) from ten oranges; a large soft drink can provide as many as 15 teaspoons of sugar in a single serve; while a takeaway coffee can contain as much as 10 grams of fat if made with full cream milk. It is not hard to see how the calories can stack up without filling you up.

Of all the things we drink, however, alcohol could be thought of as the most fattening—not because of its kilojoule content, but because it has priority as a fuel over all other nutrients. So basically, as long as there is alcohol in your system, anything else is surplus until the alcohol kilojoules are used up. Looking at it another way, just one can of beer replaces all the calories burnt by 20 minutes of brisk walking.

Your best option for extra fluid is water. Soda water, low sodium mineral water, herbal teas and decaffeinated drinks are other options. Diet soft drinks are okay—certainly they contain almost no kilojoules, but they are highly acidic (which can soften the enamel of your teeth). Plus, be aware of the caffeine content in these types of drinks, which can be considerable.

When you are trying to lose weight, it is best to think of alcohol as an indulgence. It may be enjoyable but it doesn't provide any essential nutrients and is high in kilojoules. Limit your intake as much as you can. Even when you get to the weight maintenance stage, an average daily limit of no more than two standard drinks for men and one standard drink for women is recommended.

A standard drink is:

• 100 ml wine
• A middy (285 ml) of full strength beer or a schooner of light (410 ml)
• 30 ml spirits
• 60 ml fortified wine (sherry, port, etc.)

Did you know?

Your body reacts differently to fluids compared to food. There is evidence that sugar in liquid form (such as soft drinks and fruit juices) may sneak past the brain's appetite centre. When we chew, signals are sent to the brain that food is on its way and our appetite begins to be altered before the food even hits our stomach. When we drink, however, these signals don't occur and the same level of satiety is not reached, making it easy for us to overconsume.

EXERCISE GOAL

Aim to walk at the same pace as last week (level 4 of our PRE scale), but for a total of 25 minutes on six days. *Plus* try to complete each of the two resistance workouts, focusing on the upper and lower body respectively, three times during the week.

Resistance exercises

Workout 1	Lower body exercises	'Core' strength abdominals and back
	Squats 1 set of 20	Three-quarter hover 2 x 30 seconds
	Lunges 10 each leg	Pointer 10 each side
Workout 2	**Upper body exercises**	
	Assisted push-ups 1 set of 20	Leg extensions 10 each leg
	Standing tricep extensions 1 set of 20	Ab curl 1 set of 20
	Bicep curl 1 set of 20	

NEW EXERCISE

Bicep curl

When working one muscle or group of muscles we should always try to work the opposing muscle(s) to the same extent. This maintains an equilibrium of strength and flexibility across joints and is crucial in achieving good posture and avoiding injuries. We learnt to work the back of the arm last week, therefore this week we need to add an exercise for the front of the arm. A bicep curl is the most effective and simple way to do this.

Strengthens and tones: front of the arm

How to do it:

1 Hold your hand weights (or cans) by your sides with your palms facing forward.
2 Maintain good posture through your body, keeping your torso strong and upright throughout.
3 Curl the weights up towards your shoulders, keeping your elbows close to your ribcage, and slowly return to the start position.

How many: Complete 20 curls.

Sample diary

Monday	Tuesday	Wednesday	Thursday	Friday	Saturday	Sunday
25 min walk	25 min walk	25 min walk	25 min walk		25 min walk	25 min walk
+ workout 1	+ workout 2	+ workout 1	+ workout 2		+ workout 1	+ workout 2
35 mins	35 mins	35 mins	35 mins		35 mins	35 mins

A BICEP CURL IS THE MOST EFFECTIVE AND SIMPLE WAY TO STRENGTHEN AND TONE THIS PART OF THE ARM.

FOOD FOR THOUGHT

Wholegrains—the whole story.

While there is plenty of evidence that wholegrains and cereal fibre are good for you, there are plenty of nutritious foods that are relatively low in fibre and yet full of micronutrients (such as oranges, dairy products, fish and lean meat). In our experience, many people do not like to eat unrefined foods such as brown bread, brown rice and brown pasta.

Humans did not eat large amounts of any cereal grain until the advent of agriculture, a recent event on the evolutionary clock. But once farming became established, we found increasingly ingenious ways of removing the 'brown bits' and making cereal products ever more palatable—probably too palatable for our own good!

Having said this, the benefits of eating more fibre—especially if you are battling the bulge—are obvious. In one study of nearly 3000 young adults, those who ate more fibre (about 25 grams a day) gained much less weight over the years than those who ate the least (less than 10 grams a day). What's more, their fibre intake was a better predictor of the amount of weight gain than their fat intake (the usual suspect). Why? Lots of reasons: high fibre foods take longer to eat, they are heavier and bulkier, fill you up sooner and leave you feeling more satiated. Another reason is that eating more wholegrains and fibre has been shown to improve insulin sensitivity and lower insulin levels. That means greater use of fat as a source of fuel—good news if you are trying to lose weight.

There are plenty of other reasons to encourage you to eat more wholegrains if you enjoy them. Higher fibre intake—especially from cereals—has been linked to lower risk of cancer of the large bowel, breast, stomach and mouth. What is the connection? New research shows that high insulin levels increase the multiplication of mutated cells, producing uncontrolled growth of tumours and cancers. Plus, another function of fibre is to bind carcinogenic substances and help sweep them out of the system.

Much of the goodness in grains is found just beneath the bran layer and is usually lost along with the fibre when grains are milled. Vitamins, minerals, anti-oxidants and other protective substances in wholegrains—many of which are not present in nutritional supplements—are also lost. However, some wheats are better than others—when hard wheats, such as durum wheat, are milled into flour or semolina (to make pasta), it is easier to separate the bran, and the final product contains higher quantities of micronutrients.

Wholegrain and low GI are not the same

When it comes to food labelling, there's no international definition of 'wholegrain'. It can mean different things in different countries. Food Standards Australia and New Zealand (FSANZ) have expanded the legal definition for packaging labels to allow more foods including refined wholemeal foods to include 'wholegrain' on the label. A manufacturer can label a product 'wholegrain' if the 'intact grain or the dehulled, ground, milled, cracked or flaked grain, where the constituents—endosperm, germ and bran—are present in such proportions that represent the typical ratio of those fractions occurring in the whole cereal'. So, if there's no GI rating on the label, follow our rule of thumb, if you can't see the grains, don't assume it's low GI.

Our message is to reduce your intake of highly processed and refined cereal products that produce glycemic spikes and leave you craving more. The most obvious examples are soft white bread and crackers but some foods that are high in fibre—modern wholemeal breads (where you can't see the grain) and brown rice—are also often quickly digested and absorbed. We recommend you swap some of these high GI carbs for smart low GI carbs that are slowly digested and absorbed, irrespective of their fibre content. Pasta, noodles, low GI rices and sourdough bread are good examples of low GI foods. If a food's label shows at least 3 grams of fibre per serving, consider it a good source. Experts recommend 30 grams of fibre a day. Increase your fibre intake slowly so your bowel flora has time to adapt.

Low GI sources of fibre (grams per serve)

Grain bread (lots of whole kernels visible), 1 slice	2
Porridge, 1 cup, cooked	2
Apple, 1 medium, including skin	3
Barley, ½ cup, cooked	3
Corn kernels, 100 g, canned	3
Lentils, ½ cup, cooked	3
Prunes, 5	3
Sweet potato, 120 g, boiled	3
Popcorn, 2 cups, popped	4
Pumpernickel bread, 50 g slice	4
Dried apricots, 6 halves	5
Guardian®, 1 cup	5
Peas, ½ cup, cooked	5
All-Bran®, ½ cup	10
Chickpeas, ½ cup, cooked	10

Week 7 Menu Plan

	BREAKFAST	SNACK
MONDAY	Grainy bread spread with fresh ricotta and blackberry conserve	A banana
TUESDAY	Breakfast on the Go (see page 275)	Skim milk latte
WEDNESDAY	Low GI, high fibre breakfast cereal with low fat milk and sliced banana	Mandarins
THURSDAY	Low fat toasted muesli with yoghurt and canned fruit	An apple
FRIDAY	Fruit loaf spread with light cream cheese and topped with sliced apple and a sprinkle of cinnamon	Dried pear halves
SATURDAY	Mushroom, cheese and spinach omelette with grainy toast and a glass of fruit juice	An apple
SUNDAY	Chopped banana stirred into porridge, topped with a drizzle of honey and low fat milk	Oatmeal biscuits

LUNCH	SNACK	DINNER
...asta salad with lean ...am, corn kernels, ...apsicum, shallots and ...ayonnaise with lettuce	Low fat yoghurt	Stir-fry lean beef with grated ginger and crushed garlic. Add snowpeas, broccoli florets, chopped spring onion, Chinese cabbage slices and a little finely chopped chilli. Combine soy and hoi sin sauces with honey, toss and serve with Doongara rice
...sian seafood combi-...ation with vegetables ...nd boiled noodles	Canned peaches	Panfried chicken breast with mushroom sauce (use light evaporated milk in place of cream), canned butter beans, carrots and green beans
...nicken, avocado and ...lad on grainy bread	Low fat fruit yoghurt	Boil a packet of spinach and cheese (or your favourite filling) tortellini according to packet directions. Heat some bottled tomato sauce and serve this on top of the tortellini with a sprinkle of Parmesan cheese. Serve with a large salad and vinaigrette
...rainy crackers with ...ommous, sliced tomato, ...lery and sardines	Carrot sticks with hommous	Mediterranean roast vegetables with trimmed lamb cutlets
...umpkin soup with grainy ...asted croutons and low ...: yoghurt garnish	Orange and Passionfruit Mousse (see page 321)	Mexican bean tacos: fill warm taco shells with 2–3 tablespoons Mexi-beans and top with shredded lettuce, grated reduced fat cheese and 1–2 teaspoons light sour cream
...eak sandwich: grilled ...nute steak in multigrain ...ead with lettuce, ...etroot, grated carrot, ...mato and mustard	A banana	Roasted rosemary sweet potato wedges with oven-baked fish. Brush sweet potato wedges with a little olive oil, sprinkle with dried rosemary and bake in the oven for about 20 minutes at 180ºC. Wrap fish fillets or cutlets (allowing one per person) in individual foil parcels with a slice or two of lemon and a twist of freshly ground black pepper, and bake in the oven for 10 to 15 minutes
...rdines or smoked trout, ...urdough bread and ...sh green salad with ...non and vinegar	Baked banana with passion-fruit (try it in the microwave)	Ham and Vegetable Bake (see page 282) and salad

Week 8

Many of us assign foods to a 'good' or 'bad' category and inevitably it is the foods we see as treat foods that we see as 'bad'. Yet by allowing yourself to indulge in whatever food/drink you really enjoy, you can diminish the uncontrollable desire to overeat these foods and they become a normal part of eating. Focus on the following goals this week:

FOOD GOAL

Include an indulgence occasionally.

EXERCISE GOAL

Aim to walk for a total of 25 minutes on six days but increase your pace to a brisk walk (of around level 5 of the PRE scale) for the middle 15 minutes. *Plus* try to complete each of the resistance workouts, focusing on the upper and lower body respectively, three times during the week.

ACTIVITY GOAL

Go shopping on foot and carry your bags home—a fantastic total body workout! (If you have to drive to the nearest shopping centre, park the car in the furthest parking spot and walk the rest of the way.)

FOOD FOR THOUGHT

Allow yourself something sweet!

FOOD GOAL

Include an indulgence occasionally.

Have you ever finished your main course and found yourself hankering for a little of something sweet? Do you prefer your tea and coffee with the taste of real sugar? Perhaps you feel that a sweet fix helps you work through the afternoon. Maybe you really enjoy coffee and cake with a good friend once a week. Bad habits? We don't think so.

Just because you have decided to change your eating habits doesn't mean you can't indulge once a week. Imagine yourself at a meeting and suddenly a chocolate mud cake is being offered around. It is okay to enjoy a piece of cake with everyone else, but make the decision to eat—or not eat—an active one. Do you automatically accept a piece of cake (even though you're not hungry) and eat it during the meeting, barely tasting it (passively indulging), or do you consider the look of the cake and how hungry you are and decide it could be a nice change for morning tea (active decision making)? Your thinking and actions in the second instance are more positive than in the first instance, which means you are less likely to feel guilty about indulging.

This week, we want you to look at the feelings you may have about eating certain foods. The aim is for you to make active, guilt-free choices about the foods you eat, confident in the knowledge that you can eat your favourite foods, and still work towards your goals. This is also a good time to revise your basic daily food quantities to be sure your background diet is sound. (See page 73.)

And in case you haven't done so for a while, this week, choose an indulgence that you fancy and go ahead and enjoy it!

Indulgences to savour:

3 jam tartlets

½ slice of cake

2 cream biscuits

40 g of your favourite cheese

1 snack-size (25 g) chocolate bar

2 glasses (200 ml) wine

1 can regular soft drink

2 tablespoons cream

½ small serve French fries

375 ml beer

In the era of digital cameras, it is easy to take a weekly shot of your body (full length) side on. Take it in the same place each week (such as inside a door frame) so you can easily see your weekly progress.

> ### EXERCISE GOAL
>
> Aim to walk for a total of 25 minutes on six days but increase your pace
> to a brisk walk (of around level 5 of the PRE scale) for the middle 15 minutes.
> *Plus* try to complete each of the resistance workouts, focusing on the
> upper and lower body respectively, three times during the week.

Resistance exercises

Workout 1	Lower body exercises	'Core' strength abdominals and back
	Squats 1 set of 20	Full hover 2 x 30 seconds
	Lunges 10 each leg	Pointer 10 each side
	Power lunge 20 alternate legs	
Workout 2	**Upper body exercises**	
	Assisted push-ups 1 set of 20	Leg extensions 10 each leg
	Standing tricep extensions 1 set of 20	Ab curl 1 set of 20
	Bicep curl 1 set of 20	

NEW EXERCISES
Power lunges

This is a more advanced version of the lunge you have already learnt. By adding some movement you recruit all the smaller stabiliser muscles of the legs, the postural muscles have to work hard and you increase the load the major muscles of the legs and bottom have to move. This is a fantastic exercise for toning and strengthening the lower body.

Strengthens and tones: legs and bottom

How to do it:
1 Start with your feet hip-width apart and your arms by your side. Keep your eyes looking straight ahead rather than down at the floor to help you maintain good posture.
2 Take a long step forward with one leg and sink into your lunge, similarly to your usual lunge move, but then push yourself back to standing by driving into your front heel.
3 As you complete the power lunge allow your arms to swing naturally by your sides to help with balance. Repeat on the other leg.

Remember: Keep your chest proud and upper body upright throughout so that all the work is in the legs and bottom muscles.

How many: 20, using alternate legs

Full hover

This is a more advanced level of the three-quarter hover you have already learnt.

Strengthens and tones: core abdominals—improves your posture and narrows your waist

How to do it:

1 Start in your three-quarter hover position (see page 117) and then lift your knees, straightening your legs until your body is in alignment from heel to shoulder.

2 Check that your bottom is not sticking up and that you are not allowing your lower back to sag—pull your navel in towards your spine.

3 Straighten up and keep your hips in line with your body.

Remember: Breathe normally while you maintain the position—it is very easy to hold your breath without realising.

How long: Hold for 2 sets of 30 seconds with a short rest in between.

Sample diary

Monday	Tuesday	Wednesday	Thursday	Friday	Saturday	Sunday
25 min walk	25 min walk	25 min walk	25 mins walk		25 min walk	25 min walk
+ workout 1	+ workout 2	+ workout 1	+ workout 2		+ workout 1	+ workout 2
35 mins	35 mins	35 mins	35 mins		35 mins	35 mins

FOOD FOR THOUGHT

Allow yourself something sweet!

Most people mistakenly believe that sugar is the first thing that ought to go when they are 'on a diet'—it is just 'empty calories' and is probably responsible for one's current state of overweight. We have a prudish notion that if something tastes good, it must be bad for us. However, yearning for something sweet is instinctual and hard to ignore, especially when you are actively losing weight. In our evolutionary past, honey was a significant part of hunter-gatherer diets and a lot more concentrated as a source of sugar than most of the sugary foods we eat today.

In fact, sugar is not specifically implicated in making us fat. In the Baltimore Ageing Study, for example, the best predictor of weight gain over time was a diet characterised by a lot of bread (most varieties being high GI). Those who ate a lot of sweets gained very little—about the same as those who adhered to the principles of healthy eating (lots of fruit, vegetables, wholegrains and lean protein).

It is obvious, too, that the vast array of sugar-free and 'no added sugar' foods on supermarket shelves has not solved the problem of overweight. In fact, it could be said that they have exacerbated the problem by encouraging people to think that using a sugar substitute is all it takes to cut kilojoules and control weight. If only!

Here is a word of caution, however. For example, if you give people 500 extra kilojoules as solid food, they compensate by consuming fewer kilojoules during the rest of the day. But if you feed them 500 kilojoules in a soft drink, juice or other clear liquid, they don't reduce their intake at all. All 500 kilojoules are surplus and may head straight for your hips or waist. Indeed, in a recent study, the children who became overweight were greater consumers of soft drinks and fruit juices.

In The Low GI Diet, we encourage you to enjoy refined sugar in moderation—that's about 40 to 50 grams a day—an amount that most people consume without thinking about it. Include sweetened foods that pack nutrients, not just kilojoules—dairy foods, breakfast cereals, porridge with brown sugar or jam on grainy toast. Even the World Health Organisation says, 'a moderate intake of sugar-rich foods can provide for a palatable and nutritious diet'. We want you to cut the guilt trip and allow yourself the pleasure of sweetness. To guide you, let's take a quick look at the sugar content of some common foods.

Refined sugar content of various foods

1 shortbread biscuit	3 g
1 cream filled biscuit	5 g
1 boiled lolly	5 g
1 cup sweetened fruit juice	5 g
1 rounded teaspoon sugar	6 g
1 cinnamon and sugar doughnut	7 g
1 piece plain cake	7 g
1 tablespoon jam	8 g
1 muesli bar (average)	8 g
1 piece chocolate cake	11 g
30 ml undiluted cordial	18 g
5 squares chocolate	20 g
1 tablespoon honey	20 g
1 chocolate bar (average)	35 g
375 ml can soft drink (average)	45 g

Week 8 Menu Plan

	BREAKFAST	SNACK
MONDAY	High fibre fruit smoothie: blend low fat milk, natural yoghurt, a banana, a handful of berries and 1 tablespoon psyllium husks	A small handful of raw almo
TUESDAY	Baked beans on grainy toast followed by an orange	An apple and a wedge of reduced fat cheddar
WEDNESDAY	Grilled lean bacon and tomato sandwich on sourdough bread	A handful of red grapes
THURSDAY	Traditional porridge served with low fat milk and a dollop of raspberry jam	Hot chocolate with low fat
FRIDAY	Home-made muesli (blend rolled oats, mixture of dried fruit, nuts and seeds) with low fat milk and a few sliced strawberries	Low fat fruit yoghurt
SATURDAY	Egg and bacon with toast, tomato and mushroom	An apple
SUNDAY	Omelette filled with spinach and mushrooms served with toasted sourdough bread	Skim milk latte with a smal cake

LUNCH	SNACK	DINNER
Ham sandwich on grainy bread. Lean ham and lots of salad vegies—lettuce, tomato, beetroot, grated carrot and sprouts. Flavour with mustard or chutney	A piece of fruit	Spaghetti bolognaise made with premium beef mince—serve with a large mixed salad, a shaving of Parmesan and a small glass of red wine
Tortilla wrap filled with chicken, lettuce, tomato, cucumber and salsa	A small (40 g) chocolate bar	Herbed Fish Parcel with Sweet Potato Wedges and Coleslaw (see page 303)
Tomato and barley soup with grainy bread and low fat cheese	Skim milk hot chocolate	Chicken and cashew nut stir-fry with capsicum, mushrooms, onion, ginger, garlic, chilli, Asian greens and 1 teaspoon honey. Serve with noodles or Basmati/Doongara rice
Smoked mackerel fillet with a large mixed salad and a slice of sourdough bread, plus a piece of fresh fruit	Your favourite ice-cream	Grilled lean beef steak with a steamed ear of corn and a large mixed salad dressed with a little olive oil and vinegar dressing
Roast beef sandwich on grainy bread with salad vegetables and mustard	Peaches and cream	Salad Niçoise with lettuce, blanched green beans, boiled new potatoes, hard-boiled egg, olives, spring onions, baby gherkins, anchovies and plum tomatoes. Top with fresh or canned tuna and drizzle with olive oil and lemon juice dressing
Mixed bean salad with rocket and a slice of grainy bread	A handful of red grapes	Seafood fettuccine in a tomato-based sauce and a green salad
Barbecued Lamb with Lentil Salad and Lemon Yoghurt Dressing (see page 299)	Fruit salad with natural yoghurt	Quick pita bread pizza: top a pita bread with tomato paste, chopped zucchini, capsicum, tomato and mixed herbs, sprinkle with reduced fat mozzarella and bake for 20 minutes in a hot oven. Serve with a green salad

Week 9

After two months of changing your eating and exercise habits step by step, you should be feeling and looking lighter and brighter! If, however, you are finding your energy levels are lagging, it could be that you have cut your food intake too much, particularly your intake of carbohydrates. Focus on the following goals this week:

FOOD GOAL

Ensure you are eating enough carbohydrate (from low GI sources) to give you the energy to sustain your increased exercise and activity levels.

EXERCISE GOAL

Aim to walk for a total of 30 minutes on six days at the same brisk pace as last week (around level 5 of the PRE scale) for the middle 15 minutes. *Plus* try to complete each of the resistance workouts, focusing on the upper and lower body respectively, three times during the week.

ACTIVITY GOAL

Instead of heading to the local automatic car wash, do it yourself by hand, including an internal spring clean.

FOOD FOR THOUGHT

Facts and fallacies about the GI.

FOOD GOAL

Ensure you are eating enough carbohydrate (from low GI sources) to give you the energy to sustain your increased activity and exercise levels.

While cutting out carbs might seem to bring rapid results when you weigh yourself, such weight loss is inevitably too difficult to maintain long term. You need a certain amount of carbs to function at your best, particularly given your recent increased exercise and activity levels.

Focus this week on the carb-rich foods you are eating and assess whether you are including a low GI carb in each meal. Your goal is not to load your body with a huge amount of carbohydrate in one meal, but to spread a moderate amount of slowly absorbed low GI carbs to fuel your body across the course of the day. This translates into gentle fluctuations in your blood glucose with less insulin being required to deal with the day's intake. Perhaps keep a diary for a few days and look back to check on how you are really doing. If you find you are not spreading your carb intake across the day, try following our suggested meal plans for a few days.

Sample day (low GI choices in bold to show serves spread throughout the day)

Breakfast: **natural muesli** with **low fat milk** and sliced **fresh berries**

Snack: **banana** and a **low fat yoghurt**

Lunch: **lentil** soup with **low GI bread** and reduced fat cheese

Snack: hot chocolate made with **low fat milk** and an **oatmeal biscuit**

Main meal: grilled salmon fillet with baked **sweet potato** and a green salad

EXERCISE GOAL

Aim to walk for a total of 30 minutes on six days at the same brisk pace as last week (around level 5 of the PRE scale) for the middle 15 minutes. *Plus* try to complete each of the resistance workouts, focusing on the upper and lower body respectively, three times during the week.

Most health authorities around the world agree that for health we should aim to achieve 30 minutes of walking on most days of the week. This week our goal is to meet those recommendations. You are now well on your way to better health, a leaner body and more active mind—well done!

Resistance exercises

Workout 1	Lower body exercises	'Core' strength abdominals and back
	Squats 1 set of 20	Full hover 2 x 30 seconds
	Lunges 10 each leg	Pointer 10 each side
	Power lunges 20 alternate legs	
Workout 2	**Upper body exercises**	
	Three-quarter push-ups 1 set of 20	Leg extensions 10 each leg
	Standing tricep extensions 1 set of 20	Ab curl 1 set of 20
	Bicep curl 1 set of 20	Oblique curl 20 each side

NEW EXERCISES

Three-quarter push-ups

This uses the same technique as the assisted push-ups (pages 99–100), but we make things a little more challenging by removing the help of the table (or stair). Ensure you set up with a wide hand stance and keep your bottom tucked while you lower your chest to the floor.

Oblique curl

This is a variation of the ab curl that you have already learnt (pages 136–37).

Strengthens and tones: waist and torso

How to do it:

1 From your ab curl position drop both knees down to the right.
2 Extend your left arm behind your body towards your left heel and reach for the heel as you curl the body up. Make sure you keep your shoulders square to the ceiling (you will feel like twisting in the direction of your knees) and use your right hand to lightly support the weight of your head to avoid straining your neck.
3 Repeat on the other side.

How many: 20 curls on each side

Sample diary

Monday	Tuesday	Wednesday	Thursday	Friday	Saturday	Sunday
30 min walk	30 min walk	30 min walk	30 min walk		30 min walk	30 min walk
+ workout 2	+ workout 1	+ workout 2	+ workout 1		+ workout 1	+ workout 2
40 mins	40 mins	40 mins	40 mins		40 mins	40 mins

FOOD FOR THOUGHT

Facts and fallacies about the GI.

1 Carrots have a high GI

No, they don't! They have a GI of 41 and you can eat them as a 'free food'. The reason for the confusion: the first value ever published gave them a high GI (92). Unfortunately it was based on too few subjects and the resulting average was skewed. This error made the GI concept highly controversial right from the beginning.

2 The GI doesn't consider the amount of carbohydrate in a serving of food

That's true—it is a measure of the carbohydrate quality, not quantity. Do we need to know the quantity, too? For the most part, no. If you substitute a low GI bread for others, a low GI breakfast cereal for others and a low GI rice for others, then you are achieving your goal: a low GI diet in which the carbs are slowly digested and absorbed. If you are choosing chocolate over watermelon (not a good idea really) then it is sensible to consider both quality and quantity (the glycemic load). For more on the glycemic load, see page 40.

3 Some foods have a high GI but contain little carbohydrate

True, there is a handful of foods that contain so little carbohydrate that their GI is irrelevant. This includes watermelon and rockmelon, pumpkin, parsnips and broadbeans. You can ignore their high GI.

4 Glycemic load (GL) makes more sense than GI

Not true. The GI can be more important than the GL. That's because it is critical to choose slowly digested carbs (low GI carbs) over quickly digested ones (high GI carbs), even if the GL is the same. You'll stay fuller for longer if you choose a normal portion of pasta (a low GI food) over a small serve of potato (a high GI food). Our primary goal should be improving the quality of the carbs (exchanging high GI for low GI), not reducing the quantity of carbohydrate eaten. A secondary goal—it's up to you—is to replace some of the high GI carbs with good fats or lean protein.

5 Cutting carbs is the best way to lower insulin levels

No, that's not correct. While it is true that high GI carbs produce high insulin responses, low GI carbs have the same insulin demand as high protein foods that contain no carbs. See the diagram on page 25. Moreover, people who eat more carbs have better insulin sensitivity than low carb eaters.

6 Wholemeal products have low GI values

Not true most of the time. Wholemeal cereal products, especially those derived from wheat, usually have the same GI as their white counterparts. For example, white bread's GI is 70, wholemeal bread's GI is 71. **One rule to follow is that if you can't see the grains it's probably not low GI.** When wheat bran is finely milled, digestive enzymes can attack fast. That's not to say wholemeal cereals are unhealthy. There is good evidence that wholemeal foods improve insulin sensitivity and reduce disease risk. The best choices are both low GI and high in fibre.

7 The GI doesn't work in mixed meals

Yes, it does—it works perfectly. Why the controversy? Early studies on the subject of mixed meals were carried out by vocal opponents of the GI concept. Subsequent studies—at least a dozen from all over the world—proved convincingly that the GI of single foods could be used to predict the GI of a mixed meal. Moreover, long-term studies comparing high and low GI diets show differences in measures of blood glucose control. If the GI values of single foods were not a good guide to food choices, then those differences would not be evident.

8 The GI doesn't work when you add protein or fat

Not true. When you add protein or fat to a high carbohydrate food—for example, add cheese to bread—the blood glucose response will go down. But if you then exchange the source of carbohydrate (instead of bread with cheese, you have pasta with cheese), then you can expect an even lower response. The relative ranking of carbohydrate foods according to their GI predicts the overall glycemic response even in the presence of extra protein and fat. There will be limits to this, of course—if your meal contains a lot of protein and fat and little in the way of carbs, then the GI becomes irrelevant.

9 Too many variables affect the blood glucose response to meals

It's true that there are many variables that affect your glycemic response to meals. But that criticism applies equally well to carbo-hydrate 'counting' as it does to the GI. And carbohydrate counting is highly recommended for people with diabetes. Your day-to-day variation will be influenced by many things, including things you did the day before: amount of exercise; consumption of fat, fibre and alcohol; and even amount of sleep. What's good to know is that a low GI meal at dinner or breakfast will improve your glycemic response to lunch the following day, irrespective of what you eat.

10 Choosing low GI takes precedence over any other consideration

Of course not! If you're under the illusion that chocolate's low GI is a reason to go to town on it, then think again. In recommending the GI, we don't want people to throw commonsense to the wind. The GI is not meant to be used in isolation. Reducing saturated and trans fats is vitally important. Eat lots of fruit and vegies (bar potatoes) for their vitamins, minerals, anti-oxidants and fibre. Disregard their GI except in the case of potato. Cutting down on the volume of soft drinks, ice-cream, cakes, biscuits and confectionery, irrespective of their GI, is important. That does not mean strict avoidance—remember, an indulgence a day keeps bingeing at bay. That's especially true if your indulgence is low GI to boot.

THE BEST CHOICES ARE BOTH LOW GI AND HIGH IN FIBRE

Week 9 Menu Plan

	BREAKFAST	SNACK
MONDAY	Natural muesli topped with sliced banana and natural yoghurt	Low fat drinking yoghurt
TUESDAY	Grainy toast with a skim of peanut butter	Low fat flavoured milk
WEDNESDAY	A low GI cereal with low fat milk and sliced strawberries	A pear
THURSDAY	Bircher muesli with sliced peach	A quarter of a honeydew
FRIDAY	Natural muesli with 1 tablespoon of blueberries and natural yoghurt	A small handful of almonds
SATURDAY	Banana and Ricotta Toasts (see page 317)	A handful of pistachio nuts their shells
SUNDAY	Scrambled eggs with grainy toast, grilled tomato and dry-fried mushrooms	A quarter of a rockmelon

LUNCH	SNACK	DINNER
...ushi rolls and a bowl of miso soup	Apple slices and a chunk of reduced fat cheddar	Lentil dhal with tandoori chicken, steamed Basmati rice and a tomato salad
...urkey and Peach Salsa Wraps (see ...age 283)	A quarter of a melon	Penne pasta stir-fried with smoked salmon, olives, spinach, halved cherry tomatoes, garlic and a little white wine
...asta salad with corn, spring onion, ...apsicum, cherry tomatoes, olives ...nd cucumber, and a little olive oil ...ayonnaise with sliced lean meat	Low fat fruit yoghurt	Fajitas made with lean beef or chicken and capsicum. Serve with flour tortillas, salsa, guacamole, shredded lettuce, grated reduced fat cheese and natural yoghurt
...ta bread with felafel, hommous ...nd tabbouli	Carrot and celery sticks with tzatziki dip	Stir-fry with prawns, vegies and Hokkien noodles
...ian-style clear soup with noodles ...nd seafood or chicken	A handful of cherries	Grilled or barbecued lamb kebabs served with tzatziki, spinach salad and grilled pita bread slices
...en sandwich on toasted ...mpernickel bread with ham, ...w fat cream cheese and salad ...gies	A quarter of a melon	Grilled sardines with mixed bean salsa (can of mixed beans, spring onion, fresh coriander, lemon juice, olives, olive oil and halved cherry tomatoes) and a rocket salad
...ast lamb or beef with low fat gravy ...d baked sweet potato, parsnip, ...etroot, zucchini and carrot	An apple	Bowl of vegetable and bean soup with grainy bread

Week 10

The drive to consume a certain volume of food each day is heavily ingrained in human behaviour. We tend to consume the same physical bulk of food, regardless of its kilojoule content. Therefore, if the food we choose is energy dense—a little bit contains lots of kilojoules (think biscuits)—then it is very easy to overconsume. For this reason, it is critical to lower the energy density of our diet if we want to control our weight.

FOOD GOAL

Lowering the energy density of your diet.

EXERCISE GOAL

Aim to walk for a total of 30 minutes on six days, at the same brisk pace as last week (around level 5 of the PRE scale) for the middle 15 minutes. *Plus* try to complete each of the resistance workouts, focusing on the upper and lower body respectively, three times during the week.

ACTIVITY GOAL

Try out a new active hobby. For example, join a dancing class—ballroom, salsa, line dancing, Scottish dancing or jazz; go rollerblading in the park; book in for golf lessons; or take your dog to agility classes.

FOOD FOR THOUGHT

Incidental exercise—a lesson from the past.

FOOD GOAL

Lowering the energy density of your diet.

Reducing the energy density of your diet will help you reduce your energy intake, and thereby facilitate weight loss. Energy density is a measure of how many kilojoules are contained in a food. Foods with a high energy density contain a large number of kilojoules in only a small amount of food. Chocolate is one example (22 kilojoules per gram). Foods of low energy density provide few calories for a large quantity of food. Apples have a low energy density (2 kilojoules per gram).

This week we encourage you to examine the energy density of foods that you regularly eat, with the aim of reducing the overall energy density of your diet. If you haven't looked at it before, start taking a look at the nutrition information panel on foods and work out their energy density. To calculate energy density, divide the energy (kilojoules) per 100 grams of the food by 100. A food can be considered energy dense if it has more than 5 kilojoules per gram.

Sample nutrition information panel

Nutrient	Per 100 g
Energy (kJ)	1500
Protein (g)	9.5
Fat—total (g)	3.0
—saturated (g)	1.1
Carbohydrate (g)	72.2
—sugars (g)	5.4

This food has an energy density of 1500 kilojoules per 100 grams =
15 kilojoules per gram. It has a high energy density.

Note that even though a food may be low in fat, it can still be high in
energy density. High fat foods will obviously be energy dense, but many
commercial low fat foods are high in energy density too, for example:

Energy density (kJ/100 g) of some popular low fat foods

Yoghurt, low fat, fruit	3
Bananas	4
Bread, white	10
Wheat biscuit breakfast cereal	14
Corn flakes	16
Pretzels	16
Rice crackers	17
Plain, sweet biscuits	19

How to reduce the energy density of your diet

- Combine small servings of nutritious but energy-dense foods (such
  as nuts, cheese and olive oil) with larger servings of low energy-dense
  foods (such as fruit, vegetables, pasta, rice and grainy breads).
- Base meals on vegetables and legumes using meat as an
  accompaniment and nuts as a condiment.
- Use oils (such as olive oil) where they will increase your enjoyment
  of low energy-dense foods (especially plant foods and fish) by
  improving the flavour of such dishes (for example, salads with
  dressing, roasted vegetables and panfried fish). Added oils may also

help your absorption of fat-soluble nutrients and phytochemicals
from plant foods.

- Minimise foods containing hidden animal fats (fatty meat, full fat
dairy products, some fast/processed food) and hydrogenated plant
fats (some fast/processed food, commercial cakes/biscuits).
- Avoid eating large volumes of low fat but energy-dense foods,
particularly commercially processed cereals and biscuits.
- Eat more fruit and vegetables. Large amounts of low energy-dense
foods such as fruit and vegetables help to 'dilute' the energy density of
your diet.
  — Add extra vegetables (frozen if you prefer) to stir-fried meat,
  chicken, prawns, fish or tofu.
  — Eat salad daily.
  — Include salad ingredients in sandwiches and rolls.
  — Throw some vegies onto the barbecue with meat. Try zucchini,
  corn cobs, capsicum, mushrooms, eggplant or thick slices of
  parboiled sweet potato or onion. (Use vegetable oil spray on a cold
  grill or a little olive oil to prevent sticking.)
  — Try a vegetarian main dish at least once a week.
  — For quick munching, keep celery, capsicum, baby carrots,
  cucumber, broccoli or cauliflower florets and cherry or grape
  tomatoes on hand.

**TAKE CARE NOT TO *OVER*ESTIMATE HOW MUCH YOU DO OR
*UNDER*ESTIMATE HOW MUCH YOU EAT**

EXERCISE GOAL

Aim to walk for a total of 30 minutes on six days, at the same brisk pace as last week (around level 5 of the PRE scale) for the middle 15 minutes. *Plus* try to complete each of the resistance workouts, focusing on the upper and lower body respectively, three times during the week.

Resistance exercises

Workout 1	Lower body exercises	'Core' strength abdominals and back
	Squats 1 set of 20	Full hover 2 x 30 seconds
	Squats with alternate leg extension 1 set of 20	Pointer 10 each side
	Lunges 10 each leg	
	Power lunges 20 alternating legs	
Workout 2	**Upper body exercises**	
	Three-quarter push-ups 1 set of 20	Leg extensions 10 each leg
	Standing tricep extensions 1 set of 20	Ab curl 1 set of 20
	Bicep curl 1 set of 20	Oblique curl 20 each side

NEW EXERCISE
Squats with alternate leg extension

This advanced exercise really targets the bottom by adding a lift at the top of the squat. If possible, use a mirror to help you perfect your technique and avoid leaning to one side as you lift.

Strengthens and tones: legs and bottom

How to do it:

1 Perform your squat as before (see page 89–90) , but as you rise, extend onc leg at a 45-degree angle behind you, squeezing your bottom muscles as you do so.

2 Ensure that you maintain good posture by pulling in your navel and lifting your chest. Avoid swinging your leg—rather try for a controlled fluid movement without arching the back.

3 Repeat, lifting alternate legs each time.

How many: 20, using alternate legs each time

Sample diary

Monday	Tuesday	Wednesday	Thursday	Friday	Saturday	Sunday
30 min walk	30 min walk	30 min walk	30 min walk		30 min walk	30 min walk
+ workout 1	+ workout 2	+ workout 1	+ workout 2		+ workout 1	+ workout 2
40 mins	40 mins	40 mins	40 mins		40 mins	40 mins

FOOD FOR THOUGHT

Incidental exercise—a lesson from the past.

Life today is far more challenging on our brains than it is on our bodies. Technology has made many of the everyday arduous tasks our grandparents would have done by hand far easier and less time consuming. Washing machines, dishwashers, automatic car washes, drive-through food outlets, shopping malls and the internet all make life easier. The result, however, has been that modern life makes it very difficult for us to control our weight. Imagine living one day without any of this technology—washing your clothes or scrubbing the floor by hand, walking to the shops, walking home carrying heavy bags, chopping logs for the fire, creating everything you eat from the raw ingredients and washing up by hand.

Perhaps you still do some of these things, but imagine every day being filled with this level of activity. In addition to the high levels of activity in the past, food was not so readily available or so appetising—the wide choice of foods we have now encourages us to eat more. You can see that our environment works against our ability to control our weight. While no one wants to see a return to washing by hand and chopping wood for the fire, we can take a lesson from the past and aim to become more active each and every day.

Consider your own lifestyle and environment and think about where you could build in a little more activity. It doesn't have to be much and it probably won't feel like much at the time, but all those little movements add up to a considerable increase in your energy output over the coming weeks, months and years.

Suggestions to build activity naturally into your days

At home

- Wash the car by hand.
- Iron while you watch television.
- Spend 20 minutes gardening.
- Mow the lawn.
- Clean one set of windows.
- Walk the dog.
- Stroll to your local shops.
- Spend an afternoon window shopping.
- Play with the kids.
- Vacuum the floor.

At work

- Use the printer along the hall or, even better, one floor up or down.
- Get up from your desk to speak with a colleague rather than use email.
- Stand and stretch while on the telephone.
- Go outside at lunchtime for a stroll—walking while shopping still counts!
- Use the upstairs or downstairs lavatory.
- Volunteer to buy the cappuccinos.
- Find an excuse to deliver something somewhere.
- Meeting with a colleague? Why not walk while you talk.

Week 10 Menu Plan

	BREAKFAST	SNACK
MONDAY	Half a grapefruit followed by low GI toast with avocado and sliced tomato	A handful of peanuts in the shell
TUESDAY	Natural muesli with sliced apple and low fat milk	Oatmeal biscuits with hommous
WEDNESDAY	Carton of low fat flavoured milk and a banana	Slice of raisin toast with lo cream cheese
THURSDAY	Mixed nut bar, an apple and a low fat yoghurt	Oatmeal biscuit and a ski cappuccino
FRIDAY	Toasted grainy bread with ricotta cheese and fruit jam	A handful of red grapes
SATURDAY	Poached egg with smoked salmon, toasted sourdough and spinach	A small glass of orange ju
SUNDAY	Low fat yoghurt with fruit salad and a sprinkle of mixed nuts and seeds	A glass of vegetable juice

LUNCH	SNACK	DINNER
Tuna Rice Paper Rolls (see page 284)	A nectarine	Chickpea and vegetable curry with steamed Basmati rice
Bowl of vegetable soup with grainy crackers and low fat cream cheese	A peach	Stir-fried greens with a grilled chicken breast and spiced lentils
Salad with a can of tuna, a handful of mixed beans and a little yoghurt dressing	Six raw Brazil nuts	Tortillas with refried beans, lettuce, salsa, chicken strips and natural yoghurt
Grainy bread with toasted reduced fat cheese and tomato	An apple	Spinach and ricotta lasagne with a large green salad
Indian Chicken Burgers (see page 287) with hot chilli salsa, warmed pita bread and shredded lettuce	Natural yoghurt with blueberries	Grilled lean steak with mashed sweet potato, steamed greens and carrots
Grainy crackers with cottage cheese, cucumber and sliced tomato and a cup of ready-to-serve soup	A handful of dried apricots	Asian-style noodle and seafood stir-fry with plenty of mixed vegies
Grainy bread sandwich with hard-boiled egg, olive oil mayonnaise and salad	Fruit Parfaits (see page 318)	Roast chicken with baked vegies—sweet potato, beetroot, carrot, pumpkin and squash. Drizzle with olive oil and balsamic vinegar and bake for 30 minutes

Week 11

This week, focus on these goals:

FOOD GOAL

Making the best of takeaway.

EXERCISE GOAL

This week we split the walks into one shorter, brisker walk (30 minutes maintaining a brisk pace of level 5 for 20 minutes) and one longer but gentler walk (40 minutes at a steady pace of level 4). Aim to complete each walk three times. *Plus* try to complete the full resistance workout, incorporating both upper and lower body exercises, three times during the week.

ACTIVITY GOAL

Whenever you are on a bus or a train for a short journey, choose to stand rather than sit.

FOOD FOR THOUGHT

Can takeaway food be part of a healthy diet?

FOOD GOAL

Making the best of takeaway.

Who said takeaway food can't be good for you? It definitely isn't if you eat it every night, but you can certainly put together a reasonable meal in minimal time with some astute choices and a little help from your local takeaway provider. You will need to think about frequency, however, and that is one of the goals this week. How often is it reasonable for you or your family to be eating takeaway foods for the main meal? Some would say once a month, others would say twice a week; we suggest no more than once or twice a week.

The other thing to think about is what you order. We'd like you to practise putting together a balanced meal with takeaway food this week. Here are some examples using our three-step guide to planning a balanced meal.

Planning a balanced meal with takeway food

Low GI carb	Fruit and vegetables	Protein and good fats
Home-cooked Doongara rice	Stir-fry vegetables	Braised beef and cashew nuts
Basmati rice and lentil dhal	Home-prepared green salad	Tandoori chicken
Corn cobs	Home-prepared coleslaw with canola dressing	Barbecued chicken minus the skin

EXERCISE GOAL

This week we split the walks into one shorter, brisker walk (30 minutes maintaining a brisk pace of level 5 for 20 minutes) and one longer but gentler walk (40 minutes at a steady pace of level 4). Aim to complete each walk three times. *Plus* try to complete the full resistance workout, incorporating both upper and lower body exercises, three times during the week.

Resistance exercises

This week we are going to combine the resistance training exercises into one effective workout to be undertaken three times in the week. We suggest you do the workout on the days you complete your 30-minute walk to give you more time on the other three days for a longer walk. Maximising your time in this way means that you never need to spend hours exercising yet continue to work towards your goals.

Lower body exercises

Squats	1 set of 20
Squats with alternate leg extension	1 set of 20
Lunges	10 each leg
Power lunges	20 alternating legs

Upper body exercises

Three-quarter push-ups	1 set of 20
Standing tricep extensions	1 set of 20
Bicep curl	1 set of 20

'Core' strength, abdominals and back

Full hover	1 x 30 seconds
Pointer	10 each side
Leg extensions	10 each leg
Ab curl	1 set of 20
Oblique curl	20 each side

Sample diary

Monday	Tuesday	Wednesday	Thursday	Friday	Saturday	Sunday
40 min walk 2	30 min walk 1	40 min walk 2	30 min walk 1		40 min walk 2	30 min walk 1
	+ resistance workout		+ resistance workout			+ resistance workout
40 mins	50 mins	40 mins	50 mins		40 mins	50 mins

FOOD FOR THOUGHT

Can takeaway food be part of a healthy diet?

Most people eat takeaway *sometimes*. That's okay; as we have said before, it is the frequency that matters. The real problem exists for *some* people who eat takeaway *most* of the time. With an average meal from a fast food restaurant supplying about half most people's daily energy requirements, those 'two for one' or 'upsize' meal deals, 'free fries' and 'delivered to your door' options really are better off resisted *most* of the time. So, decide on a reasonable, realistic limit for you and your family and stick to it.

On the plus side

- It is a welcome break from cooking.
- You can make upsize meals feed two people or one adult and a child.
- Kilojoule-conscious items now appear on some menus.
- You can add something nutritious (such as a salad or vegetables) at home.

On the minus side

- The menu is often limited.
- Foods are high in kilojoules, salt and saturated fat.
- Meal deals that upsize for a small cost trap you into increasing your kilojoule intake.
- The difference between a small and a large can be double the kilojoules.
- It takes so little time to eat the food from fast food restaurants (no or little chewing required)—all those kilojoules, and you are not even feeling full.

- Even just a muffin and coffee can set you back 2000 kilojoules (that is a third of the day's requirement for some people).

For our suggestions on what to choose when ordering, see pages 226–230.

Here are some more healthy takeaway options and quick-prep home alternatives:

- A regular hamburger with salad—hold the high kilojoule extras such as cheese and bacon
- Salad sandwiches and rolls with ham, salmon, silverside or egg included
- Vegetarian pizza (thin crust)—teamed with a tossed salad
- Takeaway pasta with anything other than a creamy sauce
- Oven-heat fish and chips or wedges from the freezer—check for the varieties cooked in healthy oil—served with vegetables and salad
- Vegetarian lasagne
- Fresh noodles added to pre-cut stir-fry vegetable mix (fresh or frozen) with prawns
- Canned mexican beans on low salt corn chips with dollops of avocado
- Chunks of skinless barbecued chicken added to a packet of chicken noodle soup with egg vermicelli, canned cream corn, frozen baby peas and shallots to make a chicken and corn soup
- Vegetarian kebabs

Week 11 Menu Plan

	BREAKFAST	SNACK
MONDAY	Grilled lean bacon served on a slice of toasted sourdough and topped with sliced tomato	A banana
TUESDAY	Toasted cheese and tomato sandwich from the takeaway shop and an apple	A cup of cherries
WEDNESDAY	Toasted grainy bread topped with a little peanut butter and sliced banana	An apple
THURSDAY	Fruit salad with natural yoghurt and a small handful of mixed nuts and seeds	A skim milk cappuccino and oatmeal biscuit
FRIDAY	On the run: a nut and seed bar and an apple	Low fat fruit yoghurt
SATURDAY	Scrambled egg with smoked salmon and spinach on a slice of toasted grainy bread	A pear
SUNDAY	Breakfast barley: cover the barley with water and simmer for 30–40 minutes until soft. Towards the end of cooking add a mixture of dried fruit, nuts and seeds and serve with warmed low fat milk	An apple

UNCH	SNACK	DINNER
lafel roll with felafel, tabbouli and mmous	A nectarine	Lamb salad with tzatziki: grill or barbecue a lean lamb fillet and slice. Serve on a large salad of baby spinach leaves, semi-dried tomatoes, olives, cucumber and capsicum. Drizzle with tzatziki
xed sushi box and miso soup	A small handful of raw almonds	Thai green chicken curry with a bag of Asian stir-fried frozen vegies added at home and served with home-cooked Doongara rice
ainy bread sandwich of cream eese, smoked salmon and owpea sprouts with salad	A low fat fruit yoghurt	Barbecued chicken, skin removed and meat chopped, added to a pot of chicken stock with long noodles, creamed corn and shallots
mbination long soup	Low fat flavoured milk	Mexican-style bean burrito with steamed Basmati or Doongara rice, salsa and a green salad
ast beef open sandwich on rye rdough with plenty of salad jies	A peach	Grilled fish fillet with a handful of chips, vinegar and a rocket salad
ntil, Beetroot and Feta Salad (see je 288)	A handful of pistachios in their shells	Beef and vegetable stir-fry in black bean sauce with Hokkien noodles
nday Roast with mashed sweet ato and steamed green peas, rots and brussels sprouts	Creamed Rice with Rhubarb and Strawberries (see page 320)	Vegetable soup with melted cheese on toast

Week 12

You have made major changes over the last three months and you should be feeling the rewards of your hard efforts. Now is the time to start reinforcing all the changes you have made and making sure that none of your old habits are sneaking back in on a regular basis. Focus on the following goals this week:

FOOD GOAL

Making healthy eating a habit.

EXERCISE GOAL

As last week, aim to complete a shorter, brisker walk (30 minutes, maintaining a brisk pace of level 5 for 20 minutes) on three days, and one longer but gentler walk (40 minutes at a steady pace of level 4) on three days. *Plus* try to complete the full resistance workout, incorporating more advanced exercises for the upper and lower body, three times during the week.

ACTIVITY GOAL

Become an active person by nature where you see every moment as an opportunity for movement. In other words, be the person who offers to run an errand, walk to the local shop for the papers, walk the dog or carry the shopping home. Every moment of activity counts in the long run.

FOOD FOR THOUGHT

Helping yourself towards healthier eating habits.

FOOD GOAL

Making healthy eating a habit.

There is no magic bullet for permanent weight loss, but people who have lost weight and maintained it over the long haul reveal that weight loss maintainers:

- Have a positive attitude towards changing their diet to improve health
- Possess a willingness to lose weight slowly
- Make lasting changes to their diet and exercise patterns
- Feel comfortable with, rather than restricted by, dietary changes

So how are you feeling about what you have done so far? It is time to reassess your eating habits with another food diary, to see how far you have come. As in Week 1, write down everything you eat and drink each day and compare it with the diary you first kept. Hopefully you will see some major differences. The aim is to keep it going! Remember, success is not about achieving a particular weight, but changing the way you eat and live. It is the simple changes made every day to the way we shop, cook, prepare and eat that can change our lives.

MOTIVATION IS WHAT GETS YOU STARTED.

HABIT IS WHAT KEEPS YOU GOING.

EXERCISE GOAL

As last week, aim to complete a shorter, brisker walk (30 minutes, maintaining a brisk pace of level 5 for 20 minutes) on three days, and one longer but gentler walk (40 minutes at a steady pace of level 4) on three days. *Plus* try to complete the full resistance workout, incorporating more advanced exercises for the upper and lower body, three times during the week.

Resistance exercises

You should be feeling more energetic, alive and starting to reap the rewards of all your efforts over the last weeks. This week we make the resistance exercises a little more challenging to ensure your body keeps changing.

Lower body exercises	
Squats	1 set of 20
Squats with alternate leg extension	1 set of 20
Lunges	10 each leg
Power lunges	20 alternating legs

Upper body exercises	
Full push-ups	1 set of 10
Tricep push-ups	2 sets of 10
Bicep curl	1 set of 20

'Core' strength, abdominals and back

Full hover	2 x 30 seconds
Pointer	10 each side
Leg extensions	10 each leg
Ab curl	1 set of 20
Oblique curl	20 each side

NEW EXERCISES

Full push-ups

Challenge yourself by increasing the load your body has to lift by performing your push-ups on your toes. As before, be sure to keep your bottom in line with your body (see page 167).

How many: Try to complete 10 full push-ups, then, if you need to, lower your knees to complete the second set of 10 in the kneeling position.

Tricep push-ups

This is a more challenging exercise for the triceps than the standing extensions because your resistance in the push-up is coming from your own body weight, which is undoubtedly heavier than the weight you have been using.

Strengthens and tones: back of the arm and shoulders

How to do it:

1 From your regular three-quarter push-up position (see page 167), step your hands in closer until they are directly under your shoulders. You may find it more comfortable to make a fist rather than a flat hand as this allows you to keep your wrist straighter.

2 Lower your chest towards the floor and back, with your elbows tracking close to your ribcage.

How many: Try to complete 2 sets of 10 with a short rest in between.

Sample diary

Monday	Tuesday	Wednesday	Thursday	Friday	Saturday	Sunday
40 min walk 2	30 min walk 1	40 min walk 2	30 min walk 1		40 min walk 2	30 min walk 1
	+ resistance workout		+ resistance workout			+ resistance workout
40 mins	50 mins	40 mins	50 mins		40 mins	40 mins

FIT PEOPLE BURN MORE FAT!

FOOD FOR THOUGHT

Helping yourself towards healthier eating habits.

1 Listen to your appetite

The most normal way to eat is in response to your appetite. The first step for some people is tuning in to it, eating when they are hungry and stopping when they feel full (not stuffed). It may help you to know that it is normal to eat more on some days and less on others.

2 Become aware of non-hungry eating

Eating is an extremely complex behaviour. There is a lot more to it than simply satisfying hunger or meeting nutrient needs. Food is part of socialising and celebrating, comforting and boredom filling. We eat food that is offered so as not to offend a host, we eat because we feel anxious or depressed, we finish off what the kids have left rather than waste it, we eat just because it looks good, or because it is there. All this non-hungry eating isn't wrong but it can contribute to overeating and we need to be aware of it if we are to do anything about it.

3 Eat regularly

Have you ever noticed that the hungrier you are the more tempting high kilojoule foods such as chocolate, biscuits and chips are? And the harder it is to stop at one? You will find it easier to eat normally and control your appetite by regularly grazing on low GI smart carbs.

4 Think about what to eat, rather than what not to eat

What happens if I ask you to think of a pink elephant? You imagine it, right? The future is what we imagine, so rather than thinking of what you don't want to eat, think of what you do.

5 Make overeating as difficult as possible

When you go to have a slice of bread, take out one slice, then seal up the bag and put the loaf away. Put the spreads and toppings away before you sit down to eat. Out of sight generally means out of mind. Keep those occasional foods out of sight but, better still, don't buy them routinely.

6 Make healthy foods more accessible

Put healthy foods where you will find them first:

- Washed, shiny apples and stone fruits in an attractive bowl in the fridge
- Dried fruit and nuts in an airtight jar on your bench or desk
- Pre-sliced tomato and cucumber in the fridge, ready to use on sandwiches or crackers
- Tubs of low fat yoghurt in the fridge
- A loaf of fruit bread by the toaster

These are just a few of the many ways you can increase your chances of eating the types of foods you planned to eat.

7 Don't prepare enough to have leftovers

If you cook too much and have leftovers, serve them into containers and put them in the fridge before you sit down to eat the main meal. Still finding yourself tempted to go back for seconds? Try brushing your teeth soon after finishing a meal.

8 Minimise other distractions while you are eating

Sitting in front of the television with a bag of chips or a block of chocolate, it is very easy to absentmindedly finish the lot. Focus on and savour what you are eating.

9 Stick to regular times for your meals and snacks

When you find yourself thinking about eating outside of your usual meal and snack times, try these four steps:

- Delay.
- Deep breathe.
- Drink water.
- Do something else.

10 Put some thought and planning into your meals

Preparing food is, for most of us, a necessity to eating, a fact of life. So take the time to cook—go to a class if you don't know how. Try different foods, write a shopping list, buy foods in season, get to know your local shopkeepers, shop regularly and develop a passion for good, healthy food.

THINK ABOUT WHAT TO EAT,

RATHER THAN WHAT NOT TO EAT.

Week 12 Menu Plan

	BREAKFAST	SNACK
MONDAY	High fibre cereal with sliced banana and low fat milk	Fruit snack pack
TUESDAY	Toasted sourdough with avocado, smoked mackerel and sliced tomato	Fruit salad
WEDNESDAY	Porridge with sliced banana, sultanas and low fat milk	A slice of raisin toast v low fat cream cheese
THURSDAY	High protein cereal with sliced strawberries and low fat milk	Oatmeal biscuits
FRIDAY	Boiled eggs with grainy toast soldiers	An orange
SATURDAY	Half a grapefruit followed by grainy toast with reduced fat cheese and sliced tomato	An apple
SUNDAY	Spinach and mushroom omelette with a slice of toasted soy and linseed bread	A glass of carrot and orange juice

UNCH	SNACK	DINNER
una sandwich on grainy bread ith corn, olive oil mayonnaise and ced cucumber	Low fat fruit yoghurt	Mushroom and Vegetable Stir-fry (see page 307)
entil soup and a grainy roll	A handful of peanuts in their shell	Grilled lamb cutlets with sweet potato and pumpkin mash and steamed green beans, carrots and broccoli
asted grainy bread topped with a nall can of baked beans and sliced mato	A handful of grapes	Chicken breast baked in orange juice served with boiled new potatoes and stir-fried greens
mato soup with grainy bread and w fat cheese	A quarter of a melon	Beef Kebabs with Vegetable Noodle Salad (see page 300)
nicken and salad tortilla wrap	A low fat drinking yoghurt	Vegetable and chickpea curry with Basmati rice
am, Corn and Zucchini Muffins ee page 280) with salad	Carrot sticks with hommous dip	Cover a whole fish with chopped garlic, ginger, coriander leaves and lemon juice and wrap in foil. Bake or barbecue for 30 minutes and serve with a large mixed salad
rilled sardines (canned or fresh) on urdough toast and tomato and ocado salsa	An apple	Pork and vegetable stir-fry in oyster sauce with Hokkien noodles

the Low GI Diet

PART THREE

doing it
for **life**

preventing weight regain

ARE YOU FAMILIAR WITH THE 'RHYTHM METHOD OF GIRTH control'? You gain some weight, lose it, gain some more, lose it—just like a yoyo. Unfortunately, 95 per cent of people who lose weight by 'dieting' gain it all back again. And that is exactly the reason we have devoted this section to the topic of preventing weight regain.

In 'Doing It For Life', our focus turns from weight loss to weight maintenance, from 'holding your hand' to giving you the skills and knowledge that will maximise your chances of successful long-term weight control. Not only do we help you *entrench* a healthy new lifestyle, we also give you tried and tested tools, tips and clever tricks for maintaining a healthy diet and keeping fit during different times in life—weekends, eating out, holidays, business travel, celebrations and the ever-present emotional roller coaster. When facing these challenges, the more you know in advance, the better.

Just like the 12-week Action Plan, 'Doing It For Life' has three themes that work in concert: meal planning, physical activity and behaviour modification. But it is your turn to take control and hold the reins. With practice and persistence—it will take about a year—you will find you have adopted a host of good habits and behaviours that are often unconscious and hard to break. Indeed, our aim is to have you well and truly hooked on the 'high' that comes from living the healthy low GI life.

Remember, success in the 12-week Action Plan should not be measured by the amount of weight or centimetres lost. What is more important is the extent to which your lifestyle has changed for the better, and the degree to which you have adhered to the eating and exercise guidelines.

Perhaps you lost 10 per cent of your initial weight (that's terrific!), but remember, just 5 per cent is a *significant* achievement that will markedly improve your health and vitality. We know some of you will want to lose more weight still, but it is important to spend at least the next three months preventing weight regain (maintaining your weight loss) before tackling further weight loss by repeating the 12-week Action Plan. By using this alternating three-month pattern of weight loss and weight maintenance, you take the pressure off and give your body time to adjust.

In theory, preventing weight regain should be a lot easier than the process of losing weight. After all, at this stage of the game, the energy equation is balanced, that is to say, energy intake equals energy output. During weight loss, energy intake must be less than energy output. So at this point you get to eat a little more than you have been eating during active weight loss. But beware, it is not the time to relax and let down your guard. And it is certainly not the time to stop exercising. If anything, this stage—preventing weight regain—is the most critical of all. It is going to take *at least 12 months* of persistent effort to convert your old eating and lifestyle pattern into a new and healthy one. Unfortunately, many people mistakenly believe that once the desired amount of weight is lost, the hard part is over. Before they know it, they have regained the weight they lost, often in less time than it took to lose it and with added 'interest'.

Why? There are several reasons why weight regain is very easy. Research suggests that our bodies 'remember' the previously higher weight and strive to attain it again. Hormones act to stimulate appetite and encourage excessive food intake. At your new weight, your body is also a smaller engine than it was in the past, so it requires less fuel to run. If you lost weight too rapidly and without exercising, then chances are you also lost excessive amounts of muscle, making your engine size even smaller.

Another reason why weight loss is so hard to maintain is that your resting metabolic rate (RMR), in absolute terms and on a per kilogram basis, has dropped, often by as much as 10–12 per cent. This is nature's way of helping animals adapt to the environment in which they live. If food is scarce, your body will get by with less fuel by reducing the engine revs. One *proven* benefit of The Low GI Diet is that the reduction in RMR that comes with weight loss is much smaller, around 5 per cent, instead of 10 per cent. The Low GI Diet leads to less fluctuation in blood glucose levels, and consequently your body regulates fuel better with no shortage of either glucose or fat to burn at any time.

Whatever the reason for the decline in energy expenditure, the bottom line is that you need to remain focused on eating well and exercising regularly. If you drift back into your old eating habits and couch potato lifestyle, then the writing's on the wall. Importantly, your healthy low GI diet will be easy to maintain because, unlike low carb or kilojoule-restricted diets, it is not an enormous departure from either the social or individual norm. Concentrating on the *quality* rather than *quantity* of carbs and fats gives you built-in flexibility and freedom.

Characteristics of long-term 'weight losers'

They have high levels of physical activity.

Their exercise is usually brisk walking but often includes weight lifting.

They use a pedometer to count steps per day (see pages 254–55).

They watch the total amount of food eaten.

They eat a reduced fat, not low carb, diet.

They frequently 'self-monitor' (use diet and activity diaries).

Characteristics of weight regainers

They resume their old ways.

They relax their dietary restraint.

They reduce their physical activity.

BE A FULL-TIME WEIGHT MAINTAINER

NOT A PART-TIME LOSER.

Case study: Susie's story

Susie decided to try The Low GI Diet when she was diagnosed as pre-diabetes. With the help of this book she learned how to plan her meals and managed to lose over 25 kilograms. Her weight has fallen from nearly 92 kilograms to 63 kilograms (which was her target weight) and she has maintained this weight loss for over two months now. She reports that she feels much better overall.

She says, 'Your book has taken a lot of thinking out of planning meals and my husband also sings its praises and loves the recipes. I did not feel like I was on a "diet" as such because I felt as though I was always eating— I never felt hungry. It took me a while to get used to, mainly because I wasn't a great vegie eater, but I found that using balsamic vinegar with salads helped. And I did cheat with main meals by having gravy—which helped me enjoy the cooked vegetables. Your book has definitely worked for me.' Susie also reports that she did more exercise than we recommended. Congratulations, Susie!

meal planning for weight maintenance

IT IS YOUR TURN NOW TO PLAN YOUR OWN HEALTHY low GI meals. The good news is that because you aren't trying to *lose* more weight, you can eat a little more each day. This could be an extra serve of fruit or low fat dairy food, or both if you weigh more than 100 kilograms. You might even like to have an extra indulgence occasionally. Although the goal at this stage is to maintain your current weight, it is still necessary to be choosy about your food. This means not straying too far from The Low GI Diet guidelines (pages 47–64). You can include treat foods once a day but it is absolutely critical that you meet your exercise and activity obligations.

Here's a hot tip—adding an extra serve of protein in the form of lean meat, fish or chicken is especially helpful in preventing weight regain. New studies are showing that adding 30 to 50 grams more protein to the diet helps people maintain weight loss in the long term. This equates to about 200 grams (raw weight) of lean steak, poultry or fish. The reason? Turn back to pages 128–29, where we summarised protein's magic.

If you are finding your weight loss difficult to maintain, you probably need to revise your serving sizes. You could be eating healthy foods but perhaps you are simply eating too much of some.

Babies and young children subconsciously 'listen' to their natural body signals to eat when they are hungry and to stop when they are satisfied. Many adults (and older children) have lost touch with this fundamental physiological regulation of food intake. Consequently, in an environment of highly appetising, constantly visible, energy-dense food, it is just too easy to overeat. Instead of relying on our bodies' natural signals of hunger and satiety to decide how much to eat, we use environmental and learnt behavioural cues such as finishing all that's on our plate (it is wasting food not to) or eating all that's offered (seconds anyone?).

Here are a few tips for keeping your food intake in line with your requirements.

First, revisit some of the behavioural techniques listed in Week 12 (see pages 197–99) of the 12-week Action Plan. Listen to your body's cues for food intake and fine-tune your eating behaviour.

Second, ensure that you are eating foods in the correct proportions using our three-step guide to meal planning:

1 *Start* with a low GI carbohydrate.

2 *Add* a generous serve of vegetables or fruit.

3 *Plus* add some protein with a little healthy fat for good measure.

On the following pages we show you how to build your meals around low GI carbs.

**LISTEN TO YOUR APPETITE
AND LET IT GUIDE HOW MUCH YOU EAT.**

Breakfasts

Low GI + carb	Fruit and + vegetables	Protein and = good fat	Balanced low GI meal
Muesli	Strawberries and yoghurt	Low fat milk and yoghurt	Muesli with fruit
Baked beans	Mushrooms	Poached egg	Poached eggs, mushrooms and baked beans
Rolled oats	Raisins with banana slices	Low fat milk	Raisin and banana porridge
Grainy low GI toast	Fresh, ripe, sliced tomato and lettuce	Rindless eye bacon and a smear of barbecue sauce	BLT
Low fat plain yoghurt with a drizzle of honey	Mashed ripe banana	Low fat milk with a dash of nutmeg	Banana smoothie
Sourdough toast	Tomato juice	Herrings with a squeeze of lemon	Herrings on sourdough
Grainy toast	Sliced red apple	Reduced fat cheddar	Toasted cheese and apple sandwiches
Low fat vanilla yoghurt	Fresh chopped seasonal fruit	Mixed nuts and seeds	Fruit and nut yoghurt
Fruit toast	Fruit spread or fresh sliced stone fruit	Fresh ricotta cheese	Raisin toast with ricotta and fruit
Grainy toast	Shallots, mushrooms, tomatoes and parsley	Eggs and grated reduced fat cheese	Savoury omelette on toast

Light Meals

Low GI carb +	Fruit and vegetables +	Protein and good fat =	Balanced low GI meal
Sourdough bread	Lettuce, tomato, beetroot, onion	Minute steak	Steak sandwich
Flat bread	Tabbouli salad hommous	Felafel and kebab	Felafel roll
Sweet corn cobs	Coleslaw	Barbecued chicken	Chicken and salad
Grainy bread	Lettuce, tomato, cucumber, beetroot, alfalfa, grated carrot and onion	Shaved ham	Ham and salad sandwich
Pasta	Napoletana sauce	Shaved parmesan cheese	Pasta Napoletana
Grainy low GI bread	Sliced ripe tomatoes drizzled with olive oil and balsamic vinegar plus torn basil	Canned tuna (drained) combined with garlic, capers, parsley and olive oil, plus a little hommous to spread on the bread	Tuna tapenade and tomato salad
Grainy bread	Lettuce, cucumber and white onion	Red salmon, plus a little light cream cheese to spread on the bread	Salmon and lettuce sandwich
Toasted sourdough rubbed with a clove of garlic	Slow-roasted tomatoes and field mushrooms	Baked ricotta with herbed olive oil for dressing	Garlic toast with tomatoes, mushrooms and baked ricotta
Five bean mix with diced capsicum and shallots, tossed in oil, lemon and and parsley	Salad greens, tomato, grated carrot and diced cucumber	Grated cheddar cheese	Cheese and bean salad

Main Meals

Low GI + carb	Fruit and + vegetables	Protein and = good fat	Balanced low GI meal
Corn tortilla with refried beans or Mexican beans	Shredded lettuce, tomato, diced celery and cucumber with tomato salsa	Lean minced beef, grated cheese and a dollop of mayonnaise for the salad	Beef and bean tortillas with salad
Canned brown lentils	Diced tomato, shredded English spinach and lemon juice	Lamb fillet marinated in olive oil, garlic and oregano	Barbecued Lamb with Lentil Salad and Yoghurt Dressing (see page 299)
Sweet potato	A bunch of rocket or mixed salad greens	Fillets of bream, ocean perch, flake or ling brushed with olive oil and black pepper	Sweet Potato Fish cakes (see page 285)
Basmati rice and dhal	Curry powder or paste plus cauliflower, carrot, green peas and and canned tomatoes	Diced beef or lamb browned in canola oil with garlic and onion	Indian curry and rice
Baby new potatoes, steamed and cooled	Fresh green beans (blanched), cherry tomatoes (halved) and kalamata olives, dressed with olive oil and red wine vinegar	Canned tuna in water (drained) and hard-boiled egg (quartered)	Tuna salad
Sweet potato	Strips of red capsicum and red onion plus steamed green beans	Eggs	Vegetable Frittata (see page 278) with green beans
Canned borlotti beans	Canned tomatoes, onions, garlic, carrots celery and swede	Lean diced beef browned in olive oil	Beef and bean casserole

Low GI carb	+	Fruit and vegetables	+	Protein and good fat	=	Balanced low GI meal
Steamed Doongara or Basmati rice		Asian stir-fry frozen vegetable mix or fresh snowpeas, baby corn, carrot, onion and Asian greens		Chicken, beef, lamb or pork strips stir-fried in peanut oil with chilli plum sauce		Stir-fry with rice
Steamed corn on the cob		Mixed salad		Skinless barbecued chicken		Chicken with salad
Spaghetti		Onion, garlic, mushrooms and capsicum with a jar of tomato pasta sauce		Lean minced beef		Spaghetti bolognaise

Make breakfast a priority

Your mother was right—breakfast really is the most important meal of the day. It is particularly important for weight control, not only because it recharges your brain, but because it speeds up your metabolism after an overnight 'fast'.

Those who eat the biggest breakfasts eat *fewer* kilojoules over the whole day. Why? It is possible that a prolonged interval between dinner and the next meal triggers counter-regulatory hormones that increase eating behaviour. Furthermore, the longer you maintain your 'fast' or delay breakfast, the more insulin resistant you become. This means that whatever you eat next will produce an elevated insulin response, driving greater carbohydrate oxidation and reducing the burning of fat. All of the people on the National Weight Control Registry in the United States (a registry of people who have lost at least 14 kilograms and kept it off for at least 12 months) were found to be having breakfast on most days of the week. You can study their habits more closely by visiting the website at www.nwcr.ws.

One meal for the whole family

Our readers and clients often tell us that one of the side benefits of eating better is that their partner or family is doing so, too. Sometimes it seems as if the others were just waiting for someone to take the lead. What does this tell us about trying to lose weight? Family support is a vital part of eating and living well. If one person in a household changes their eating habits, the whole household may have to adapt. All the more reason to stay clear of untested fad diets. Here are some tips for harmonious family eating.

Aim to prepare the same meal for the whole family

Separate meals will only serve to alienate the person who is trying to change. If there is a diversity of tastes within the family, prepare a range of foods and allow them to serve themselves at the table.

The Ten Golden Rules of preventing weight regain

1 Never skip meals (or you will reduce your metabolic rate).

2 Eat a really good breakfast.

3 Eat at least three to four times a day.

4 Limit television to less than 12 hours per week.

5 Choose low GI carbs at every meal.

6 Eat lean protein sources at every meal.

7 Don't skimp on the fats—just choose healthy ones.

8 Eat seven serves of fruit and vegies every day.

9 Schedule moderate physical activity for 30–60 minutes on six days out of seven.

10 On the seventh day, relax and enjoy.

Eat dinner together

As we all know, there is something uniting about sharing a meal together. Think about making meals special with extra touches such as using your favourite china, lighting candles, having flowers on the table or putting on some background music. Eating together will also improve the quality of your children's diet. Kids who eat with their family on most days have significantly better nutrient intakes and are far more likely to eat the recommended amounts of fruit and vegetables; their diets also contain less saturated fat and have a lower GI.

Turning off the television and having dinner table conversations are some of the best things you can do for your kids' intellectual development.

Growing good food habits in your children

1   Don't restrict their kilojoules.
2   Serve sensible portions (about the size of their fist).
3   Allow all foods, including desserts.
4   Involve them in shopping and food preparation.
5   Make a general rule: three bites of every food on the plate.
6   Limit soft drinks and fruit juices; replace with low fat milk.
7   Don't keep soft drinks in the house; purchase them only outside the home.
8   Limit fast food to twice per week.

Involve others in food choices and meal planning

Talk about it with each other. Ask, 'What are the most important foods to you?', 'Which type of low fat milk would you like to try?', or 'Here's a list of recommended snacks, which would you prefer?'

Make family lifestyle changes

For example, take a stroll together after dinner, have a television-free night once a week, or try having meals outdoors.

Don't buy food you want to avoid

If your kids are clamouring for foods that you are trying to avoid, give them the money that you would normally spend on those treats. Let them decide what they want to buy with it.

Enjoy special treats together when the occasion arises

Food is a traditional part of most celebrations and treats will be even more special if you reserve them for these times.

Eat well on weekends and holidays

Do you manage to maintain healthy eating habits diligently through the week but let things slide when you get to the weekend? Or have you been holding out for holidays to indulge in your favourite snack foods, takeaways, cake shops and restaurants? The problem with this approach is that it can be difficult to resume your hard-earnt good habits after the break. While it is good to have one day free of restrictions and obligations, any longer makes it likely you will slip back to old, familiar ways. So instead of denying yourself your favourite meal, enjoy it once a week, whatever the occasion, and approach holidays and weekends as an extension of your new healthier lifestyle.

One of the hardest places to make healthy choices is on the road. It might seem easy to pull into the 'drive-thru' for a bite to eat, but you will save money if you plan a proper stop. Choose from the menu sensibly and enjoy the break from routine. Alternatively, if you know there is a rest stop or beauty spot en route, plan ahead and enjoy a roadside picnic. A lookout, walking track or park can give you the opportunity not only to refuel your batteries, but to stretch those legs and breathe in some fresh air to help break the drive. Pack some sandwiches (individually wrapped and packed in a plastic container so they don't get squashed) and some easy-to-eat fruit such as apples, bananas or grapes. Some icy bottled water is also a good idea, especially during summer.

A self-catered holiday—in an apartment or holiday house—will give you far more control over your food choices, but, understandably, you won't want to spend all your time preparing food! So make it easy with a little forethought and preparation. Consider taking an appliance you can use for quick meals such as a sandwich maker or portable press grill. Or take the blender to make smoothies for breakfast or for a delicious snack. If there will be lots of sitting around, perhaps you could take that popcorn maker or vegetable juicer that never gets much use. Kebab skewers and barbecue tools can be very handy, too.

If you are self-catering, you might take all the food with you or plan a trip to the supermarket when you first arrive. You will find it easier if you have thought of some easy meals beforehand and written yourself a shopping list.

Meals to make anywhere

- Make a home-made pizza from Lebanese bread spread with cheese and toppings.
- Combine a can of tuna, chopped tomatoes and some antipasto vegetables for an easy pasta sauce.
- Burritos can be made out of avocado, tortillas and a can of Mexican beans.

Snacks to have on hand when you're away

- Fresh fruit—try some locally grown produce
- Unsalted nuts and dried fruit
- A low saturated fat dip such as hommous or mashed avocado, scooped up with carrot sticks and celery
- Low fat fruit yoghurts

Simple barbecue meals

A barbecue is an easy, popular meal while you're out and about or away on holidays.

- Try pieces of marinated lean steak or green king prawns.
- Add some vegetables to the barbecue: mushrooms, halved tomatoes, sliced potato, corn on the cob (in its sheath), pineapple, capsicum and onions.
- For dessert, try barbecued bananas in their skin (for a treat, add some chocolate hazelnut spread!).
- A prepared salad such as coleslaw or tabbouli can be purchased, or make your own combination of fresh salad vegetables and add the dressing just before serving.

> **Tip:** If you are unsure if you will find a barbecue or there are fire restrictions in place, just take along a barbecued chicken.

Plan a picnic

Whether you are out on a day trip, feeding a horde of kids, or just looking for something different to offer friends, pack it all up in a basket and head for the great outdoors. You will enjoy the break from routine and expend some energy in the process. Here are some tasty ideas:

- Olives, marinated mushrooms, marinated capsicum and eggplant, semi-dried tomatoes and a home-made pasta salad
- Vegetable frittata, a handful of salad greens and tiny new potatoes with vinegar and mint
- Lean cold meats such as turkey breast, ham, silverside, pastrami or marinated chicken drumsticks
- Smoked trout or salmon, fresh oysters, prawns or Balmain bugs
- Tabbouli, hommous, pita bread and thin slices of tender roast lamb with a chickpea or lentil salad
- Fresh fruits such as grapes, sliced mango and strawberries
- A piece of nice cheese and fresh sourdough bread
- Cool mineral or soda water with a twist of lime or lemon

Day-trip survival kit

Besides taking along items such as sunscreen and insect repellent, pack up an insulated bag or esky with this collection:

- Cold bottled water
- Fresh sandwiches with easy, simple fillings such as sliced cheese and pickle, ham and mustard and turkey breast with cranberry jelly
- Washed and dried fresh fruit such as small crisp apples or grapes

Eating out the low GI way

Whether you think it is compatible with healthy eating or not, statistics tell us that at some point you are going to be eating out or buying takeaway food. Eating out can really test your resolve as far as healthy eating goes. Like any food choice, however, the more often we eat out, the more important it is that we choose healthy options. If you only eat out once a month you needn't be too fussy, but if it's three to four times a week, good choices are critical. Here are our survival tips to help you when you're eating out.

Don't go ravenously hungry

If you are planning a big night out, don't starve yourself through the day. All that does is reduce your metabolic rate. Eat a light breakfast and lunch and, before you go, have a quick snack—try a slice of grainy bread. This takes the edge off your appetite and you will be less likely to overeat.

Take an extra walk

When you know you will be eating and drinking more than usual, take some extra exercise, preferably beforehand. If it is feasible, walk to the restaurant. At the very least, try not to park right outside the restaurant.

Before you order

Ask for water as soon as you arrive and guzzle some down before your meal. It will begin filling your stomach.

Bypass the bread

Send the bread basket away (unless it is exceptional or low GI).

Remember 1,2,3

No, we are not talking about three-course meals, rather the three basic parts to a healthy, balanced meal:

1 Low GI smart carbs

2 Vegetables or salad

3 Protein—choose from meat, seafood, poultry or a vegetarian alternative such as tofu

Ensure that what you are selecting provides all three parts.

Keep it simple

Often simple fare is the healthiest. You know where you stand with green salad, oysters au naturel, steak, roast lamb or a fresh fruit plate.

Halve it

Order an entrée for your main course or specify entrée sizing. Alternatively, eat *only half* of everything on your plate.

Hold the fries

Tell the waiter to hold the fries. In some restaurants, French fries, chips, wedges, pommes noisettes—whatever they are called—come with the meal whether ordered or not. Their high energy density, high GI and high saturated fat content make them weight control enemy number one.

Pace yourself

Never order all courses at once. Try ordering one at a time and then see how you feel before ordering the next course. This gives the receptors in your stomach time to send a satiety signal to your brain.

Save sauce for the side

Ask for the sauce separately. There are lots of advantages in doing this. Number one: if it is not to your taste, you haven't spoilt your entire meal. Number two: you might end up getting more real food on your plate— like more prawns in your salad. And, of course, if the sauce is terribly fatty or oily, at least you can control the amount you have.

Take your time

Relax and enjoy the food that is being prepared for you, not by you.

If you don't want it, leave it

It is okay to leave some food on your plate. If you don't want to go home feeling like a stuffed walrus, put your knife and fork down as soon as you feel comfortably satisfied.

Be discerning with drinks

Make water your first choice. Ask for some routinely whether you feel like it or not. Chances are you will drink it if it is in front of you. Go easy on the sugary drinks because they tend to bypass satiety mechanisms. Drink no more than one to three glasses of alcohol. Remember, alcohol has almost twice as many kilojoules as carbohydrate.

Spoons for two

The Low GI Diet is not about deprivation, so if you really feel like it, go ahead and have a dessert, but why not share it with someone?

Walk it off

After a restaurant meal, walk home or back to the office and climb the stairs rather than using the lift.

Finding the low GI choice on the menu

Indian food

The traditional accompaniment for Indian dishes is steamed Basmati rice, which is a classic low GI choice. Lentil dhal offers another low GI accompaniment, but make sure they don't add the oil topping (tadka).

Unleavened breads such as chapatti or roti may have a lower GI than normal bread but it will boost the carbohydrate content of the meal and increase the GL.

Our suggestions:
- Tikka (dry roasted) or tandoori (marinated in spices and yoghurt) chicken
- Basmati rice
- Cucumber raita
- Spicy spinach (saag)

Japanese food

Japanese sushi rice (koshihikari) has a low GI, and any refrigerated rice has a lower GI than when it is freshly cooked. The vinegar used in preparation of sushi helps keep the GI low (acidity helps slow stomach emptying), and so do the viscous fibres in the seaweed. Typical ingredients and flavours to enjoy are shoyu (Japanese soy sauce), mirin (rice wine), wasabi (a strong horseradish), miso (soybean paste), pickled ginger (oshinko), sesame seeds and sesame oil. Go easy on deep-fried dishes such as tempura.

Japanese restaurants are great places to stock up on omega-3 fats, as dishes such as sushi and sashimi made with salmon and tuna contain high amounts of beneficial polyunsaturated fatty acids.

Our suggestions:
- Miso soup
- Sushi
- Teppanyaki (steak, seafood and vegetables)
- Yakitori (skewered chicken and onions in teriyaki sauce)
- Sashimi (thinly sliced raw fish or beef)
- Shabu-shabu (thin slices of beef quickly cooked with mushrooms, cabbage and other vegetables)
- Side orders such as seaweed salad, wasabi, soy sauce and pickled ginger

Thai food

Thai food is generally sweet and spicy and contains aromatic ingredients such as basil, lemongrass and galangal. Spicy Thai salads which usually contain seafood, chicken or meat are a delicious light meal. For starters, avoid the deep-fried items such as spring rolls.

One downside to Thai cuisine is the coconut milk, which really raises the saturated fat content of Thai curry. So don't feel you have to consume all of the sauce or soup. The traditional accompaniment to Thai food is plain, steamed Jasmine rice, but this is very high GI so you are better off if you can reduce the quantity. Noodles are always on the menu as well, but avoid fried versions. Boiled rice noodles may be an option. Limit yourself to a small helping or, if you are having takeaway, you could cook up some Doongara rice at home as an accompaniment.

Our suggestions:
- Tom yam—hot and sour soup
- Thai beef or chicken salad
- Wok-tossed meats or seafood
- Stir-fried mixed vegetables
- Small serve of steamed noodles or rice
- Fresh spring rolls (not fried)

Italian food

The big plus with Italian restaurants is the supply of low GI pasta with an array of sauces. Good choices are arrabiata, puttanesca, Napoletana and marinara sauces (without cream). Despite what you may think, most Italians don't sit down to huge bowls of pasta, so don't be afraid to leave some on your plate (or order an entrée size)—the GI may be low but a large serve of pasta will have a high GL. Other good choices include minestrone and vegetable dishes, lean veal and grilled seafood. Steer clear of crumbed and deep-fried seafood.

Our suggestions:
- Minestrone
- Veal escalopes in tomato-based sauce
- Prosciutto (paper-thin slices of smoky ham) wrapped around melon
- Barbecued or grilled seafood such as calamari or octopus

- Roasted or char-grilled fillet of beef, lamb loin or poultry
- Green garden salad with olive oil and balsamic vinegar
- Sorbet, gelato or simply a fresh fruit platter
- Entrée-size pasta with seafood and tomato or stock-based sauce

Greek and Middle Eastern food

In Mediterranean cuisine, olive oil, lemon, garlic and onions and other vegetables abound. Many dishes are char-grilled and specialities such as barbecued octopus or grilled sardines are excellent choices. You will find regular bread replaced with flat bread or Turkish bread, while potatoes are replaced with wholegrains such as bulgur (in tabbouli) and couscous.

Among the small appetising mezze dishes, you could pick and choose what you like. Many of the choices are healthy, such as hommous, baba ghanoush, olives, tzatziki and dolmades.

Our suggestions:
- Mezze platter with Lebanese bread
- Souvlaki (char-grilled skewers of meat with vegetables)
- Kofta (balls of minced lamb with bulgur wheat)
- Greek salad of fresh lettuce, tomato, olives, feta and capsicum, with balsamic dressing or oil and lemon
- Fresh fruit platter
- Felafel with tabbouli and hommous with a flat bread

Tips for those who routinely eat at restaurants

1 *Walk* to the restaurant if possible.

2 Order water as soon as you arrive.

3 Send the bread basket away (unless it's *exceptional*).

4 Order green salad, oysters au naturel or soup for entrée.

5 Order an entrée for your main course (or specify entrée size).

6 Alternatively, eat *only half* of everything on your plate.

7 Tell the waiter to hold the hot chips.

8 Share dessert with a dining companion.

9 Drink no more than one to three glasses of alcohol.

10 Walk back to the office or climb the stairs.

Staying on track while travelling for business

Whether you love it or hate it, regular business travel necessitates some thought and planning to avoid disrupting your healthy lifestyle routine.

Breakfast

There is no reason why breakfast away from home shouldn't be as good, if not better, than what you normally have. You may even have more time on your hands to enjoy it. A buffet breakfast can be a great place to sample some different breakfast foods from around the world. The biggest hazard is overeating—because it's all there in front of you, it's easy to have more than you need. Good options include:

- Fruit—fruit or fresh juice is always available and this is a great way to boost your daily fruit intake. Try a fruit you've never had before with yoghurt on top.
- Cereal with low fat milk—dry packet cereals need careful selection. Muesli, fruit and yoghurt is a more sustaining option.
- Cooked breakfast—go with the grainy bread for toast, skip the butter or margarine, and top it with poached or scrambled eggs. This gives you protein without too many kilojoules and can make everything more sustaining. Side orders such as mushrooms and tomato add micronutrients without excessive calories.

Lunch

Lunch these days is mostly a light affair, but if it isn't, try to make your evening meal light. By light we mean big on salad and vegetables. In fact, it's generally vital to include vegetable matter with lunch if you are to meet the daily recommendation of at least five serves a day. Add protein for sustenance but don't be heavy handed with high GI carbs at lunch if you want to minimise a post-lunch dip in energy levels. If you are on the go, stop at a suitable place that sells grainy bread, salad mixes and fresh fruit.

Dinner

Have a look at our recommendations on pages 223–30 for good choices when you are eating out. Stick with simple options for dinner—grilled steak, chicken breast, fish or seafood with vegetables or salad. While ordering, think about how much energy you have used during the day, and order to match that.

Snacks

For a start, empty the mini bar and stock it with a couple of low fat yoghurts and a few bananas or apples. Another solution is to prepare snacks in advance and take enough to last you through the trip. Dried fruit and nuts make lightweight, nutritious snacks.

Activity tip

While away on business, confined to hotel rooms and meeting rooms, it can be hard to find any time for activity. We suggest you pack a skipping rope and find 15 minutes a day to exercise in your hotel room. Alternatively, if the firestairs are accessible and safe, ask for a room on the second or third floor and use them as you come and go.

Stress eating—can you cope?

Are you a stress eater—someone who raids the cookie jar or the freezer when the going gets tough, the deadlines loom and the obligations mount up? When you are disappointed in something or someone, or grieving the loss of anything, does food help fill the void? Afterwards you feel let down, guilty, more stressed and the cycle begins to repeat itself. Does this pattern sound familiar?

You are not alone. About 50 per cent of people feel hungry when stressed and women struggle with it more than men. And it is not just a failure of will power—it's a case of hormones. Science can now explain the phenomenon of 'emotional' eating. When we are in immediate physical danger, the hormone cortisol is flushed into the blood stream as part the fight-or-flight response. A less marked but prolonged rise occurs when we are simply under pressure to perform—stressed. Cortisol's function is to help us cope with the challenge by mobilising fuels (glucose and fat) for exceptional physical performance. Another action of cortisol is to increase our appetite—after all, eating will provide more fuel for meeting the next challenge.

This direct connection between cortisol and hunger spells trouble, especially if you're dieting. Dieters have cortisol levels about 20 per cent higher than less restrained eaters. The constant challenge to restrict energy intake is a cause of stress in itself. Researchers at Yale University found that women with the highest levels of cortisol ate double the amount of energy-dense food (think doughnuts or chocolate) than those with low cortisol levels. Furthermore, stress actually makes those foods taste better, enhancing the flavour of sweet, fatty foods.

Cortisol's actions would have been entirely appropriate in the past when we ran for our lives as hunter-gatherers, when fear of wild animals was a constant threat. But these days, the challenges we face are mental rather than physical and we don't need all those extra kilojoules to perform cognitive feats. The difficulty today in our rush-rush world is that we often feel under constant pressure. Indeed, in one survey, nearly 30 per cent of people admitted that they have a 'red alert' day almost daily. It is no coincidence that the increase in overweight people is matched with rising rates of stress—the two are linked physiologically.

One of cortisol's downstream effects is to increase insulin levels and thereby promote fat storage around the waist rather than elsewhere. That is because fat around the stomach is easy to convert to instant energy compared with fat that is stored in the thighs or under the skin. Fat stored in the belly is 'emergency' energy. Even thin women with high cortisol levels have been found to have a pot belly. Unfortunately, you won't be drawing on that emergency supply when your mind, not your legs, is doing the running. If both cortisol and insulin stay high for several hours, they drive glucose burning instead of fat burning.

How to pull yourself together

You guessed it—exercise! Not just because it burns excess energy but because it releases the 'feel good' chemicals that negate anxiety and stress. A quick bout of exercise can even stop a surge in cortisol and reduce food cravings in their tracks. For example, if you are in the office, a quick run up the stairs may be all it takes to blunt the cortisol spike.

Cutting stress in its tracks

Step 1: Recognise that stress, anxiety and worry make you hungry.

Step 2: Recognise there's a physical reason behind it.

Step 3: Give in to the hunger but make it a low GI, high protein snack (see suggestions opposite).

Step 4: Get on your bike or into your joggers and move it.

Step 5: Increase your heart rate until it's really pumping for at least 20 minutes.

Step 6: Afterwards savour the feeling of invigoration that only exercise can give.

Cortisol emergency fixes

apple slices with peanut butter

strawberries dipped in chocolate hazelnut spread

a sweet yoghurt topped with berries

a good cheese with celery sticks

a handful almonds and muscatel raisins

a handful of chocolate sultanas

a biscuit or two if that's what it takes

A FALL IN CORTISOL MEANS

A WORLD OF DIFFERENCE IN ATTITUDE

AND A MORE PRODUCTIVE YOU.

Apart from exercise, there are a few other simple tricks to deal more effectively with stress on a long-term basis:

1 Listen to music while you work.

2 Keep a serene or smiling Buddha on your desktop.

3 Listen to a relaxation tape while driving to and from work.

4 Connect with a good friend or group of friends.

5 Do a yoga class.

6 Have a massage.

7 Take a bath.

8 Get seven to eight hours' sleep (the sleep-deprived have higher cortisol levels).

All-night diners

Night eating syndrome was first reported 50 years ago but scientists are now taking a new look at it. One to 2 per cent of the population are thought to suffer some of the symptoms of this condition. More common among overweight people, it may be as high as one in four among obese invidividuals.

In recent studies at the University of Pennsylvania, sufferers were monitored in sleep laboratories and compared with matched-for-weight 'control' subjects who did not report night eating. Characteristically, the signs and symptoms of the all-night diners were:

- Having little or no appetite for breakfast
- Their first meal is delayed for several hours after waking
- Increased appetite at night
- Eating more in the evening
- Consuming more than half of the daily energy intake after 8 p.m.
- Trouble falling asleep or staying asleep (insomnia)
- Waking frequently (more than one to two times a night) and then eating
- Feeling tense, anxious or guilty while eating
- A tendency to eat carb-rich foods (sugars, starches)

The preferred snack of the night eaters studied was a peanut butter sandwich (about 1500 kilojoules with carbohydrate as the dominant energy source). What's more, they remembered what they ate, unlike people with the rare night-time eating disorder linked to sleep-walking. In contrast to binge eaters who have short intense bursts of eating, night eaters eat continuously throughout the evening and night. They do not purge or use laxatives.

The causes of night eating are not well understood, but it appears to involve a disturbance of the body's internal clock. Even though the normal sleep/wake cycle is intact, appetite is clearly highest at night. It seems to be triggered by stress or depression but there may be a genetic predisposition. There is even a suggestion that the pituitary gland in the brain is malfunctioning, causing defective secretion of stress hormones such as cortisol. Some researchers suggest that sufferers are self-medicating with food, unconsciously aware that carbohydrates stimulate the 'feel good' chemicals such as serotonin.

What can you do about it?

If you think you have night eating syndrome, then it is important that you contact your doctor and ask for a full physical examination and a referral to an eating disorder specialist. There are medications that can help reset the body's natural circadian (daily) rhythm and lift feelings of depression. Optimal treatment for night eating syndrome is still being developed but a dietitian can help with healthy, low GI meal plans that will leave you less vulnerable to the night-time munchies.

what you need to do— activity and exercise

ONCE YOU HAVE BEEN THROUGH A WEIGHT LOSS PHASE, exercise and activity become more important than ever. The single most important difference between long-term weight losers and weight gainers is the amount of physical activity they build into their day. Quite simply, exercise has to be your first priority. At the end of your 12-week Action Plan you should be fitter and capable of doing a little more than you were able to at the start. The aim in the 'Doing It For Life' phase is to maintain the same activity level of Week 12 (see pages 192–96) but build in different forms of exercise so that you don't become bored. Setting new goals and enjoying what you do are critical.

FOOD MINUS EXERCISE EQUALS FAT!

To appreciate the importance of exercise and activity, let's take a look at the big picture. It is not how much fat or energy is used during a single bout of activity, but how it all adds up over the months and years. The fact is that most of us gain weight very slowly over the years—on average gaining 0.5 to 1 kilogram every year. So ten years down the track, you weigh 5–10 kilograms more. Similarly, small amounts of activity may seem unimportant in the short term—you can't detect a change on the scales—but they add up over the long term. In the table below, consider how many kilos of fat you potentially 'save' if you take five minutes here and five minutes there to be active. Every little bit counts!

Take five minutes every day to:	Potential saving in kilos of fat*	
	in 1 year	in 5 years
Take the stairs instead of the lift	3.7	18.5
Weed one patch of the garden	0.6	3.0
Rake the lawn	0.6	3.0
Vacuum the lounge room	0.7	3.5
Walk 150 m from the car to the office	0.7	3.5
Carry the groceries 150 m back to the car	0.9	4.5

*Figures are based on a 70 kg (11 stone) person.

This shows us that all those seemingly small actions where we *choose* to take the more active option really do add up in the long run. It won't hurt you to park your car at the furthest end of the car park. It might not feel as if climbing one flight of stairs makes a difference. But it does—you can save yourself 1 or 2 kilos of fat over the course of a year. Similarly, even if you have just five minutes rather than 30 minutes to fit in some exercise, do it anyway. It is abundantly clear why active people find it much easier to prevent weight regain.

Keep an activity diary for a week and record any exercise you do in addition to active choices you have made. Review it at the end of the week and see how well you have done and whether you are being as active as you can be.

Karen's diary (example)

Monday: Walked the dog (30 minutes), used the stairs instead of the escalator in the shopping centre and walked 5 minutes to the local shop for more milk instead of taking the car.

Tuesday: Raining so didn't walk the dog. Spent most of the day at my desk—only activity was a short walk to the cafe for lunch.

Wednesday: Attended a yoga class.

Thursday: Walked the dog (30 minutes), spring-cleaned the house for the whole afternoon—exhausted, but feel a great sense of achievement.

Friday: Went to an indoor cycling class at my local health club—loved it! Much better than sitting on a bike in the gym on my own. Felt so good I walked home afterwards—20 minutes.

Saturday: Took the dog for a long walk (60 minutes) first thing this morning. Went shopping for the afternoon—on my feet for 4 hours. Carried my shopping home (a 15-minute walk) instead of taking the bus.

Sunday: Lazy day at home and didn't do much activity other than press the buttons on the television remote!

Review:

Karen had a fairly good week activity-wise. She accumulated 160 minutes, walking, not counting all the walking of an afternoon's shopping, as well as a yoga class, an indoor cycling class and the extra energy expended in taking the stairs, cleaning the house and carrying shopping bags. Looking back at her week, however, Karen realises there were two days when she did almost no activity or exercise.

She enjoyed her fitness class so much that she has decided to add a second class on a Tuesday night to ensure she is active for six days of the week and has chosen to keep Sunday as her day of rest and recuperation.

Tom's diary (example)

Monday–Friday: Left the car at home and walked to the train station (10 minutes), which meant a short 5-minute walk to the office at the other end. At lunchtime, instead of eating at my desk, I bought a sandwich and walked to the nearby park (5 minutes there and 5 minutes back) and enjoyed a 20-minute break—the fresh air and break from my desk actually helped to keep me focused for the afternoon whereas I usually have an 'energy slump' after lunch. Adding in the walk to and from the train station each day I have accumulated 40 minutes of walking into my day! I'm amazed at how much better I feel without adding exercise time commitments to my day.

Saturday: Took the kids to the park in the afternoon armed with a frisbee and a football—comfortably spent an hour having fun and the kids loved it, too.

Sunday: Washed and vacuumed the car by hand with a little help from the kids (enticed with some extra pocket money). It only took us half an hour but the car looks great and saved me some money on the usual car wash charge (despite having to bribe the kids).

Review:

Tom works in an office and although he played sport and was much more active when he was younger, he has found it increasingly difficult to find the time for exercise while working long hours and spending time with his young family. Tom had decided to try to fit in an accumulated 30 minutes of activity into his day—let's take a look at how he achieved this. He built 40 minutes of accumulated activity into his day by walking to the train station instead of taking his car and going for a short stroll at lunchtime. Adding to this the extra activities with the kids at the weekend, Tom has drastically increased his weekly activity.

In short, building exercise into your life is vital. There really couldn't be a more powerful means of improving your health while looking and feeling better. There is much controversy in scientific research regarding nutrition, but there is unanimity over the benefits of exercise.

This does not mean you need to go and join the gym or start pounding the streets every night. There are lots of options, and finding what sort of exercise is suitable and enjoyable to you is the key to success. Use the exercise selector on pages 249–54 to help you work out which form of exercise will suit you best.

Types of exercise

While exercise works through three different systems, as illustrated on the next page, many forms of exercise work more than one system and sometimes all three. Cycling, for example, is primarily an aerobic exercise, but also involves resistance training for the legs as they have to push against a force. Yoga is usually thought of as primarily improving flexibility, yet holding the poses involves a good deal of resistance training using your body weight as resistance.

In your initial 12-week Action Plan we focused on aerobic exercise (walking) and resistance training in the form of key exercises you could

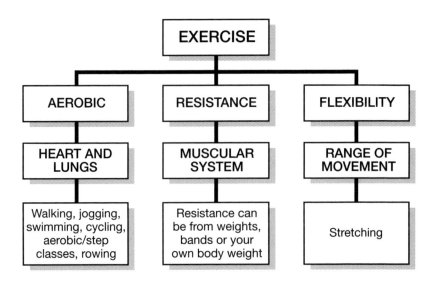

do at home. Both these forms of exercise are most effective in helping you to lose body fat and they continue to be important from now on in assisting you to prevent a regain of weight. This doesn't mean that flexibility training is any less important—you should always stretch at the end of your exercise session—but spending more time on the types of exercise that will specifically help your weight control is just good time management. Let's take a look at some popular forms of exercise and see where they fit in with this model.

Walking and jogging

We chose walking as the suggested form of exercise in the 12-week Action Plan for good reason—it is undoubtedly one of the best forms of exercise you can do for your health and almost anyone can do it. Continuing with your walking program may be all you want to do at this point and that is fine.

If you are ready to step up your fitness a little more, you can raise the intensity, building up to a jog, or increase the time you spend walking.

Aerobics classes

As the name suggests, these are primarily aerobic workouts although many will also incorporate some resistance exercises and a good class will always include a stretch at the end. Group fitness classes are an excellent way to motivate you to exercise a little harder—the combination of uplifting music, guidance from a qualified instructor and the group atmosphere makes classes fun and effective. Don't be put off by the old 'leg-warmers and thong leotards' image! Times have changed and there are now classes to suit everyone—choose from aerobics, step, boxing, martial arts or circuit training. Classes are run in health clubs, leisure centres, universities and local halls all around the country.

Cycling

If you love to get outdoors and to exercise alone, then cycling may be for you. Cycling is primarily aerobic exercise but also involves some resistance training for the legs. The downside is that you will need to invest in a decent bike and helmet—cycling shorts and shoes are also a good idea. Once you are geared up and ready to go, this is an excellent form of exercise to keep burning the kilojoules and preventing weight regain. Of course this needn't be a solo activity—try getting the whole family involved on the weekend or join a cycling group in your area for organised routes and social contact. The other option is to go along to an indoor group cycling class at your local health club. These are instructor-led with motivating music to inspire you to give your best.

Rowing and kayaking

A good option if you live near the water and like to be outdoors. Rowing and kayaking mainly provide aerobic exercise, but since you are also using both upper and lower body strength you incorporate a good deal of resistance training at the same time.

Tennis, squash and other racket sports

These sports provide effective aerobic exercise, plus the social aspect helps you to keep it up. If you have never played before, book yourself in for a program of lessons—then you'll meet fellow beginners to play with on a regular basis.

Golf

While not as intense as some of the other forms of exercise, golf does take a long time to play and can be a great way to assist your weight loss. Of course, you need to walk to gain the benefits so leave the golf buggy at the clubhouse!

Weight training

The people who really need to weight train are not the young guns spotted pumping iron at your local gym, but the rest of us. As you already know, increasing your muscle mass raises your metabolic rate and helps you burn more fat all of the time, but did you know that weight training also strengthens your bones and can help to prevent weight gain as we age? This means that weight training is important for women approaching menopause, those at risk of osteoporosis, seniors and anyone who wants to control their weight. Health clubs now have sophisticated equipment that ensures you train effectively and safely—or you can work with resistance bands or join a weights-based group exercise class.

Team sports

If you enjoy the competition and camaraderie of team sports, then find a local team playing whatever sport you fancy. You could try soccer, netball, hockey, basketball, rugby or baseball. All these are great aerobic training and clubs often have a training program that also incorporates resistance and flexibility training.

Pilates and yoga

These classes focus more on flexibility but have a good element of resistance training—as you will know if you have ever tried to hold a yoga pose or taken part in a Pilates class. They have very little aerobic benefit, however, and, while they are a good addition to your exercise program, ensure that you also include some form of aerobic training. That said, there are different forms of both classes—for example, Ashtanga yoga is far more energetic and demanding than other more relaxing and meditative forms of yoga.

Swimming

Water provides 15 times more resistance than air. For this reason working out in water can be extremely effective. If you are very overweight or suffer from arthritis or other injury, getting in the water offers a safe and effective means of exercising. The water supports your body weight, your muscles work against the resistance of the water and you won't feel sore afterwards (muscle soreness comes mainly from muscles lengthening under resistance—in water the opposing muscle takes over so muscles only ever have to contract against the resistance). You can choose from swimming laps or joining an aqua aerobics class in which an instructor will lead you through a series of exercises in the water.

Dancing

Dance classes are a fabulous way to get active. Not only are they lots of fun but many are also a great way to meet new friends and socialise. Any kind of dancing is suitable—choose from jazz, salsa, Scottish dancing, line dancing, ballet and ballroom—the choice is endless. See what appeals to you and what is available in your area. The advertisements in the back of your local newspaper are a good starting point.

Setting an example for the kids

We know we can't force kids to exercise but you can lead by example. If they see you lounging on the sofa every night, eating chips and watching television for hours, then, inevitably, they copy that behaviour. Kids of active parents/guardians are far more likely to be active themselves—if not now, at least in the future. You may even persuade them to exercise with you!

Get the kids moving, too

1 Restrict periods of extended inactivity such as watching television or videos or playing computer games.
2 Invent projects to create at home (like a go-cart or a bird feeder).
3 Don't encourage sedentary behaviour over activity. (You may have to delete 'sit down and be quiet' from your vocabulary.)
4 Make sure the kids aren't watching you watching television.
5 Let them see you being active.
6 Don't chauffeur them, let them use public transport.
7 Don't confine them to the four walls of home or school.
8 Don't restrict spontaneous decisions to be active.
9 Put the ride-on toys and trampoline where they catch attention.
10 Prepare food with their help. They could help you with a special dish.

**WHATEVER TYPE OF EXERCISE YOU DECIDE ON,
THE TWO IMPORTANT FACTORS ARE THAT YOU ENJOY THE
EXERCISE AND YOU DO IT REGULARLY.**

The exercise selector

The key to making exercise a regular part of your life is to find something that you enjoy and look forward to. That's not to say that there won't be times when you have to motivate yourself to get to your exercise session, but finding the motivation will be infinitely easier if you are then rewarded by a fun, enjoyable session that leaves you invigorated. If you hate running and are not an early morning person, then choosing to get up for a 6 a.m. run before work just will not last beyond the first couple of weeks. Similarly, if you live in a rural area, more than 30 minutes' drive from the nearest fitness centre, then attending a group fitness class will again become difficult to maintain in the long run. Use the following questionnaire to help you to identify which form of exercise might suit you best.

- For each question highlight the answer row that applies to you with a fluorescent pen.
- Then for each activity column, add up your scores and enter the total at the bottom.
- This is your total score for each activity.

	Walking/ jogging	Aerobics	Cycling	Kayaking
PERSONAL DETAILS				
Age				
Under 35	0	0	0	0
35–49	0	0	0	0
50–59	2	3	3	1
60+	4	7	7	2
Body frame				
Small/medium	0	0	0	0
Large	3	2	0	0
EXERCISE QUESTIONNAIRE				
Are you more than a little overweight?				
No	0	0	0	0
Yes	4	4	3	3
Are you an indoor or outdoor person?				
Indoor	7	0	6	8
Outdoor	0	1	1	0
Are you self-conscious about exercising in public?				
No	0	0	0	0
Yes	5	8	4	0
How competitive are you?				
Highly	3	1	5	3
Moderately	0	1	4	3
Not very	0	0	2	0
Are you prepared to pay more than $30 a week to exercise?				
Yes	0	0	0	0
No	0	8	2	0
Are you suffering limiting injuries to any of the following:				
Legs/ankles/knees?	9	9	4	0
Shoulders/arms?	1	7	2	7
Hip?	9	9	3	1
Back?	5	10	5	5

Weight training	Ball games	Yoga/ Pilates	Swimming	Dancing	Circuit training	Skipping/ stepping
0	0	0	0	0	0	0
0	4	0	0	1	0	3
1	5	0	0	3	1	5
9	6	0	0	4	4	8
0	0	0	0	0	0	0
0	2	2	0	2	2	4
0	0	0	0	0	0	0
0	6	4	0	4	3	5
0	4	0	4	0	0	0
1	0	4	2	0	1	5
0	0	0	0	0	0	0
3	5	3	4	7	0	0
1	0	8	3	8	2	8
0	2	4	3	5	1	5
0	8	0	3	0	0	0
0	0	0	0	0	0	0
8	4	4	1	4	0	0
1	7	3	1	7	5	9
6	5	4	3	2	4	4
1	7	6	3	7	3	8
2	6	3	2	6	4	5

	Walking/ jogging	Aerobics	Cycling	Kayaking
EXERCISE QUESTIONNAIRE				
Are you NOT within easy reach (say 15 minutes) of any of the following:				
Pool/lake/sea?	0	0	0	10
Park/open space?	5	0	0	0
Fitness centre?	0	5	0	0
Sports facilities?	0	0	0	0
Safe bike routes?	0	0	10	0
How much time can you give 3–4 days a week for exercise?				
<20 mins	4	9	3	6
20–40 mins	0	2	0	2
>40 mins	0	0	0	0
How do you prefer to exercise?				
Alone	0	0	0	0
With a friend	1	9	3	1
In a group	2	0	6	3
TOTAL TEST SCORE				

Calculate your **interest score** for each activity

- If you think you would definitely enjoy carrying out the activity regularly give yourself an interest score of 100.
- If you think you may enjoy carrying out the activity regularly give yourself an interest score of 90.
- If the activity doesn't appeal to you, give yourself an interest score of 80.

Insert your interest score for each activity into the corresponding space opposite.

Weight training	Ball games	Yoga/ Pilates	Swimming	Dancing	Circuit training	Skipping/ stepping
0	0	0	10	0	0	0
0	0	0	0	0	0	0
9	4	5	0	3	0	0
0	10	0	0	0	0	0
0	0	0	0	0	0	0
5	10	5	10	10	3	3
0	4	0	4	2	0	0
0	0	0	0	0	0	0
0	10	3	0	5	1	0
0	0	4	2	0	1	3
8	0	0	2	0	1	6

	Walking/jogging	Aerobics	Cycling	Kayaking	Weight training	Ball games	Yoga/Pilates	Swimming	Dancing	Circuit training	Skipping/stepping
Interest score											

Calculate a **final score** for each activity by subtracting the **total test score** from the **interest score** for each activity.

	Walking/jogging	Aerobics	Cycling	Kayaking	Weight training	Ball games	Yoga/Pilates	Swimming	Dancing	Circuit training	Skipping/stepping
Final score (Interest score *minus* total test score)											

The activity with the highest final score will generally be the most appropriate form of exercise for you. If there are several activities at the top falling within about 5 points of each other, choose the one you think you would prefer, or combine them for a varied program. It is a good idea to combine at least a couple of activities to maintain your interest in your program and challenge your body in different ways.

Using a pedometer

A pedometer is a neat little tool that is highly effective in helping you achieve a walking goal. Inexpensive and available at good sports shops and department stores, it looks a bit like a pager which you clip to your waistband or belt in the morning. It counts the number of steps you take during the day, which can be a real eye-opener as to how active you really are—you may well be completely shocked at how few steps you actually take during a normal day!

There are now guidelines to advise us on how many steps we should be aiming for and these are shown below. You may have to build yourself slowly up to these levels. Wear your pedometer for the first week of 'Doing It For Life' and, at the end of each day, record the number of steps you took. Work out your average daily steps at the end of the week and add 30 per cent. This is your new goal for the next two to three weeks. Once you are achieving the new step goal easily, add a further 30 per cent. Repeat this process, taking as long as you need at each stage, until you are meeting the goals below.

- For optimum health: aim to achieve 7500 steps per day.
- For weight loss during the 12-week Action Plan: aim to achieve 10 000 steps per day.
- To prevent weight regain: aim to achieve 12 500 steps per day.

Of course, the pedometer only counts the actual walking that you do and not other activities. The following table gives you an idea of how many steps are equivalent to 15 minutes of certain activities. Using these guidelines, you can reduce your daily step goal on days when you complete some other exercise or activity.

15 minutes of activity	Equivalent number of steps
Moderate sexual activity	500
Standing while watering lawn or garden	600
Vigorous sexual activity	750
Clearing and washing dishes	900
Standing while cooking at the barbecue	950
Standing while playing with kids	1100
Carpentry—general workshop	1200
Playing frisbee	1200
Ten-pin bowling	1200
Playing golf at the driving range	1200
Food shopping with a trolley	1400
General house cleaning	1400
Bicycling moderately (18 km/h)	1600
Raking the lawn	1600
Playing actively with kids	1600
Sweeping	1600
Paddle boat peddling	1600
Horse riding	1600
Playing table tennis	1600
Washing the car by hand	1850
Spreading soil with a shovel	1950
Cleaning gutters of house	2000
Walk/run while playing vigorously with kids	2000
Digging or cultivating the garden	2000
Mowing the lawn with a hand mower	2350
Moving furniture	2350
Carrying bricks	3150
Using heavy tools—e.g. shovel or crow bar	3150

What about joining a health club?

Health clubs are a great way to build exercise into your life—you have expert advice from qualified instructors, group fitness classes to choose from, a program designed for you in the gym and many also have a pool, squash courts or an associated running club.

Nevertheless your first visit can be a little daunting. Do your research first and find a club that meets your needs:

- Is it within a 15-minute drive from either your home or work?
- If you have young children, is there a crèche?
- What are the opening hours—if you want to go in the early morning or late evening are there classes at these times?
- If you think you would enjoy swimming or aqua classes, is there a pool?
- Will an instructor provide a gym program to get you started?
- What are the membership fee options and what is the get-out clause if you wish to cease membership?

What about a personal trainer?

There is no doubt that employing a personal trainer is a terrific way to improve your fitness and progress towards your goals. A good trainer will provide an individualised, progressive program as well as much-needed motivation and support. Many personal trainers now provide services for a reasonable rate and you can choose to use a health club or train outdoors. A good way to bring the cost down is to train with a small group of three or four others with similar fitness levels. For more information on personal trainers, see page 264.

What if I don't have access to a personal trainer or health club, or can't afford it?

Use the 'buddy system'—you can get all the support and motivation you need from exercising with a buddy who has similar goals. Having an appointment to go walking or swimming with a friend makes it harder to be distracted or find an excuse to put it off. Remember, you are also offering the same motivation and support to your buddy so that you are both more likely to succeed.

Practical ways to reduce television watching

1 Make a rule and enforce it: no more than 12 hours per week.
2 Schedule the programs you will watch for the week.
3 Rearrange the furniture so there is more room for movement.
4 Do stretches and floor exercises while you watch.
5 Put the television in a naturally light room to discourage daytime viewing.
6 Turn on the stereo instead.
7 Play now—do homework later. (The kids love this!)
8 During the commercial breaks, try to get a small chore done.
9 Anything is better than nothing.
10 Combine television watching with the ironing (not just mum's job, either).

How much do you need to do?

Try to do something active on most days and add the following:

- Three cardiovascular sessions—this could be a group fitness class, cycling, a brisk walk or swimming.
- Two resistance workouts—either continue with your program from Week 12 of the Action Plan or join a weights-based group fitness class, or have a program designed for you at your local health club. Yoga and Pilates classes will also improve your strength and muscle tone, though to a lesser extent.

If you do regular exercise you:

- Will tend to have lower blood pressure
- Will feel more energetic
- Are less likely to have a heart attack or develop diabetes
- Will reduce your insulin requirements if you have diabetes
- Will find it easier to stop smoking
- Will be better able to control your weight
- Can increase levels of 'good' HDL cholesterol
- Will sleep better
- Will have stronger bones and muscles
- Are less likely to develop colon cancer
- Will feel happier, more confident and relaxed
- Can ease depression

looking forward to the one-year mark

A YEAR OF FOLLOWING THE LOW GI DIET WILL GIVE you a new lease of life. Having lost at least 5 to 10 per cent of your initial body weight, you will be fitting into clothes one or two sizes smaller, you will look and feel terrific and you will feel an undeniable buzz every time you have done your exercise for the day. Most importantly, you will have maintained the weight you lost and developed the confidence and know-how that ensures you keep it off for the rest of your life. Sure, there will be times when you gain a little, but that's normal and it shouldn't faze you, as you know you can repeat the Action Plan and shed the kilos at any stage. You will have learnt exactly what it takes to keep your weight under control through the recommendations in this chapter. It is not just about eating but also physical activity and balancing the energy equation. You have adopted a lifestyle, not a 'diet'.

The amount of weight you have lost may not take you back to your weight at age 18 or 25 but it doesn't matter. The weight you lose in this first year is what makes the world of difference to your health and well-being. While it might not be uppermost in your mind right now, living the healthy low GI life will be giving you lots of value-added benefits, such as reducing the likelihood that you will develop diabetes, heart disease, arthritis, cancer and a number of other diseases. Your quality of life will remain high as the years advance, and you will be in the best shape possible to meet the challenges and pleasures of middle and older age. Putting your health first gives you the best possible chance of achieving not only lifelong dreams, but everything else life puts on your plate.

**READ THE LANGUAGE OF YOUR BODY—
NOTICE WHEN YOU FEEL MOST ALIVE
AND DO MORE OF THAT.**

Find a good dietitian

Dietitians have professionally recognised qualifications in human nutrition. They can provide specific advice tailored to your current eating habits and food preferences, and will work with you to set realistic and achievable goals. They will help you understand the relationship between food and health and guide you in making dietary choices that optimise your lifestyle. Dietitians practise as individual professionals and are available through most public hospitals and in private practice. To find a dietitian visit 'Find a Dietitian' at www.daa.asn.au or call 1800 812 942.

What to expect when you see a dietitian

Your first visit to a dietitian will generally take about an hour and will begin with collecting personal details, such as your weight and medical history, usual eating patterns and activity levels, and your goals and expectations. This information helps the dietitian to assess your needs and provide information and education relevant to you.

Find a good personal trainer

If you belong to a health club you should be able to find a personal trainer there. For working out in your own home or outdoors, look in your local newspaper or search online for someone in your area. Ask to see their qualifications—they should have a Certificate IV in training. Any good trainer will offer you at least one complimentary session to 'try before you buy'—to make sure you like the style of your trainer and can work well with him or her before you sign up for a number of sessions.

TWENTY MINUTES OF EXERCISES
GIVES YOU A MOOD BOOST AND A NATURAL HIGH.

What to expect when you see a personal trainer

In your first session, a good personal trainer will quiz you on your current lifestyle, your goals and your expectations from working with him or her. He or she will then work out a program to best guide you towards reaching those goals.

Discuss payment options with the trainer in your first session. You should expect to have at least the first session free of charge to see if you are a compatible team. If you are not sure, try out another trainer.

Do you need to see a doctor?

If you have done your best with a serious attempt at weight loss over three months, even with the additional help of a dietitian or personal trainer, and still feel dissatisfied with the amount of weight loss, we recommend a visit to your doctor. If you are markedly overweight— if your waist circumference is over 102 centimetres (male) or 88 centimetres (female)—he or she may refer you to an endocrinologist who specialises in obesity management. Apart from medication, there are surgical interventions to help those who are extremely overweight.

What you need to know about using drugs to treat weight concerns

First of all, you should be aware that your doctor won't even consider prescribing any drug therapy until you have actively pursued a dietary and physical activity change for at least three months. If, at the end of that period, you have lost little weight (say, less than 5 per cent of your initial weight), then drug therapy *might* be an option. Your doctor will consider the risks against the benefits in your individual case. Even when drug therapy is initiated, however, it is never used as sole therapy, but as an adjunct to a diet and exercise program.

Drugs for the treatment of obesity have had a bad reputation and many doctors are reluctant to use them. This is unfortunate because appropriate drug treatment can be life-saving. In the past, drugs were used inappropriately, weight regain was common and some drugs were associated with addiction and serious side effects. Nowadays, most of these drugs have been withdrawn from use. Those that are used today have been subjected to large international clinical trials and are safer than the drugs prescribed ten or 20 years ago.

There are two principal drugs currently available throughout much of the world, including Australia, New Zealand, the USA and the UK, for the management of obesity. The first is called orlistat. It is a lipase inhibitor, a substance that blocks the digestion of fat (lipids). In practice, 10 to 30 per cent of fat eaten is not absorbed and is excreted in the faeces. Over the course of six to 12 months, orlistat has been shown to produce a 10 per cent weight loss compared to only 6 per cent weight loss in patients who took the placebo. This might not seem to be a big difference, but it can make a huge difference to blood glucose and blood lipid levels and therefore reduce the risk of developing diabetes and cardiovascular disease. During treatment with orlistat, it is absolutely essential to eat a low fat diet to reduce the severity of the gastrointestinal side effects. These include flatulence with discharge, oily evacuation and faecal incontinence. Not to be taken lightly! Fortunately, the side effects lessen with time and most people stick to the treatment. A general vitamin supplement should be taken alongside orlistat because fat-soluble vitamins can be malabsorbed along with the fat.

The second drug commonly prescribed for treating overweight people is sibutramine. It is an appetite suppressant, acting on the nerve pathways in the brain to inhibit food intake. It has been subjected to widespread international trials and is safe for use in uncomplicated obesity. It should not be prescribed to people with any form of heart disease or who have had a stroke. It can also interfere with the metabolism of other drugs such as antidepressants and blood pressure medication, so caution is needed.

How about alternative treatments?

Alternative treatments have become increasingly popular in all areas of health and wellbeing. Walk in to any health food store and you are faced with a plethora of supplements all claiming to help you to lose weight. The advertising and marketing of these products are powerfully persuasive—often picturing before and after photos of people who have reportedly transformed their bodies entirely just by using the advertised product. Is there any truth behind these claims?

The short answer is, unfortunately, no. If there were an easy answer to weight loss then not so many of us would be struggling! One reason supplements may seem to work in the short term is the so-called placebo effect—if you believe strongly enough that something will help you to lose weight, it probably will—not because the supplement is achieving the action it claims to do, but because with this perceived helping hand you manage to reduce your energy intake, at least for a short while.

Nevertheless, there are a small number of products that do plausibly aid weight loss and show promise for the future, although even these few will never provide the miracle cure. At best they may be useful as an adjunct treatment to the type of lifestyle modifications we have laid out in this book—these will always be the cornerstone of achieving better health and, in the process, successful weight control.

One problem with supplements is that if they are successful in assisting weight loss, then inevitably there will be side effects. This is true whether the supplement is a drug or a 'natural' product. Don't be fooled by the word 'natural'—this does not necessarily mean safe. In fact, many herbal products can be extremely dangerous because there is little control over how much of the active ingredient is present, unlike drugs, which are strictly regulated to provide a standardised dose. This can mean you either don't get enough of the active ingredient to make a difference, or you get too much, raising the risk of unpleasant side effects.

Many over-the-counter weight loss products contain different combinations of the same ingredients. These include the following:

Ma Huang (ephedra)

Ma Huang is the Chinese name for the plant ephedra. The active ingredient is ephedrine, and in Europe supplements containing ephedrine and caffeine combinations have been popular for weight loss. In Australia and the USA, however, Ma Huang and ephedrine have been banned due to their serious side effects, including elevated blood pressure and heart rate, insomnia, agitation, dry mouth and gastrointestinal upsets. In the light of these safety concerns it is prudent to avoid the supplement until further research has been conducted.

Herbs reported to reduce appetite and/or raise metabolic rate

These include brindleberry, gymnema, bladderwrack, dandelion, calendula, blue flag, ginseng, kelp and garcinia cambogia. None of these extracts has been conclusively shown to be effective. One possible exception is a fruit acid extracted from the rind of brindleberry, called HCA (hydroxycitric acid), which may enhance weight loss when combined with a low energy diet. A more recent, more rigorous study, however, found no such effect.

Fibre—often as guar gum or psyllium

Since fibre absorbs water in the gut and swells, it can help you to feel full after a meal. There is little evidence, however, that taking fibre in supplement form will help you to lose weight. You will find it best to stick with a high fibre, low GI diet which has proven health benefits.

Chitosan

Chitosan comes from the shells of crustaceans and has been shown to bind fat. The theory is that it can therefore bind fat in your gut, preventing absorption. Unfortunately this does not seem to happen in real life and these claims remain unsubstantiated.

Chromium picolinate

We need small amounts of the mineral chromium for correct carbohydrate and fat metabolism, and, in particular, making sure that insulin works effectively. In a rather giant leap it was therefore suggested that taking chromium in supplement form would reduce insulin resistance and encourage fat burning while preserving lean muscle. A small amount of evidence does show an improvement in insulin action in people with type 2 diabetes, but the majority of studies have shown no effect. The picolinate form found in most supplements has been shown to damage DNA in rats and while it is not known if this occurs in humans, we should at least exercise caution until further research is carried out.

Carnitine and choline

These supplements claim to assist in fat mobilisation. While they are involved in fat transport within the body there is no evidence that taking them in supplement form can help you to lose body fat. Furthermore, these are found naturally in meat and dairy foods so can be consumed easily in your normal diet.

Capsaicin

This is the chemical responsible for the spicy bite to chilli peppers and cayenne powder. There is some evidence that capsaicin can raise your metabolic rate and this research led to a short craze in the UK of eating hot curries in an attempt to lose weight! While the effect can be measured when consumed in supplement form, the increase is so minor as to have no promising effect on weight loss.

To summarise, none of the currently available supplements has proven efficacy and safety. You are more likely to lighten your wallet than lighten your weight on the scales. Even those that hold some promise can only help as part of a total lifestyle modification program. Our advice is to save your money and put all your energies into changing the factors that we know will count in the long run—what you eat and how often you move!

the Low GI Diet

PART FOUR

recipes for
light meals
and brunches,
mains,
savoury snacks
and sweet treats

IN THIS SECTION YOU'LL FIND 50-PLUS RECIPES AND MEAL ideas to help you put the GI to work in your kitchen—and throughout your day. We have chosen recipes that will give you a healthy balance of all the nutrients your body needs.

We have analysed the recipes, and the nutrient profile* includes the GI, energy, fat, protein, carbohydrate and fibre per serve.

GI: An emphasis on low GI carbs such as pasta, legumes, sweet potato, wholegrains, fruit and dairy ensures most of our recipes have a low GI. The value we give is our best estimate of the range in which the GI of each recipe falls.

- Low GI < 55
- Medium or moderate GI 56–69
- High GI > 70

ENERGY DENSITY: The kilojoule count per serve of each recipe indicates its energy density. This is important to weight control because

---

* Recipes have been analysed using nutrient analysis software, FoodWorks® (Xyris Software), based on Australian and New Zealand food composition data.

it's easy to overconsume kilojoules when your diet is based on energy-dense foods. By incorporating lots of vegetables, salads, fruits and high fibre foods into recipes, they retain a lower energy density.

FATS: The type of fat is more important than the total amount. Most of us need to eat more of certain kinds of fats for optimal health. These fats include the omega-3 fats found in fish and seafood and omega-neutral monounsaturated fats found in olive and canola oils.

PROTEIN: Sufficient protein in the diet is important for weight control. Compared to carbohydrate and fat, protein makes us feel more satisfied immediately after eating and reduces hunger between meals. Protein also increases our metabolic rate for 1–3 hours after eating. This means we burn more energy by the minute compared with the increase that occurs after eating carbohydrates or fats. Even though this is a relatively small difference it may be important in long-term weight control.

CARBOHYDRATE: Many of our recipes have a carbohydrate base but the emphasis is always on low GI because the slow digestion and absorption of these foods will fill you up, trickle fuel into your engine at a more useable rate and keep you satisfied for longer. The actual amount of carbohydrate consumed at each meal may be relevant to those with diabetes and those who monitor their blood glucose levels.

FIBRE: Experts recommend a daily fibre intake of 30 grams, but most people fall short of that, averaging 20–25 grams. The Low GI Diet will bring you a lot closer to the target because most of our recipes are brimming with fibre. This means they'll not only keep you regular but will help lower your blood glucose, your cholesterol levels and reduce your risk of many chronic diseases.

light meals
and brunches

Breakfast on the Go

A quick and healthy breakfast drink.

Per serve

kJ/Cal 1500/353   **Protein** 27 g   **Fat** 4 g (saturated 1 g)

Carbohydrate 55 g   **Fibre** 3 g   **GI** Low

Preparation time 5 minutes

Cooking time nil   **Serves** 2

500 ml low fat milk or soy beverage

½ cup low fat natural yoghurt

½ punnet strawberries, hulled and chopped (optional)

1 large, ripe banana, roughly chopped

1 egg

1 tablespoon honey

1 tablespoon All-Bran® or wheat germ or psyllium husks

1 Combine the ingredients in a blender.

2 Process until smooth and frothy.

3 Pour into two glasses, drink and go!

Fruity Porridge Oats

You can make the dried fruit mixture in advance. Keep it in the refrigerator for 3–4 days and use as required. It can be served hot or cold on the porridge.

Per serve

kJ/Cal 1075/255 **Protein** 8 g **Fat** 3 g (saturated <1 g)

Carbohydrate 48 g **Fibre** 4 g **GI** Low

Preparation time 5 minutes (plus soaking time)

Cooking time 20 minutes **Serves** 4

100 g dried fruit (mixture of prunes, apricots, pears, apples, sultanas)

2 × 2.5 cm slices lemon rind

½ teaspoon cinnamon

2 cloves

300 ml unsweetened apple juice

125 g porridge oats

1½ cups (375 ml) low fat milk

1 Place the dried fruit, lemon rind, cinnamon and cloves in a bowl. Pour over the apple juice, cover and leave in the refrigerator to soak overnight to bring out the flavours.

2 Transfer the ingredients to a heavy-based saucepan and bring to the boil, then reduce the heat and leave to simmer gently for about 15 minutes, stirring occasionally.

3 Put the oats in a saucepan with the milk and bring to the boil (making sure it doesn't boil over) then reduce the heat and simmer for 5 minutes.

4 Serve the porridge in small bowls topped with a spoonful or two of the dried fruit compote (warm or cold as preferred).

Egg and Bacon Tarts

These tarts are delicious, simple and healthy to make for a cooked breakfast or brunch. The high fat content makes them a weekend treat.

Per serve

kJ/Cal 1640/386   **Protein** 28 g   **Fat** 18 g (saturated 6 g)

Carbohydrate 30 g   **Fibre** 4 g   **GI** Low

Preparation time 10 minutes

Cooking time 20–25 minutes   **Serves** 2

4 slices grainy bread

spray olive or canola oil

4 small eggs

2 rashers short-cut rindless bacon, trimmed of all fat and finely diced

¼ cup grated reduced fat cheese

1 tablespoon parsley, chopped

1 Preheat the oven to 180°C.

2 Trim any thick or hard crusts from the bread and flatten each slice by rolling gently with a rolling pin.

3 Spray a medium-cup muffin pan with the oil and gently push each slice of bread into its own cup to line it. Spray again.

4 Break an egg into each cup—don't worry if it overflows a little. Top each with some bacon, cheese and parsley.

5 Bake for 20–25 minutes or until set.

Vegetable Frittata

A lovely light lunch, this frittata is also great for picnics. It is a good source of folate and rich in beta-carotene. Offer fresh sourdough bread alongside.

> **Per serve (with salad)**
> **kJ/Cal** 790/190 **Protein** 12 g **Fat** 9 g (saturated 3 g)
> **Carbohydrate** 14 g **Fibre** 4 g **GI** Low

Preparation time 20 minutes
Cooking time 45 minutes **Makes** 4 wedges

1 teaspoon olive oil
1 small onion, finely chopped
1 clove garlic, crushed
2 cups (300 g) grated sweet potato
2 zucchinis, grated
¼ cup basil leaves, shredded
⅓ cup grated reduced fat cheese
salt and freshly ground black pepper, to taste
4 eggs, lightly beaten
150 g cherry tomatoes, halved

To serve
100 g mixed salad leaves
squeeze of lemon juice

1 Preheat the oven to 180°C. Lightly grease a 20 cm round cake tin and line the base with non-stick baking paper.

2 Heat the olive oil in a non-stick frypan and cook the onion and garlic for 4 minutes, or until soft. Add the sweet potato and zucchini and cook, stirring, for 3 minutes until softened slightly.

3 Transfer the vegetable mixture to a bowl and cool slightly. Mix in the basil and cheese, and season with salt and pepper. Stir to combine evenly. Fold in the eggs, and pour the mixture into the prepared tin. Smooth the surface.

4 Arrange the cherry tomatoes over the mixture, cut side up, and press in gently. Bake for 45 minutes, until set and golden. Leave in the tin until just cool enough to handle, then turn out and quickly invert right-side-up onto a plate.

5 Cut the frittata into wedges and serve with salad leaves, lightly dressed with lemon juice.

Salmon and Dill Omelette with Tomato Salad

This omelette is a fantastic source of omega-3 fats, thanks to the salmon and eggs. Serve with salad and rye bread.

Per serve (with bread and salad)

kJ/Cal 3260/767   **Protein** 42 g   **Fat** 45 g (saturated 12 g)
Carbohydrate 47 g   **Fibre** 10 g   **GI** Low

Preparation time 15 minutes
Cooking time 5 minutes   **Serves** 2

4 eggs, at room temperature

2 tablespoons low fat milk

1 tablespoon fresh dill, chopped

salt and freshly ground black pepper, to taste

2 teaspoons monounsaturated, salt-reduced margarine

30 g baby spinach leaves

100 g smoked salmon, cut into thin strips

¼ cup (25 g) grated Parmesan

Tomato salad

200 g cherry or grape tomatoes, halved

100 g snowpea sprouts, ends trimmed

1 large Lebanese cucumber, cut into small chunks

2 tablespoons commercial fat free dressing

1 ripe avocado, thinly sliced

To Serve

4 slices rye bread

1 Whisk together the eggs, milk, dill, salt and pepper in a bowl.

2 Place 1 teaspoon margarine in each of two small non-stick frypans. (If you don't have 2 small frypans, make one large omelette to share.) Heat over a medium heat until the margarine starts to bubble. Pour the egg mixture evenly among the two pans and reduce the heat to low. Cook for 2 minutes or until the omelette is almost set.

3 Place half the spinach, salmon and Parmesan on one side of each omelette. Carefully fold the other side of the omelette over the filling.

4 Meanwhile, to make the salad, place the tomatoes, snowpea sprouts and cucumber in a bowl. Add the dressing and toss gently to combine. Add the avocado.

5 Serve the omelettes with the salad and bread.

Ham, Corn and Zucchini Muffins

Best eaten the day they are made, these muffins are an excellent source of fibre.

Per muffin
kJ/Cal 1314/309   **Protein** 15 g
Fat 4 g (saturated 1 g)   **Carbohydrate** 51 g
Fibre 6 g   **GI** Medium

Per serve (with salad)
kJ/Cal 1480/348   **Protein** 16 g
Fat 7 g (saturated 2 g)   **Carbohydrate** 53 g
Fibre 7 g   **GI** Medium

Preparation time 20 minutes

Cooking time 20 minutes   **Makes** 6 muffins

1 cup (150 g) self-raising flour

1 cup (160 g) wholemeal self-raising flour

1 teaspoon baking powder

2 tablespoons caster sugar

1 x 310 g can corn kernels, drained

1 zucchini (about 125 g), coarsely grated

100 g lean leg ham, finely chopped

⅓ cup (30 g) grated Parmesan

¼ cup fresh chives, chopped

2 eggs

⅔ cup (160 ml) low fat milk

½ cup (125 g) low fat natural yoghurt

To serve

100 g mixed salad leaves or mesclun

1 red capsicum, cut into short, thin strips

100 g snowpeas, cut into long, thin strips

2 tablespoons vinaigrette

1 Preheat the oven to 200°C and lightly grease a 6 x 1 cup (250 ml) muffin pan.

2 Sift the flours and baking powder into a large bowl. Stir in the sugar, corn, zucchini, ham, Parmesan and chives.

3 Whisk the eggs, milk and yoghurt together. Add to the dry ingredients and use a large metal spoon to mix until just combined. Spoon the mixture evenly among the greased pans. Bake for 20 minutes or until light golden brown on top and a skewer inserted in the centre comes out clean.

4 Meanwhile, combine the salad ingredients. Serve with the warm muffins.

Fried Rice

The rice for this dish can be cooked and cooled a day ahead. Store in an airtight container in the refrigerator.

Per serve

kJ/Cal 1930/460 **Protein** 32 g **Fat** 11.3 g (saturated 3 g)
Carbohydrate 55 g **Fibre** 4 g **GI** Low

Preparation time 15 minutes (plus cooling time)
Cooking time 25 minutes **Serves** 4

1¼ cups (250 g) Basmati rice
1 tablespoon olive oil
3 eggs, at room temperature
1 red capsicum, finely chopped
250 g small cooked, peeled prawns
120 g leg ham, chopped
1 cup (155 g) frozen peas
4 shallots, thinly diagonally sliced
1 cup bean sprouts
2 tablespoons salt-reduced soy sauce

1 Cook the rice in a large saucepan of boiling water for 10–12 minutes or until tender. Drain well. Spread out in a single layer over two baking trays. Set aside to cool completely.

2 Heat half the oil in a large non-stick wok or frypan over a medium heat. Whisk the eggs until frothy. Pour into the wok or pan and swirl to cover the base. Cook for 2 minutes or until the egg is set. Carefully loosen the edges and turn out onto a board. Set aside to cool. Roll up the omelette and cut into thin strips. Set aside.

3 Heat the remaining oil in the wok over a high heat. Add the capsicum, prawns, ham and peas. Cook, tossing, for 2 minutes. Add the shallots and toss for 1 minute. Add the cooled rice and toss until heated through. Add the bean sprouts and soy sauce. Toss to combine and serve.

Ham and Vegetable Bake

This is a terrific recipe for kids—both to make and eat! It is an easy dish that can be eaten hot, warm or cold, and it is great for picnics, too.

Per serve

kJ/Cal 1240/292 **Protein** 18 g **Fat** 10 g (saturated 4 g)

Carbohydrate 30 g **Fibre** 6 g **GI** Low

Preparation time 10 minutes

Cooking time 40 minutes **Serves** 6

4 eggs

1 x 400 g can salt reduced corn kernels, drained

2 slices (50 g) leg ham, diced

½ cup grated reduced fat tasty cheese

2 zucchinis, grated

2 carrots, grated

1 onion, grated

½ cup (160 g) wholemeal self-raising flour

1 Preheat the oven to 150°C and grease a large lasagne dish.

2 Lightly whisk the eggs in a large mixing bowl. Add the corn, ham, cheese, zucchini, carrot and onion, then sift in the flour and mix thoroughly to combine.

3 Spoon the mixture into the lasagne dish and press down to flatten the top. Bake for 40 minutes until browned and set.

Turkey and Peach Salsa Wraps

Rich in protein and low in fat, these wraps make a delicious and nutritious lunch. Use canned peaches when fresh peaches are not in season—just make sure they are well drained.

Per wrap

kJ/Cal 959/226   **Protein** 25 g   **Fat** 4 g (saturated 1 g)
Carbohydrate 21 g   **Fibre** 4 g   **GI** Medium

Preparation time 15 minutes
Cooking time nil   **Makes** 2 wraps

1 peach, peeled and chopped
½ Lebanese cucumber, chopped
2 teaspoons mint, chopped
1 shallot, sliced
30 g iceberg lettuce leaves
2 sheets wholemeal lavash bread
150 g turkey slices

1 Combine the peach, cucumber, mint and shallots.

2 Spread the lettuce leaves over two-thirds of the lavash bread. Arrange the turkey slices over the lettuce.

3 Spoon the peach salsa over the turkey. Roll up to enclose the filling. If not serving immediately, wrap in paper or foil and store for up to 5 hours. Keep cool.

Tuna Rice Paper Rolls

If you like, use mint instead of coriander in these Vietnamese-style rolls, or leave it out altogether. Plain soy sauce makes a quick dipping sauce if you don't have the other ingredients. A good source of omega-3 fats, these rolls are also high in protein and rich in beta-carotene and vitamin C.

Per serve (3 rolls)
kJ/Cal 680/160   **Protein** 24 g   **Fat** 3 g (saturated 1 g)
Carbohydrate 8 g   **Fibre** 3 g   **GI** Medium

Preparation time 30 minutes
Cooking time nil   **Makes** 12 rolls

12 x 23 cm round rice paper sheets

1 x 425 g can tuna in spring water, drained and flaked

1 carrot, grated

2 shallots, finely sliced

2 cups (200 g) mung bean sprouts

½ cup (15 g) coriander leaves

1 red capsicum, finely sliced

Dipping sauce
1 tablespoon fish sauce

2 tablespoons lime juice

1 tablespoon sweet chilli sauce

1 Pour about 3 cm of tepid water into a large shallow dish. Dip one rice paper sheet in the water and soak for about 5 seconds, until just soft and pliable.

2 Drain and pat dry with paper towel. Place some of the tuna, carrot, shallots, sprouts, coriander and capsicum across one end of the sheet. Fold the end over, then the sides in. Roll up to enclose the filling securely. Repeat with the remaining rice paper sheets and filling ingredients.

3 Combine the fish sauce, lime juice and sweet chilli sauce. Serve in a small bowl for dipping.

Sweet Potato Fish Cakes

Per serve (2 fish cakes with salad)

kJ/Cal 911/214   **Protein** 21 g   **Fat** 4 g (saturated <1 g)

Carbohydrate 22 g   **Fibre** 5 g   **GI** Low

Preparation time 20 minutes (plus chilling time)

Cooking time 15–20 minutes   **Makes** 12 fish cakes

750 g sweet potato, peeled and cut into 2 cm pieces

500 g boneless white fish fillets

2 teaspoons olive oil

1 leek, finely chopped

1 red capsicum, finely chopped

2 garlic cloves, crushed

2 tablespoons fresh parsley, chopped

salt and freshly ground black pepper, to taste

spray olive oil

To serve

100 g mixed salad leaves or mesclun

1 Lebanese cucumber, cut into chunks

2 ripe tomatoes, cut into chunks

2 tablespoons commercial fat free dressing

1 Steam or microwave the sweet potato until tender. Meanwhile, line a steamer basket with non-stick baking paper. Place the steamer basket over a wok or pan of just simmering water (make sure the water doesn't touch the basket), cover, and steam the fish for 5–10 minutes until cooked.

2 Heat the oil in a non-stick frypan over a medium heat. Add the leek, capsicum and garlic and cook, stirring often, for 6–7 minutes or until the leek is soft. Set aside.

3 Place the sweet potato in a bowl and mash until smooth. Use a fork to flake the fish into very small pieces. Add the leek mixture, fish and parsley to the sweet potato and stir well to combine. Season with salt and pepper. Cover and refrigerate until well chilled.

4 Shape the mixture into 12 patties. Place on two baking trays lined with non-stick baking paper. Refrigerate for 30 minutes. Preheat the oven to 200°C.

5 Spray both sides of the fish cakes lightly with oil. Bake for 15–20 minutes or until warmed through and light golden. Combine the salad ingredients and serve with the fish cakes.

Chilli Chickpea Patties

This recipe is based on felafel—those tasty little chickpea balls used in making Lebanese rolls. Typically they are deep fried but this variation keeps the fat content down by baking them. Serve them with Eggplant and Bean Purée (page 314), salad greens and tomato slices or with the traditional hommous and tabbouli. These patties freeze well.

Per serve—3 patties per serve
kJ/Cal 570/135 **Protein** 7 g **Fat** 3 g (saturated <1 g)
Carbohydrate 19 g **Fibre** 5 g **GI** Low

Preparation time 10 minutes
Cooking time 30 minutes **Makes** 12 small patties

1 × 400 g can chickpeas (drained)

1 medium onion, peeled and roughly chopped

1 clove garlic, crushed

2 slices of grainy bread, roughly torn

1/4 cup chopped parsley

2 teaspoons ground cumin

¼–1/2 teaspoon chilli powder (to taste)

1 egg, beaten

1 Preheat the oven to 180ºC.

2 Place the chickpeas, onion, garlic, bread, parsley, coriander, cumin and chilli powder in the bowl of a food processor. Blend in short bursts until almost smooth.

3 Add the beaten egg and process again until the mixture is thoroughly combined.

4 Shape into small patties (about 1½ tablespoons each) with wet hands.

5 Place the patties on a lined baking tray and bake for 30 minutes or until lightly browned.

Indian Chicken Burgers

If you like, replace the tikka masala paste with any of your favourite Indian-style pastes. The cooked chicken patties are ideal to take on picnics or to work.

Per serve (patty)	
kJ/Cal 940/221	**Protein** 23 g
Fat 10 g (saturated 2 g)	**Carbohydrate** 10 g
Fibre 4 g	**GI** Low

Per serve (burger)	
kJ/Cal 1920/460	**Protein** 32 g
Fat 12 g (saturated 2 g)	**Carbohydrate** 52 g
Fibre 8 g	**GI** Medium

Preparation time 20 minutes

Cooking time 10 minutes   **Makes** 6

500 g chicken breast fillets, chopped

1 bunch coriander, leaves picked

1 x 400 g can chickpeas, rinsed and drained

1 garlic clove, chopped

2 tablespoons tikka masala paste

2 teaspoons olive oil

To serve

1 x 430 g packet (45 cm long) Turkish bread, cut into 6 portions

100 g salad mix

3 small tomatoes, thinly sliced

½ cup (125 g) low fat natural yoghurt

4½ tablespoons mango chutney

1 Place the chicken, coriander, chickpeas, garlic and tikka masala paste in a food processor. Process until the mixture is finely chopped and well combined. Shape the mixture into 6 patties. Refrigerate until required.

2 Heat the oil in a large non-stick frypan over a medium heat. Add the chicken patties and cook for 4–5 minutes on each side or until cooked through and light golden. Meanwhile, split and toast the Turkish bread portions.

3 Top the bases of the Turkish bread with the salad mix and tomatoes, then add a chicken patty each. Spoon over the yoghurt and chutney. Then add the tops of the Turkish bread and serve.

Lentil, Beetroot and Feta Salad

Per serve (salad only)

kJ/Cal 665/156 **Protein** 12 g

Fat 5 g (saturated <1 g) **Carbohydrate** 12 g

Fibre 5 g **GI** Low

Per serve (with bread)

kJ/Cal 1120/264 **Protein** 16 g

Fat 6 g (saturated 1 g) **Carbohydrate** 32 g

Fibre 7 g **GI** Low

Preparation time 15 minutes

Cooking time nil **Serves** 4

1 x 400 g can brown lentils, rinsed and drained

100 g reduced fat feta, cubed

125 g baby spinach leaves

1½ tablespoons lemon juice

1 teaspoon extra-virgin olive oil

1 teaspoon honey

1 cup (180 g) canned baby beets, drained and quartered

salt and freshly ground black pepper, to taste

4 thick slices sourdough rye bread

1 Combine the lentils, feta and spinach in a large bowl.

2 Place the lemon juice, oil and honey in a screwtop jar, and shake until well combined.

3 Drizzle the dressing over the lentil mixture and turn gently to coat.

4 Arrange the lentil mixture on serving plates, and add the beets. Season with salt and pepper, and serve immediately with the bread.

Thai-style Tofu and Noodle Soup

An excellent source of folate and vitamin C and a good source of calcium, magnesium and potassium, this soup is a meal in itself. The tofu doesn't need cooking, but adding it in at the beginning helps it to absorb the flavours. Lemongrass is available either fresh or in jars, from large supermarkets. Choose fresh if you can—for the best flavour. Mung bean vermicelli, sometimes called cellophane noodles or bean thread vermicelli, is available in the Asian food section of supermarkets.

Per serve
kJ/Cal 935/220   **Protein** 16 g   **Fat** 7 g (saturated 1 g)
Carbohydrate 21 g   **Fibre** 7 g   **GI** Low

Preparation time 20 minutes
Cooking time about 5 minutes   **Serves** 4

100 g mung bean vermicelli

4 cups (1 L) vegetable stock

1 tablespoon finely chopped lemongrass

1½ teaspoons finely grated ginger

1½ teaspoons finely chopped red chilli

350 g firm tofu, cut into 1.5 cm cubes

1 bunch asparagus, cut into 5 cm lengths

1 small head broccoli (about 300 g), cut into small florets

125 g baby corn, cut in half lengthways and crossways

2 shallots, finely sliced

fresh coriander leaves, to serve

1 Place the vermicelli in a large heatproof bowl and cover with boiling water. Leave to stand for 10 minutes.

2 Meanwhile, pour the vegetable stock into a large saucepan. Add the lemongrass, ginger, chilli and tofu. Bring to the boil.

3 Add the asparagus, broccoli and corn. Return to the boil, then cook for 2 minutes.

4 Drain the noodles then divide between four serving bowls and top with the vegetables, tofu and stock. Sprinkle each bowl with shallots and coriander leaves and serve immediately.

mains

Pasta with Char-grilled Chicken, Lemon and Basil

Per serve

kJ/Cal 2100/494   **Protein** 30 g   **Fat** 10 g (saturated 2 g)

Carbohydrate 70 g   **Fibre** 7 g   **GI** Low

Preparation time 15 minutes

Cooking time about 10 minutes   **Serves** 4

2 chicken breast fillets

spray olive oil

300 g short pasta, such as penne or spirals

1 cup (150 g) fresh or frozen green peas

300 g can corn kernels, well drained

1 tablespoon extra-virgin olive oil

2 tablespoons lemon juice

salt and freshly ground black pepper, to taste

½ cup basil leaves, shredded

1 Spray the chicken breast fillets lightly with oil and cook on a preheated char-grill or frypan for 5 minutes on each side, or until cooked through. Cool the chicken slightly, then slice thinly across the grain.

2 Meanwhile, cook the pasta in a large saucepan of boiling salted water according to packet directions, or until al dente. Add the peas and corn to the pasta for the last minute of cooking.

3 Drain the pasta, peas and corn, then return to the pan. Drizzle with the extra-virgin olive oil and lemon juice, and add the chicken. Season well with salt and pepper then toss to combine.

4 Spoon onto serving plates and top with the basil leaves. Serve immediately.

Chicken Stuffed with Spinach and Cheese

This meal is high in folate, niacin, beta-carotene and fibre.

Per serve

kJ/Cal 2117/498   **Protein** 55 g   **Fat** 18 g (saturated 6 g)
Carbohydrate 26 g   **Fibre** 10 g   **GI** Low

Preparation time 15 minutes

Cooking time 25–30 minutes   **Serves** 4

4 chicken breast fillets (about 200 g each)

4 slices reduced fat Swiss cheese (15 g each), cut into thin strips

80 g mushrooms, thinly sliced

40 g baby spinach leaves

4 wooden toothpicks

2 teaspoons olive oil

salt and freshly ground black pepper, to taste

1⅓ cups (330 ml) Italian tomato cooking sauce

⅓ cup fresh basil leaves, finely shredded

To serve

1 bunch baby carrots, washed

240 g green beans, trimmed

2 cobs fresh sweet corn, halved

1 Preheat the oven to 180°C. Cut a deep slit (making sure not to cut all the way through) along the length of each chicken breast. Fill each evenly with the cheese, mushrooms and spinach. Secure the opening with toothpicks.

2 Heat the oil in a large non-stick frypan over a medium–high heat. Season both sides of the chicken breasts with salt and pepper. Cook for 2–3 minutes on each side or until well browned.

3 Transfer the chicken to a shallow ovenproof dish and pour over the cooking sauce. Bake for 15–20 minutes or until the chicken is cooked through.

4 Meanwhile, steam the carrots, beans and sweet corn.

5 Remove the toothpicks and place the chicken breasts on serving plates. Pour over the sauce and sprinkle with the basil. Serve with the vegetables.

Chicken and Rice Salad

This tasty meal is a good source of magnesium, niacin, vitamin C and vitamin A.
Before serving, try scattering over some toasted cashew nuts.

Per serve
kJ/Cal 1326/312 **Protein** 21 g **Fat** 5 g (saturated 1 g)
Carbohydrate 45 g **Fibre** 2 g **GI** Medium

Preparation time 20 minutes
Cooking time 12 minutes **Serves** 4

2 (300 g) chicken breast fillets
1 cup (200 g) Basmati rice
1 tablespoon soy sauce
¼ teaspoon sesame oil
1 red capsicum, cut into thin strips
100 g snowpeas, sliced diagonally
1 carrot, grated
2 shallots, sliced diagonally
2 tablespoons lemon juice

1 Gently simmer the chicken in a saucepan of boiling water for 12 minutes, until tender. Remove from the pan. When cool enough to handle, cut into thin strips.

2 Meanwhile, cook the rice in a large saucepan of boiling water for about 10 minutes, until tender. Drain, rinse under cold water to stop the cooking, then drain completely.

3 Place the chicken on a plate. Combine the soy sauce and sesame oil and drizzle over the chicken. Toss to coat.

4 Combine the rice and vegetables in a large bowl. Drizzle over the lemon juice and toss to combine. Add the chicken to the rice, and mix through gently. Serve immediately, or refrigerate until serving time.

Chinese Combination Soup for One

You can buy boiled wontons, lean barbecue pork and Chinese chicken stock in Chinese markets and Asian produce stores. Frozen wontons are also available in larger supermarkets. In this recipe, you can use any other Asian greens or vegetables such as handful of raw bean sprouts, baby corn or champignon mushrooms instead of the choy sum if you prefer. For a seafood combination soup use 2 or 3 prawns, 2 or 3 diced white fish cubes and 2 or 3 small pieces of squid instead of the pork and add a seafood stock.

Per serve
kJ/Cal 1860/445 **Protein** 36 g **Fat** 10 g (saturated 4 g)
Carbohydrate 50 g **Fibre** 4 g **GI** Low

Preparation time: 10 minutes

4 boiled wontons

40 g (small handful) egg noodles, blanched and drained

½ bunch choy sum, washed, leaves separated and blanched

6 slices of lean barbecue pork

2 cups (250 ml) hot Chinese chicken stock (or regular chicken stock)

To serve
1 tablespoon finely chopped shallots

1 tablespoon chopped fresh coriander

½ teaspoon finely chopped red chilli (optional)

1 Place the wontons, egg noodles, choy sum and pork in a single-serve large Chinese bowl. Ladle the stock over. Garnish with shallots and coriander and chilli if desired.

Tandoori Chicken with Cumin-flavoured Rice

You can make this using a whole chicken as we have here or with chicken pieces if you prefer to reduce the cooking time.

Per serve (with cumin-flavoured rice)
kJ/Cal 2120/505   **Protein** 45 g   **Fat** 16 g (saturated 4 g)
Carbohydrate 44 g   **Fibre** 1 g   **GI** Low

Preparation time 20 minutes (plus 6–8 hours for marinating)
Cooking time about 50 minutes   **Serves** 4

1 medium chicken (about 800 g), cleaned and skin removed

1 teaspoon chilli powder

2 teaspoons lemon juice

salt to taste

3 teaspoons margarine

Marinade
250 ml low fat plain yoghurt

1 teaspoon garam masala

1 teaspoon ground cumin

2 small red chillies, finely chopped (or to taste)

3 teaspoons finely grated ginger

3 teaspoons finely diced garlic

1 teaspoon lemon juice

To serve
3–4 tablespoons chopped coriander leaves

1 onion, finely sliced into rings

1 lemon cut into wedges

1 To prepare the chicken, combine the chilli powder, lemon juice and salt in a small bowl. Place the chicken in a shallow glass or ceramic dish. Using a sharp knife, make incisions on breast and leg pieces of the chicken. Rub the chilli mixture over the chicken, cover and set aside.

2 To make the marinade, combine the yoghurt in a bowl with the rest of the marinade ingredients and stir until thoroughly combined. Spoon the marinade mix all over the chicken, pushing it into the slits. Cover and place the chicken in the refrigerator for 6–8 hours to marinate. Turn occasionally to make sure all sides are coated in the mixture.

3 Preheat the oven to 200°C. Place the chicken on a wire rack over a large baking dish and roast for about 40–50 minutes, or until the chicken is cooked—the juices will run clear when you insert a skewer. Alternatively, skewer the chicken and cook it in a hot clay oven (tandoor) or barbecue it on an open hot grill. When the chicken is almost cooked, baste with melted margarine and roast for another 3 minutes.

4 While the chicken is cooking, prepare the cumin-flavoured rice (see below).

5 Serve with onion rings, chopped coriander, lemon wedges and cumin-flavoured rice.

Cumin-flavoured Rice

1 cup (200 g) Basmati rice
1½ cups (375 ml) water
1 teaspoon canola oil
2 teaspoons cumin seeds

1 Wash the rice well then place in a bowl, cover with cold water and soak for 30 minutes. Drain.

2 Heat the oil in a heavy-based pan, add the cumin and let it 'sputter' until aromatic. Add the rice and water, stir and bring to the boil. Reduce the heat to very low, cover the pan and cook for about 15–20 minutes or until all the water has evaporated.

Eggplant and Zucchini Pilaf with Lamb

Per serve
kJ/Cal 2110/496   **Protein** 30 g   **Fat** 10 g (saturated 3 g)
Carbohydrate 70 g   **Fibre** 7 g   **GI** Medium

Preparation time 15 minutes
Cooking time 30 minutes   **Serves** 4

2 large red capsicums (about 200 g each), cut into 2.5 cm pieces

1 eggplant (about 300 g), cut into 2.5 cm pieces

2 large zucchinis (about 350 g each), cut into 2.5 cm pieces

4 teaspoons olive oil

salt and freshly ground black pepper, to taste

1 brown onion, finely chopped

2 garlic cloves, crushed

1½ cups (300 g) Basmati rice, rinsed

2½ cups (625 ml) salt-reduced chicken stock

2 lamb backstraps (about 200 g each)

1½ tablespoons fresh parsley, finely chopped

1 Preheat the oven to 230°C and line a large roasting pan with non-stick baking paper.

2 Place the capsicum, eggplant, zucchini and 2 teaspoons of oil in a bowl. Season with salt and pepper and toss well to coat. Spread in a single layer over the lined pan. Bake for 25–30 minutes or until very tender and light golden brown.

3 Meanwhile, heat 1 teaspoon of oil in a large, non-stick, heavy-based saucepan over a medium heat. Add the onion and garlic and cook, stirring often, for 7–8 minutes or until the onion is soft. Increase the heat to high and add the rice. Cook, stirring, for 1 minute. Add the stock, cover, and bring to the boil. Reduce the heat to low and cook, covered, for 10 minutes. Remove from the heat and set aside, covered, for 10 minutes.

4 Brush the lamb with the remaining oil and season with salt and pepper. Preheat a char-grill pan or frypan over a medium–high heat. Add the lamb and cook for 3–4 minutes on each side for medium, or until cooked to your liking. Set aside for 5 minutes, then slice diagonally.

5 Use a fork to fluff up the rice and separate the grains. Add the roasted vegetables and the parsley to the rice and toss gently to combine.

6 Divide the rice among serving plates and top with the lamb.

Barbecued Lamb with Lentil Salad and Lemon Yoghurt Dressing

Per serve

kJ/Cal 1900/447   **Protein** 49 g   **Fat** 16 g (saturated 4 g)

Carbohydrate 21 g   **Fibre** 11 g   **GI** Low

Preparation time 10 minutes (plus marinating time)

Cooking time 15 minutes   **Serves** 2

1 tablespoon olive oil

1 clove garlic, crushed

a few sprigs of fresh oregano, roughly torn

zest of 1 lemon

300–400 g lamb fillet or backstrap

1 Combine the olive oil, garlic, oregano and lemon zest in a bowl. Add the lamb fillets or backstrap and marinate for at least 30 minutes. Brown the marinated lamb in a frypan over medium–high heat or on the barbecue until just cooked. Remove, cover and set aside.

Dressing

juice of 1 lemon

½ cup low fat natural yoghurt

salt and freshly ground pepper, to taste

2 Meanwhile, combine the lemon juice with the yoghurt in a small jar, leaving aside a squeeze of the lemon juice. Season with salt and pepper. Put on the lid and shake to combine.

Salad

1 tablespoon olive oil

1 x 400 g can brown lentils, drained

2 medium tomatoes, diced

35 g baby spinach leaves, shredded

3 To make the salad, heat the olive oil in a frypan over a medium heat and add the lentils, stirring to warm through. Add the tomatoes and spinach and a squeeze of lemon juice, and stir to combine. Remove from the heat.

4 Slice the lamb across the grain (about 1.5 cm thick).

5 Spoon the lentil salad onto serving plates. Top with the sliced meat and pour over the dressing.

Beef Kebabs with Vegetable Noodle Salad

Not only is this dish an excellent source of iron and zinc, it also contains vitamin C to enhance absorption of these nutrients. If time permits, you can marinate the meat on skewers overnight.

Per serve

kJ/Cal 1735/408   **Protein** 36 g   **Fat** 7 g (saturated 3 g)

Carbohydrate 50 g   **Fibre** 4 g   **GI** Low

Preparation time 20 minutes (plus marinating time)

Cooking time 10–15 minutes   **Serves** 4

500 g lean rump steak, cut across the grain into thin strips

16 wooden skewers, soaked in cold water for 15–20 minutes

⅓ cup (80 ml) plum sauce marinade

1 x 450 g packet Hokkien noodles

1 red capsicum, cut into short, thin strips

100 g snowpeas, cut into thin strips

1 Lebanese cucumber, cut into thin strips

1 bunch coriander, leaves picked

¼ cup (60 ml) salt-reduced soy sauce

¼ cup (60 ml) fat free French dressing

1 Thread the beef strips evenly among the skewers, then place the skewers in a shallow glass or ceramic dish. Pour over the marinade and turn to coat. Set aside for 1 hour to marinate.

2 Preheat a barbecue char-grill or frypan over a medium heat. Place the noodles in a large heatproof bowl and cover with boiling water. Set aside for 5 minutes. Drain well, set aside to cool slightly, then separate the noodles. Add the capsicum, snowpeas, cucumber and coriander, and toss to combine.

3 Whisk the soy sauce and dressing together. Add to the salad and toss to combine.

4 Cook the beef skewers for 2–3 minutes on each side or until cooked through. Serve with the noodle salad.

Mediterranean Beef Stew

Per serve

kJ/Cal 1280/305   **Protein** 35 g   **Fat** 12 g (saturated 4 g)

Carbohydrate 8 g   **Fibre** 4 g   **GI** Low

Preparation time 30 minutes

Cooking time about 2 hours   **Serves** 4

1 tablespoon olive oil

600 g trimmed beef suitable for a casserole, cut into 2.5 cm cubes

2 large onions, thinly sliced

1 clove garlic, crushed

½ cup red wine

1 cup Italian peeled tomatoes

1 large bay leaf

freshly ground black pepper, to taste

½ cup dried porcini mushrooms, rehydrated in ½ cup warm water

12 baby carrots, scrubbed and tops trimmed

1 teaspoon fresh thyme, finely chopped

1½ tablespoons fresh parsley, finely chopped

1 Preheat the oven to 180°C

2 Heat the oil in a large flameproof casserole dish then brown the cubes of beef on all sides, cooking a few at a time. Transfer the browned meat to a plate and set aside.

3 Reduce the heat then add the onions and cook for 3 or 4 minutes until they are soft and golden. Stir in the crushed garlic and add the meat cubes.

4 Add the wine, tomatoes and the bay leaf and season with freshly ground black pepper to taste. Bring to a simmer then cover with a tightly fitting lid, transfer to the middle shelf of the oven and cook for 1 hour.

5 Remove from the oven and stir in the mushrooms, the water they have been soaking in, the carrots and herbs and mix well. Return to the oven and cook for a further 30 minutes or until the carrots are soft.

6 Serve over noodles or Basmati rice with a salad or green vegetables.

Claypot Rice with Minced Pork, Eggplant and Spinach

For this recipe you need a 2-person claypot (1.25 litre capacity).

If you don't have a claypot, use a cast-iron enamel pot.

Per serve

kJ/Cal 2155/515   **Protein** 31 g   **Fat** 18 g (saturated 4 g)

Carbohydrate 51 g   **Fibre** 10 g   **GI** Medium

Preparation time 15 minutes

Cooking time 15 minutes   **Serves** 2

spray olive oil

2 cups freshly steamed Basmati or Doongara rice (made with 100 g uncooked rice)

1 bunch Chinese water spinach or English spinach, chopped and stir-fried

1 tablespoon olive oil

300 g baby eggplant, sliced

200 g minced pork

1 tablespoon finely chopped garlic

1 tablespoon finely chopped fresh ginger

2 tablespoons finely chopped shallots

1 tablespoon dark soy sauce

1 tablespoon rice wine

1 tablespoon Chinese black rice vinegar

2 teaspoons sugar

1 teaspoon Sichuan peppercorns, roasted and crushed

1 teaspoon chilli powder

50 ml (2½ tablespoons) Chinese chicken stock or water

1 Prepare the claypot by spraying thoroughly inside with olive oil.

2 To prepare the minced pork and eggplant, heat a wok and add the olive oil. Stir-fry the sliced eggplant till soft. Add the pork, garlic, ginger, shallots, soy sauce, rice wine, rice vinegar, sugar, peppercorns and chilli powder. Stir-fry for 2 minutes, then add the stock or water and simmer for 2 minutes.

3 Place the steamed rice in the prepared claypot. Spoon the pork and eggplant mixture over the rice and arrange the chopped spinach on top. Cover with the lid.

4 Place the claypot on the cooktop, bring to a high heat for 3 to 4 minutes, then reduce the heat and continue cooking gently for a further 5 minutes or until the edges of the rice are crispy and sizzling. Serve immediately.

Herbed Fish Parcels with Sweet Potato Wedges and Coleslaw

High in protein and low in fat, this meal is a far cry from fish and chips. It is also loaded with beta-carotene, potassium and magnesium.

Per serve

kJ/Cal 1186/279   **Protein** 34 g   **Fat** 8 g (saturated 1 g)

Carbohydrate 22 g   **Fibre** 5 g   **GI** Low

Preparation time 30 minutes
Cooking time 40 minutes   **Serves** 4

500 g sweet potato, peeled and cut into wedges

spray olive oil

1 teaspoon Cajun spice mix

4 x 150 g white fish fillets

2 teaspoons dill, chopped

2 teaspoons lemon rind, finely grated

freshly ground black pepper, to taste

Coleslaw

250 g cabbage, finely shredded

1 carrot, grated

½ red onion, finely chopped

¼ cup flatleaf parsley, chopped

1 tablespoon whole egg mayonnaise

2 tablespoons lemon juice

1 Preheat the oven to 200°C and line a large baking tray with non-stick baking paper.

2 Spray the sweet potato wedges lightly with oil, and sprinkle with the Cajun spice mix. Toss to coat. Arrange in a single layer on the lined tray, and bake for 25 minutes.

3 Meanwhile, tear 4 squares of non-stick baking paper. Place a fish fillet on each sheet and sprinkle with the dill and lemon rind. Season with pepper. Fold and wrap the baking paper securely to enclose the fish, then place on a baking tray. Add to the oven and cook for 15 minutes (so the sweet potatoes cook for 40 minutes in total).

4 For the coleslaw, combine the cabbage, carrot, onion and parsley in a large bowl. Add the mayonnaise and lemon juice; toss to combine. Serve the coleslaw with the fish and wedges.

Angelhair Pasta with Chilli Seafood Sauce

This recipe will please not only pasta lovers but anyone interested in a nutrient-dense dish, kind to the body and a joy to the palate.

Per serve

kJ/Cal 2170/515   **Protein** 40 g   **Fat** 15 g (saturated 2 g)

Carbohydrate 47 g   **Fibre** 3 g   **GI** Low

Preparation time 15 minutes

Cooking time 35 minutes   **Serves** 6

350 g small clams, scrubbed and rinsed

350 g mussels, scrubbed, beards removed, and rinsed

350 g medium-sized prawns, peeled and deveined

350 g scallops

1 tablespoon extra-virgin olive oil

2 large cloves garlic, minced

3 large shallots, finely chopped

3 tablespoons finely chopped flatleaf parsley

¾ cup (200 ml) dry white wine

1 × 400 g can tomatoes

350 g angelhair pasta

chilli flakes, to taste

2 tablespoons extra-virgin olive oil, extra

1 Soak the clams and mussels in cold water for 5 minutes. Discard any with opened shells. Drain and set aside. In a separate bowl, rinse and drain the prawns and scallops. Set aside.

2 In a wide, deep frypan, warm the olive oil, then add the garlic and shallots. Sauté for 1–2 minutes, until the shallots become soft (avoid burning the garlic). Stir in the parsley. Pour in the wine and cook over a medium–high heat for 3 minutes. Add the tomatoes and their liquid. Bring the mixture to a boil, then simmer, uncovered, for 15–20 minutes, stirring frequently.

3 Add the clams and the mussels to the sauce. Once their shells start opening (time varies with size—about 2–6 minutes), add the prawns, scallops and chilli flakes, to taste. Continue cooking for about 3 minutes.

4 Meanwhile, bring about 4 litres of water to the boil. Add the pasta and cook for 2 minutes. Use a wooden spoon to separate the strands. When the pasta is cooked al dente, drain and place in a large, warmed serving bowl. Drizzle the extra olive oil over the pasta and stir thoroughly.

5 Add the sauce to the pasta and mix thoroughly. Serve at once.

Prawn and Mango Salad with Chilli Lime Dressing

This salad is loaded with potassium and is a good source of zinc. The fat it contains is largely monounsaturated. It is best made just before serving.

Per serve

kJ/Cal 1518/357   **Protein** 26 g   **Fat** 13 g (saturated 3 g)

Carbohydrate 31 g   **Fibre** 7 g   **GI** Low

Preparation time 15 minutes

Cooking time 3 minutes (plus cooling time)   **Serves** 4

6 baby potatoes (about 70 g each), quartered

750 g cooked whole prawns, peeled and deveined

100 g snowpea sprouts, ends trimmed

1 cup fresh mint leaves, torn

⅓ cup (80 ml) sweet chilli sauce

¼ cup (60 ml) lime juice

1 mango, flesh cut into short, thin slices

1 avocado, thinly sliced

1 Place the potato in a shallow, microwave-safe dish. Pour over about 2 tablespoons of water, cover, and cook on high for 3 minutes or until tender. Set aside to cool.

2 Place the cooled potatoes, prawns, snowpea sprouts and mint leaves in a bowl and toss to combine.

3 Whisk the sweet chilli sauce and lime juice together for the dressing.

4 Divide the salad among serving plates. Top with the mango and avocado slices. Drizzle over the dressing and serve.

Mushroom and Vegetable Stir-fry

Per serve
kJ/Cal 1410/335 **Protein** 9 g **Fat** 3 g (saturated <1 g)
Carbohydrate 65 g **Fibre** 4 g **GI** Moderate

Preparation time 15 minutes
Cooking time 15 minutes **Serves** 4

1½ cups (300 g) Basmati rice, rinsed

1 bunch baby bok choy

2 teaspoons peanut or vegetable oil

1 small red onion, halved and thinly sliced

1 red capsicum, cut into thin strips

250 g mushrooms, sliced

2 garlic cloves, crushed

2 teaspoons ginger, grated

1 teaspoon red chilli, chopped

1 tablespoon salt-reduced soy sauce

1 Bring 2¼ cups of water to the boil in a large, tightly covered saucepan. Stir in the rice and quickly replace the lid. Reduce the heat to as low as possible and cook for 10 minutes. Remove from the heat and leave to stand, still covered, for 5 minutes.

2 Meanwhile, cut the bok choy in half to separate the leaves from the stems. Cut the leaves into wide shreds, and finely slice the stems.

3 Heat the oil in a wok and add the onion. Stir-fry over a moderately high heat for 2 minutes, until just tender. Add the capsicum and bok choy stems and stir-fry for 3 minutes.

4 Add the mushrooms, garlic, ginger and chilli, and stir-fry for 3 minutes, until the mushrooms are just soft. Drizzle with soy sauce and toss to combine. Serve immediately with the rice.

Moroccan-style Lentil and Vegetable Stew with Couscous

Per serve

kJ/Cal 1172/276   **Protein** 14 g   **Fat** 3 g (saturated <1 g)

Carbohydrate 44 g   **Fibre** 8 g   **GI** Moderate

Preparation time 25 minutes

Cooking time 50 minutes   **Serves** 4

2 teaspoons olive oil

1 onion, chopped

2 cloves garlic, crushed

2 teaspoons grated fresh ginger

2 teaspoons ground cumin

2 teaspoons ground coriander

1 cup (250 ml) vegetable stock

1 x 400 g can chopped tomatoes

400 g cauliflower, cut into small florets

1 eggplant, cut into 2 cm cubes

150 g green beans, cut into 4 cm lengths

1 x 400 g can green lentils, rinsed and drained

1 cup (150 g) couscous

1 Heat the oil in a large saucepan over a medium heat. Add the onion and cook for 5 minutes until soft and lightly golden. Add the garlic, ginger and spices and cook for 30 seconds, stirring.

2 Add the stock and tomatoes. Stir to combine, scraping the bottom of the pan. Add the cauliflower, eggplant and beans, stir to combine, and bring to the boil. Reduce the heat to medium–low and simmer, covered, for 30 minutes, until the vegetables are tender. Uncover and cook for a further 10 minutes.

3 Stir in the lentils and cook for 5 minutes to heat through.

4 Meanwhile, bring 1¼ cups (310 ml) of water to the boil in a medium-size saucepan. Add the couscous, cover tightly and turn off the heat. Leave to stand for 5 minutes, then uncover and fluff up the grains with a fork.

5 Serve the spicy vegetable stew over the couscous.

Tagine of Sweet Potato, Pumpkin, Prunes and Chickpeas

This is a delicious vegetarian dish that can be put together when there isn't much in the fridge. Serve it on its own or with couscous or rice if you wish.

Per serve

kJ/Cal 1210/290 **Protein** 11 g **Fat** 7 g (saturated 1 g)
Carbohydrate 42 g **Fibre** 10 g **GI** Low

Preparation time 15 minutes
Cooking time 30 minutes **Serves** 4

1 tablespoon olive oil

1 onion, finely chopped

1 garlic clove, crushed

1 teaspoon ground cumin

1 teaspoon ground coriander

½ teaspoon turmeric

300 g sweet potato, peeled and cut into 2 cm chunks

300 g butternut pumpkin, peeled and cut into 2 cm chunks

1 × 400 g can diced tomatoes in tomato juice

1 cup (250 ml) vegetable stock

1 × 400 g can chickpeas, drained

100 g pitted prunes

2 medium-sized zucchinis, sliced into rounds

1 Heat the oil in a large frypan over a medium heat, add the onion and garlic and sauté lightly for about 3 minutes or until soft and golden. Add the cumin, coriander and turmeric and stir until aromatic.

2 Add the sweet potato and pumpkin and stir to coat in the spices. Stir in the tomatoes, stock and chickpeas. Cover and simmer gently for 15 minutes, then add the prunes and zucchini. Cover and simmer for a further 10 minutes, or until all the vegetables are tender.

3 Serve with couscous or Basmati rice.

Chickpea Curry

Per serve

kJ/Cal 910/215 **Protein** 10 g **Fat** 8 g (saturated <1 g)
Carbohydrate 23 g **Fibre** 8 g **GI** Low

Preparation time 10 minutes
Cooking time about 30 minutes **Serves** 4–6

1 tablespoon canola oil

1 large onion, finely chopped

1 clove garlic, finely diced

1 teaspoon finely grated ginger

2 tomatoes, chopped

1 teaspoon ground cumin

1 teaspoon ground cloves, or to taste

3 teaspoons ground coriander

3 teaspoons ground chilli, or to taste

salt to taste (optional)

2 × 400 g cans chickpeas, drained

¾ cup water

2 teaspoons tamarind paste

freshly ground black pepper, to taste

2 teaspoons garam masala

1 teaspoon sugar

1 Heat the oil in a heavy-based pan and gently cook the onions until soft and golden (about 5 minutes). Add the garlic and ginger and cook for a further 5 minutes, then add the chopped tomatoes, cumin, cloves, coriander and chilli. Season with salt if desired.

2 Add the chickpeas and water and bring to the boil, then reduce the heat and stir in the tamarind paste, pepper, garam masala and sugar. Simmer uncovered for 15 minutes. Serve hot.

savoury snacks and sweet treats

Herbed Salmon Spread

This spread is rich in omega-3 fats and delicious with grainy crackers or low GI bread. If you prefer, you could replace the salmon with tuna. It will keep in the refrigerator for up to three days.

Per serve

kJ/Cal 637/150   **Protein** 15 g   **Fat** 10 g (saturated 4 g)

Carbohydrate 1 g   **Fibre** <1 g   **GI** Low

Preparation time 10 minutes

Cooking time nil   **Serves** 4

1 x 200 g can salmon (red or pink) in spring water, drained

1 x 200 g reduced fat fresh ricotta

½ teaspoon lemon rind, finely grated

2 teaspoons lemon juice

1 tablespoon chives, chopped

1 tablespoon flatleaf parsley, chopped

salt and freshly ground black pepper, to taste

1 Place the salmon in a bowl and flake with a fork. Add the ricotta, lemon rind and juice and herbs. Mash with a fork until well combined.

2 Season to taste.

Bruschetta with Basil and Tomatoes

Per serve
kJ/Cal 429/101   **Protein** 4 g   **Fat** 1 g (saturated <1 g)
Carbohydrate 18 g   **Fibre** 3 g   **GI** Low

Preparation time 10 minutes

Cooking time about 5 minutes   **Makes** 4

4 slices sourdough bread (preferably day-old)

1 garlic clove, peeled and halved

2 medium tomatoes, diced

½ small red onion, finely chopped

¼ cup basil leaves, shredded

1 teaspoon balsamic vinegar (optional)

salt and freshly ground pepper, to taste

1 Toast the bread on both sides until golden brown. Rub with the cut garlic clove, and set aside to cool.

2 Combine the tomatoes with the onion and basil. Drizzle with the balsamic vinegar (optional) and season with salt and pepper.

3 Spoon the tomato mixture onto the sourdough toast slices and serve immediately.

Eggplant and Bean Purée

This eggplant purée is a nutritious and tasty addition to sandwiches, or can be enjoyed spread on grainy crackers or wholemeal pita bread.

<table>
<tr><td>

Per serve

kJ/Cal 260/61   Protein 5 g

Fat 3 g (saturated <1 g)   Carbohydrate 3 g

Fibre 4 g   GI Low

</td><td>

Per serve (with vegetables)

kJ/Cal 320/75   Protein 5 g

Fat 3 g (saturated <1 g)   Carbohydrate 6 g

Fibre 5 g   GI Low

</td></tr>
</table>

Preparation time 20 minutes

Cooking time 40 minutes (plus cooling time)   **Serves** 6

1 large eggplant (about 400 g), cut in half lengthways

1 x 400 g can soybeans, rinsed and drained

1 teaspoon ground cumin

1 clove garlic, crushed

2 tablespoons lemon juice

1 red capsicum, cut into sticks

1 Lebanese cucumber, cut into rounds

1 carrot, cut into sticks

1 Preheat the oven to 190°C and line a baking tray with lightly oiled foil.

2 Place the eggplant cut side down on the foil. Bake for 35 minutes, until the eggplant is soft.

3 Cool the eggplant until just warm, then scoop the flesh out of the skin and place in a food processor. Add the soybeans, cumin, garlic and lemon juice, and process until smooth.

4 Serve with the vegetables for dipping.

Apricot and Almond Cookies

These cookies will keep in an airtight container for three to four days.

> **Per cookie**
> kJ/Cal 382/90   **Protein** 2 g   **Fat** 4 g (saturated <1 g)
> **Carbohydrate** 13 g   **Fibre** 1 g   **GI** Low

Preparation time 15 minutes

Cooking time 15 minutes   **Makes** about 16 cookies

100 g dried apricots, diced

100 g almond meal

½ cup (115 g) caster sugar

⅓ cup (50 g) plain flour

2 egg whites, at room temperature

1 Preheat the oven to 170°C and line two baking trays with non-stick baking paper.

2 Place the apricots, almond meal, sugar and flour in a bowl and mix well to combine.

3 Whisk the egg whites until frothy. Add to the apricot mixture and mix until well combined.

4 Use slightly wet hands to shape tablespoonfuls of the mixture into balls. Place on the lined trays and use a spoon to press out slightly.

5 Bake for 12–15 minutes, swapping the trays around once, until the biscuits are set and light golden on the bottom. Leave to cool on the trays for 5 minutes before transferring to a wire rack to cool completely.

Muesli and Honey Slice

This slice will keep in an airtight container for three to four days.

> **Per piece**
> **kJ/Cal** 650/153   **Protein** 3 g   **Fat** 7g (saturated 1 g)
> **Carbohydrate** 21 g   **Fibre** 2 g   **GI** Low

Preparation time 10 minutes
Cooking time 20–25 minutes   **Makes** 16 pieces

½ cup (125 ml) honey

100 g monounsaturated, salt-reduced margarine

2 eggs

2 cups (240 g) natural muesli

½ cup (75 g) self-raising flour

1 Preheat the oven to 170°C and line a 16 x 26 cm slab pan with non-stick baking paper.

2 Place the honey and margarine in a small saucepan. Stir over a low heat until the margarine melts and the mixture is well combined. Set aside to cool. Pour into a bowl and whisk in the eggs.

3 Combine the muesli and flour in a bowl. Add the cooled honey mixture and stir well to combine. Pour into the lined pan and smooth the surface. Bake for 20–25 minutes or until set and golden. Set aside in the pan to cool.

4 Cut the slice into 16 pieces. Store in an airtight container.

Banana and Ricotta Toasts

Other fruity toppings for ricotta toasts include sliced strawberries,
peach or nectarine slices and pear slices with walnuts.

Per serve
kJ/Cal 727/171   **Protein** 6 g   **Fat** 3 g (saturated 2 g)
Carbohydrate 29 g   **Fibre** 3 g   **GI** Low

Preparation time 5 minutes
Cooking time 5 minutes   **Makes** 4 toasts

100 g low fat fresh ricotta
1 tablespoon honey
pinch ground cinnamon
4 slices grainy bread
2 small bananas, diagonally sliced
extra honey, to serve
extra cinnamon, to serve

1 Use electric beaters to beat the ricotta, honey and cinnamon until almost smooth.

2 Toast the bread until golden.

3 Spread the ricotta mixture evenly on the bread.

4 Top with the bananas. Drizzle over a little extra honey and a sprinkle of cinnamon and serve immediately.

Fruit Parfaits

If you like, use low fat vanilla yoghurt instead of Frûche. The almond bread referred to is a very thin, sweet biscuit, similar to Italian biscotti, but wafer-thin. It is available from the biscuit or gourmet section of the supermarket.

Per serve

kJ/Cal 1090/256   **Protein** 12 g   **Fat** 4 g (saturated <1 g)

Carbohydrate 38 g   **Fibre** 4 g   **GI** Low

Preparation time 20 minutes

Refrigeration time 30 minutes   **Makes** 4 parfaits

150 g raspberries (fresh or thawed frozen)

1 tablespoon orange juice

90 g almond bread

4 nectarines or peaches, sliced

400 g vanilla reduced fat fromage frais (Frûche)

1 Place the raspberries in a bowl, then add the orange juice. Mash with a fork, and stir to make a chunky sauce.

2 Break the almond bread into bite-size pieces. Layer the nectarines (or peaches), raspberry sauce, almond bread and fromage frais in parfait glasses.

3 To let the flavours blend, refrigerate the parfaits for 30 minutes before serving.

Blueberry Cheesecakes

Per serve

kJ/Cal 875/206   **Protein** 10 g   **Fat** 13 g (saturated 5 g)

Carbohydrate 12 g   **Fibre** 2 g   **GI** Low

Preparation time 20 minutes

Refrigeration time 1 hour   **Makes** 4 cheesecakes

300 g low fat ricotta

1 tablespoon honey

1 teaspoon finely grated orange rind

1 cup (150 g) frooh blucberries

⅓ cup (40 g) walnuts, finely chopped

4 strawberries, sliced

1 Line 4 x ½ cup (125 ml) capacity ramekins with plastic wrap.

2 Place the ricotta, honey and orange rind in a bowl and mash with a fork.

3 Combine two-thirds of the blueberries with the ricotta mixture and divide between the ramekins. Press in firmly and smooth the surface.

4 Sprinkle over the walnuts. Smooth out with the back of a spoon and press the nuts into the mixture. Refrigerate for 1 hour, to firm and chill.

5 To serve, invert onto a plate and peel away the plastic wrap. Top each cake with a sliced strawberry, and serve with the remaining blueberries.

Creamed Rice with Rhubarb and Strawberries

There is almost no fat in this dessert. The rhubarb mixture will keep in an airtight container in the refrigerator for three to four days.

Per serve
kJ/Cal 1030/242   **Protein** 8 g   **Fat** 0 g
Carbohydrate 50 g   **Fibre** 4 g   **GI** Low

Preparation time 10 minutes (plus cooling time)
Cooking time 25 minutes   **Serves** 4

1 bunch rhubarb, ends trimmed and cut into 3 cm pieces

¼ cup (55 g) caster sugar

1 punnet strawberries, hulled and halved

½ cup (100 g) Doongara rice

2 tablespoons caster sugar, extra

2 cups (500 ml) skim milk

pinch ground cinnamon

1 Place the rhubarb and sugar in a medium-size, heavy-based saucepan. Stir constantly over a medium heat for 5 minutes until the rhubarb starts to soften. Add the strawberries and cook for a further 5 minutes or until the rhubarb and strawberries are tender. Remove from the heat and set aside to cool.

2 Meanwhile, place the rice, extra sugar and 1¼ cups (310 ml) of the skim milk in another medium-size, heavy-based saucepan. Stir over a low heat until the sugar dissolves, then increase the heat and bring to a simmer. Reduce the heat to low, cover, and cook for 12 minutes.

3 Remove from the heat and stir in the remaining milk, then cover and set aside for 10 minutes. Stir in a pinch of cinnamon and serve with the rhubarb mixture.

Orange and Passionfruit Mousse

This dessert is a good source of calcium and phosphorus and contains less than 1 gram of fat per serve. It will keep in the refrigerator for up to two days.

Per serve

kJ/Cal 505/119   **Protein** 7 g   **Fat** <1 g (saturated <1 g)

Carbohydrate 23 g   **Fibre** 1 g   **GI** Low

Preparation time 15 minutes

Cooking time 2 minutes (plus chilling and setting time)   **Serves** 6

⅔ cup (160 ml) freshly squeezed orange juice

⅓ cup (80 g) caster sugar

2 teaspoons powdered gelatine

⅓ cup (80 ml) fresh passionfruit pulp

1 x 375 ml can light evaporated milk, chilled

extra passionfruit, to serve (optional)

1 Place the orange juice and sugar in a small saucepan. Heat until hot, not boiling. Remove from the heat and stir in the gelatine until it dissolves. Pour the mixture into a small heatproof bowl and set aside to cool slightly. Stir in the passionfruit pulp.

2 In a large bowl use electric beaters to whisk the evaporated milk until light and fluffy. Add the orange juice mixture and stir to combine. Cover the bowl and chill for 1–1½ hours, stirring often, or until the mousse starts to thicken and set slightly. (Stirring will help the passionfruit to suspend in the mousse rather than sinking to the bottom.)

3 Spoon the mousse mixture into individual serving dishes. Refrigerate for a further 3–4 hours or until set.

4 Serve the mousse drizzled with extra passionfruit, if desired.

Fragrant Rice Pudding with Plums

This dessert is a rich source of carbohydrate, so it's best served after a simple meal such as grilled meat or fish with salad.

> **Per serve**
> **kJ/Cal** 1258/296   **Protein** 10 g   **Fat** 4 g (saturated 2 g)
> **Carbohydrate** 52 g   **Fibre** 4 g   **GI** Low

Preparation time 10 minutes
Cooking time 20 minutes   **Serves** 4

100 g Basmati rice
500 ml low fat milk
1½ tablespoons caster sugar
1 cardamom pod, lightly crushed
rind of 1 small orange, finely grated
½ teaspoon vanilla essence
½ cinnamon stick
8 plums
30 g pistachios, chopped, to serve

1 Cook the rice in a saucepan of boiling water for 5 minutes. Drain and return to the pan with the milk, sugar, cardamom pod, orange rind, vanilla essence and cinnamon stick.

2 Bring to the boil, then reduce the heat to low and cook, stirring regularly, for about 15–20 minutes, until the rice is tender and creamy and the liquid is almost all absorbed. Stir constantly towards the end of the cooking time to prevent catching on the bottom.

3 Meanwhile, place the plums in a medium-sized saucepan and cover with water. Slowly bring to the boil. Reduce the heat to very low and simmer for 10 minutes. Lift the fruit from the cooking liquid with a slotted spoon, cool slightly and slip off the skins.

4 Discard the cinnamon stick and cardamom pod from the rice, and serve immediately with the plums, sprinkled with pistachios.

your
low GI diet
pantry

What to keep in your pantry

Asian sauces Hoi sin, oyster, soy and fish sauces are a good basic range.

Barley One of the oldest cultivated cereals, barley is very nutritious and high in soluble fibre. Look for products such as pearl barley to use in soups, stews and pilafs.

Black pepper Buy freshly ground pepper or grind your own peppercorns.

Bread Low GI options include grainy, stoneground wholemeal, pumpernickel, sourdough, English-style muffins, flat bread and pita bread.

Breakfast cereals These include traditional rolled oats, natural muesli and low GI packaged breakfast cereals.

Bulgur wheat Use it to make tabbouli, or add to vegetable burgers, stuffings, soups and stews.

Canned evaporated skim milk This makes an excellent substitution for cream in pasta sauces.

Canned fish Keep a good stock of canned tuna packed in spring water, and canned sardines and salmon.

Canned fruit Have a variety of canned fruit on hand, including peaches, pears, apples and nectarines—choose the brands labelled with 'no added sugar' fruit juice syrup.

Canned vegetables Sweet corn kernels and tomatoes can help to boost the vegetable content of a meal. Tomatoes, in particular, can be used freely because they are rich in anti-oxidants, as well as having a low GI.

Couscous Ready in minutes, serve with casseroles and braised dishes.

Curry pastes A tablespoon or so makes a delicious curry base.

Dried fruit These include sultanas, apricots, raisins, prunes and apples.

Dried herbs Oregano, basil, ground coriander, thyme and rosemary can be useful to have on stand-by in the pantry.

Honey Try to avoid the commercial honeys or honey blends, and use the Australian 'pure floral' honeys. These varieties have a much lower GI, and include Yellowbox and Red Rum. Bioactive components in these honeys appear to reduce their GI naturally.

Jam A dollop of good-quality jam (with no added sugar) on toast contains fewer kilojoules than butter or margarine.

Legumes Stock a variety of legumes (dried or canned), including lentils, split peas and beans. There are many bean varieties, including cannellini, butter, borlotti, kidney and soy beans.

Mustard Seeded or grainy mustard is useful as a sandwich spread, and in salad dressings and sauces.

Noodles Many Asian noodles such as Hokkien, udon and rice vermicelli have low to intermediate GI values because of their dense texture, whether they are made from wheat or rice flour.

Nuts Try a handful of nuts (about 30 g/1 oz) every other day. Try them sprinkled over your breakfast cereal, salad or dessert, and enjoy unsalted nuts as a snack as well.

Oils Try olive oil for general use; some extra-virgin olive oil for salad dressings, marinades and dishes that benefit from its flavour; and sesame oil for Asian-style stir-fries. Canola or olive oil cooking sprays are handy too.

Pasta A great source of carbohydrates and B vitamins. Fresh or dried, the preparation is easy. Simply cook in boiling water until just tender, or al dente, drain and top with your favourite sauce and a sprinkle of Parmesan cheese.

Quinoa This grainy cooks in about 10–15 minutes and has a slightly chewy texture. It can be used as a substitute for rice, couscous or bulgur wheat. It is very important to rinse the grains thoroughly before cooking.

Rice Basmati, Doongara or Japanese koshihikari varieties are good choices because they have a lower GI than, for example, jasmine rice.

Rolled Oats Besides their use in porridge, oats can be added to cakes, biscuits, breads and desserts.

Sea salt Use in moderation.

Spices Most spices, including ground cumin, turmeric, cinnamon, paprika and nutmeg, should be bought in small quantities because they lose pungency with age and incorrect storage.

Stock Make your own stock or buy ready-made products, which are available in long-life cartons in the supermarket. To keep the sodium content down with ready-made stocks, look out for a low salt option.

Tomato paste Use in soups, sauces and casseroles.

Vinegar White wine or red wine vinegar and balsamic vinegar are excellent as vinaigrette dressings in salads.

What to keep in your refrigerator

Bacon Bacon is a valuable ingredient in many dishes because of the flavour it offers. You can make a little bacon go a long way by trimming off all fat and chopping it finely. Lean ham is often a more economical and leaner way to go. In casseroles and soups, a ham or bacon bone imparts a fine flavour without much fat.

Bottled vegetables Sun-dried tomatoes, olives, char-grilled eggplant (aubergine) and capsicum (pepper) are handy to keep as flavoursome additions to pastas and sandwiches.

Capers, olives and anchovies These can be bought in jars and kept in the refrigerator once opened. They are a tasty (but salty) addition to pasta dishes, salads and pizzas.

Cheese Any reduced fat cheese is great to keep handy in the fridge. A block of Parmesan is indispensable and will keep for up to a month. Reduced fat cottage and ricotta cheeses have a short life so are best bought as needed, and they can be a good alternative to butter or margarine in a sandwich.

Condiments Keep jars of minced garlic, chilli or ginger in the refrigerator to spice up your cooking in an instant.

Eggs To enhance your intake of omega-3 fats, we suggest using omega-3-enriched eggs. Although the yoke is high in cholesterol, the fat in eggs is predominantly monounsaturated, and therefore considered a 'good fat'.

Fish Try a variety of fresh fish.

Fresh herbs These are available in most supermarkets and there really is no substitute for the flavour they impart. For variety, try parsley, basil, mint, chives and coriander.

Fresh fruit Almost all fruit make an excellent low GI snack. When in season, try fruit such as apples, oranges, pears, grapes, grapefruit, peaches, apricots, strawberries and mangoes.

Meat Lean varieties are better—try lean beef, lamb fillets, pork fillets, chicken (breast or drumsticks) and minced beef.

Milk Skim or low fat milk is best, or try low fat calcium-enriched soy milk.

Vegetables Keep a variety of seasonal vegetables on hand such as spinach, broccoli, cauliflower, Asian greens, asparagus, zucchini (courgette) and mushrooms. Capsicum (pepper), spring onions and sprouts (mung bean and snowpea sprouts) are great to bulk up a salad. Sweet corn, sweet potato and yam are essential to your low GI food store.

Yoghurt Low fat natural yoghurt provides the most calcium for the fewest calories. Have vanilla or fruit versions as a dessert, or use natural yoghurt as a condiment in savoury dishes. However, if using yoghurt in a hot meal, make sure you add it at the last minute, and do not let it boil or it will curdle.

What to keep in your freezer

Frozen berries Berries can make any dessert special, and by using frozen ones it means you don't have to wait until berry season in order to indulge. Try berries such as blueberries, raspberries and strawberries.

Frozen yoghurt This is a fantastic substitute for ice-cream and some products even have a similar creamy texture, but with much less fat.

Frozen vegetables Keep a packet of peas, beans, corn, spinach or mixed vegetables in the freezer—these are handy to add to a quick meal.

Ice-cream Reduced or low fat ice-cream is ideal for a quick dessert, served with fresh fruit.

the Low GI Diet

PART FIVE

the GI table

THE FOLLOWING TABLE GIVES A COMPREHENSIVE, UP-TO-date listing of the GI of hundreds of popular foods in alphabetical order along with our suggestion of how freely you should eat each food.

The table will help you to select lower GI varieties in each food category and therefore enable you to lower the GI of your overall diet.

Not all foods have had their GI values measured. This list, therefore, although extensive, is not complete. If you don't see a GI value for a food or drink, then contact the manufacturer to ask them if they have had this product GI tested. Not all food manufacturers are aware of GI testing yet, and some may have GI values for their products, but may not allow them to be published.

The GI values in the table are correct at the time of publication. However, the formulation of commercial foods can change and the GI may be altered.

G This symbol on food packaging is your guarantee that the product
has had its GI accurately tested by an accredited laboratory and meets
strict nutritional criteria. For more information go to www.gisymbol.com
The GI database at www.glycemicindex.com has all the latest values and
GI testing results.

★ Some foods contain very little or no carbohydrate and, as a result, do
not give a glycemic response when eaten. These foods are marked
with this symbol and do not have a GI. We have still given these foods
a recommendation (or otherwise) for their role in The Low GI Diet.

▼ Foods marked with this symbol may be high in saturated fat. We
recommend that you check the food label for saturated fat content
and limit your intake of foods for which saturated fat accounts for
more than 20 per cent of the total fat content. With fresh foods, such
as meat and seafood, remove visible fat and prepare using small
amounts of polyunsaturated or monounsaturated fats if desired.

∴ If you see this symbol next to a GI value, this means that the value is
an average result for that particular food. The average may be of ten
studies or of only two to four studies.

FOOD   GI VALUE

A
Aero Chocolate Mousse, Nestlé®	37	Enjoy in moderation
Alba gelati, sucrose-free, chocolate	37	Low GI, low fat dessert
Alba gelati, sucrose-free, vanilla	39	Low GI, low fat dessert
Alfalfa sprouts	★	An everyday food
All-Bran®, breakfast cereal, Kellogg's®	34⊹	An excellent choice
All-Bran® Fruit 'n' Oats, breakfast cereal, Kellogg's®	39	An excellent choice
Angel food cake, plain	67▼	Okay now and again
Apple, fresh	38⊹	Great anytime
Apple, dried	29	Great for snacks—in moderate amounts

APPLE JUICE
Apple juice, no added sugar	40⊹	
Apple juice, clear, no added sugar, Wild About Fruit® ©	44	
Apple juice, cloudy, no added sugar, Wild About Fruit® ©	37	
Apple and Blackcurrant juice, pure, Berri	45	Enjoy in moderation—about one glass a day
Apple and Cherry juice, pure, Wild About Fruit® ©	43	
Apple and Mandarin juice, pure, Wild About Fruit®	53	
Apple and Mango juice, pure, Wild About Fruit® ©	47	
Granny Smith, pure, Ducat's	44	

Apple muffin, home-made	46▼	Now and then—GI varies with each recipe
Apricot Delight Log, fruit bread, Bakers Delight	56	A good choice for breakfast or snacks
Apricot-filled fruit bar, wholemeal pastry, Mother Earth	50▼	Okay for an occasional snack
Apricot fruit spread, reduced sugar, Glen Ewin	55	Enjoy in moderation
Apricots, canned in light syrup	64	Go easy—fresh is best
Apricots, dried	30	A nutritious snack or addition to meals
Apricots, fresh	57	Great anytime
Arborio, risotto rice, white, boiled	69	A fair choice
Artichokes, globe, fresh or canned in brine	★	An everyday food
Asparagus	★	An everyday food
Australia's Own Natural Rice milk	92	Go slow
Avocado	★	Good fat, eat in moderation

B
Bagel, white	72	Take it easy
Baked beans, canned in tomato sauce	49⊹	A healthy convenience food

BAKERS DELIGHT FRESH BREADS
Apricot Delight Log	56	
Cape Seed Loaf	48	
Country Grain Loaf	61	Choose lower GI types for everyday eating
Linseed and Soy Loaf	55	
Tiger Loaf, white bread	71	

⊹ average   ★ little or no carbs   ▼ high in saturated fat

FOOD   GI VALUE

B

Food	GI Value	
Wholemeal Block Loaf	71	Choose lower GI types for everyday eating
Bamboo shoots	★	An everyday food
Banana, raw	52÷	Everyday food—the less ripe, the lower the GI
Banana cake, home-made	51÷▼	Go easy—GI varies with recipe; energy dense
Banana Smoothie Drink, low fat, So Natural	30	A low fat snack or light meal
Barley, pearled, boiled	25÷	A star performer—very low GI
Barley, rolled, raw	66	Fibre rich, has a lower GI when served as porridge
Basmati rice, white, boiled	58	A good choice
Bean curd, tofu, plain, unsweetened	★	An excellent source of lean protein
Bean sprouts, raw	★	An everyday food

BEANS

Food	GI Value	
Black, boiled	30	
Black-eyed beans, soaked, boiled	42	
Borlotti, canned, drained, Edgell	41	
Butter, canned, drained, Edgell	36	
Butter, dried, boiled	31÷	
Cannellini	31	
Dark red kidney, canned, drained	43	
Four bean mix, canned, drained, Edgell	37	
Green	★	
Haricot, cooked, canned	38÷	Natural super foods—low GI and nutritious
Haricot, dried, boiled	33÷	
Lima, baby, frozen, reheated	32	
Mung	39	
Pinto, canned, drained	45	
Pinto, dried, boiled	39	
Red kidney, canned, drained, Edgell	36	
Romano	46	
Snake	★	
Soy, canned, drained	14÷	
Soy, dried, boiled	18	
Beef	▼★	Eat it lean
Beer, Tooheys New Draught (4.6% alcohol)	66	Go slow—drink in moderation, if at all
Beetroot, canned	64	A good source of anti-oxidants

BISCUITS

Food	GI Value	
Digestives, gluten-free, Nutricia	58▼	
Digestives, regular	59÷▼	Indulgence foods—limit your intake
Golden Fruit, Griffins New Zealand	77▼	
Highland Oatcakes, Walker's	57▼	

÷ average   ★ little or no carbs   ▼ high in saturated fat

FOOD	GI VALUE	
B		
Highland Oatmeal™	55▼	
Maltmeal Wafer, Griffins New Zealand	50▼	
Milk Arrowroot	69▼	
Morning Coffee	79▼	
Oatmeal	54▼	
Rich Tea®	55▼	
Shortbread, plain	64▼	
Shredded Wheatmeal	62▼	
Snack Right® Fruit Bar, Apple and Blackberry	43	
Snack Right® Fruit Bar, Apricot and Raisin	46	
Snack Right® Fruit Bar, Wild Berry	55	Indulgence foods—limit your intake
Snack Right® Fruit Bites, Apple and Sultana	45	
Snack Right® Fruit Bites, Wild Berry	52	
Snack Right® Fruit Roll, Apple and Blackberry	43	
Snack Right® Fruit Roll, Spicy Apple and Sultana	45	
Snack Right® Fruit Slice, Mango and Passionfruit	49	
Snack Right® Fruit Slice, Mixed Berry	50	
Snack Right® Fruit Slice, Spicy Apple and Sultana	45	
Snack Right® Fruit Slice, Sultana	48	
Snack Right® Fruit Slice, Sultana and Chocolate	45	
Vanilla Wafer, plain	77▼	
Black beans, boiled	30	A super food
Black-eyed beans, soaked, boiled	42	A great choice
Black rye bread, Riga®	76	Take it easy
Blueberry muffin, commercially made	59▼	Occasional treat
Bok choy	★	An everyday food
Borlotti beans, canned, drained, Edgell	41	Excellent in salads, stews and soups
Bran Flakes, breakfast cereal, Kellogg's®	74	Go slow
Bran muffin, commercially made	60▼	Now and then
Brawn	★▼	Occasionally in moderation
BREAD		
Apricot Delight Log, Bakers Delight	56	
Bagel, white	72	
Black rye bread, Riga®	76	
Bürgen® Fruit Loaf	44	Choose lower GI varieties for everyday eating
Bürgen® Oat Bran and Honey bread ©	49	
Bürgen® Rye bread ©	51	
Bürgen® Soy-Lin, soy and linseed bread ©	36	
Cape Seed Loaf, Bakers Delight	48	

✢ average   ★ little or no carbs   ▼ high in saturated fat

FOOD   GI VALUE

B

Food	GI Value
Continental fruit Loaf	47
Country Grain and Organic Rye, Country Life ©	48
Country Grain Loaf, Bakers Delight	61
Cripps 9 Grain Sandwich loaf ©	43
Cripps 9 Grain Toast loaf ©	43
Fruit and Spice Loaf, thick sliced, Buttercup	54
Gluten-free Multigrain Bread, Country Life	79
Golden Hearth Organic Heavy Grainy bread	53
Hamburger bun, white	61
Helga's™ Classic Seed Loaf	68
Helga's™ Traditional Wholemeal Bread	70
Hyfibe™, white sandwich bread, Tip Top®	70
Kaiser rolls, white	73
Lebanese bread, white, Seda Bakery	75
Linseed and Soy Loaf, Bakers Delight	55
Molenberg, New Zealand	80∻
Multigrain Sandwich Bread, Tip Top®	65
9 Grain, multigrain bread, Tip Top® ©	43
Organic stoneground wholemeal sourdough bread, Bill's Bakery	59
PerforMAX, multigrain bread, Country Life ©	38
Pita bread, white	57
Pumpernickel bread	50∻
Regular, sliced white bread	71
Rye Hi-soy and Linseed, Country Life ©	42
Schinkenbrot, dark rye bread, Riga®	86
Spelt multigrain bread, Pav's Allergy Bakery	54
Sourdough rye bread	48
Sourdough wheat bread	54
Sunblest, white bread, Tip Top®	71
Tiger Loaf, white bread, Bakers Delight	71
Wholemeal Block Loaf, Bakers Delight	71
Wholemeal Sandwich Bread, Tip Top®	71
Wonder White®, Buttercup	80

Choose lower GI varieties for everyday eating

BREAKFAST CEREALS

Food	GI Value
All-Bran®, Kellogg's®	34∻
All-Bran® Fruit 'n' Oats, Kellogg's®	39
Bran Flakes, Kellogg's®	74
Coco Pops®, Kellogg's®	77∻

Choose lower GI varieties for everyday eating

∻ average   ★ little or no carbs   ▼ high in saturated fat

FOOD   GI VALUE

B

Food	GI Value
Corn Flakes®, Kellogg's®	77
Corn Pops®, Kellogg's®	80
Crunchy Nut Corn Flakes, Kellogg's®	72
Froot Loops®, Kellogg's®	69
Frosties®, Kellogg's®	55
Fruitful Lite, Hubbard's	61
Gluten-free Muesli, Freedom Foods, with 1.5% fat milk	39
Golden Wheats, Kellogg's®	71
Goldies, Whole Wheat, Kellogg's®	70
Good Start, muesli wheat biscuits, Sanitarium®	68
Guardian®, Kellogg's®	37
Healthwise™ for Bowel Health, Uncle Tobys	66
Hi-Bran Soy and Linseed Weet-Bix®, Sanitarium®	57
Hi-Bran Weet-Bix®, regular, Sanitarium®	61
Honey Goldies, Kellogg's®	72
Honey Rice Bubbles®, Kellogg's®	77
Honey Smacks®, Kellogg's®	71
Just Right®, Kellogg's®	60
Just Right Just Grains®, Kellogg's®	62
Komplete®, Kellogg's®	48
Lite-Bix, Sanitarium®	70
Mini Wheats®, Blackcurrant, Kellogg's®	72
Mini Wheats®, Wholewheat, Kellogg's®	58
Muesli, Gluten-free, Freedom Foods, with 1.5% fat milk	39
Muesli, Lite, Sanitarium® (New Zealand)	54
Muesli, Natural, Sanitarium®	40
Muesli, Natural, Sanitarium® (New Zealand)	57
Muesli, Naytura Premium	65
Muesli, Oven-crisp, Vogel's®	52
Muesli, Swiss Formula, Uncle Tobys	56
Nutri-Grain™, Kellogg's®	66
Oat bran, raw, unprocessed	55✸
Oat Bran Weet-Bix®, Sanitarium®	57
Oat 'n' Honey Bake, Kellogg's®	77
Oats, rolled, raw, Lowan®	59
Porridge, instant, made with water, Uncle Tobys	82
Porridge, made from steel-cut oats with water	52
Porridge, Multi-grain, made with water, Monster Muesli	55
Porridge, regular, made from oats with water	58✸

Choose lower GI varieties for everyday eating

✸ average   ★ little or no carbs   ▼ high in saturated fat

FOOD   GI VALUE

B

Food	GI Value	
Puffed buckwheat	65	
Puffed Wheat, Sanitarium®	80	
Rice Bran, Extruded, Ricegrowers	19	
Rice Bubbles®, Kellogg's®	87÷	
Rice Krispies®, breakfast cereal, Kellogg's®	82	
Ricies™, Sanitarium®	95	
Semolina, cooked	55÷	
Shredded Wheat	75÷	
Skippy Cornflakes™, Sanitarium®	93	
Soy Tasty, Sanitarium®	60	
Soytana®, Vogel's®	58	Choose lower GI varieties for everyday eating
Special K®, regular, Kellogg's®	56	
Sultana Bran, Kellogg's®	73	
Sultana Goldies, Kellogg's®	61	
Sustain®, regular, Kellogg's®	68	
Toasted Muesli, Purina	43	
Ultra Bran Soy and Linseed, Vogel's®	41	
Vita-Brits®, Uncle Tobys	68	
Vita-Pro®, gluten-free, Vogel's®	52	
Weet-Bix®, regular, Sanitarium®	69÷	
Wheat-bites™, Uncle Tobys	72	

BREAKFAST CEREAL BARS

Food	GI Value	
Crunchy Nut Corn Flakes Bar, Kellogg's®	72	
Fibre Plus bar, Uncle Tobys	78	
Fruity-Bix bar, Fruit and Nut, Sanitarium®	56	
Fruity-Bix bar, Wild Berry, Sanitarium®	51	Now and then; choose lower GI, lower saturated fat varieties
K-Time® Just Right® breakfast cereal bar	72	
Rice Bubbles® Treat bar, Kellogg's®	63	
Sustain® bar, Kellogg's®	57	
Breton wheat crackers	67▼	Go slow
Broad beans	79	No problem in moderation
Broccoli	★	An everyday food
Broken rice, white, cooked in rice cooker	86	Take it easy
Brussels sprouts	★	An everyday food
Buckwheat, boiled	54÷	A nutritious alternative to rice
Buckwheat, pancakes, gluten-free, packet mix, Orgran	102	Go slow
Build-Up, drink powder, vanilla with fibre, in water, Nestlé®	41	A nutrition supplement
Bulgur, cracked wheat, ready to eat	48÷	Delicious in salads such as tabbouli
Bun, hamburger, white	61	Eat in moderation—use grainy rolls instead

÷ average   ★ little or no carbs   ▼ high in saturated fat

FOOD	GI VALUE	

B **BÜRGEN® BREADS**

Bürgen® Fruit Loaf	44	
Bürgen ® Mixed Grain ©	52	
Bürgen® Oat Bran and Honey bread ©	49	
Bürgen® Rye bread ©	51	Nutritious low GI breads for everyday eating
Bürgen® Soy-Lin, soy and linseed bread ©	36	
Bürgen® Wholemeal and Grain ©	43	

BÜRGEN® BREAKFAST CEREALS

Bürgen® Fruit and Muesli ©	51	
Bürgen® Rye Muesli ©	41	An everyday food
Bürgen® Soy-Lin Muesli ©	51	
Burger Rings, Barbeque Flavoured®	90▼	Go slow
Butter beans, canned, drained, Edgell	36	A great choice
Butter beans, dried, boiled	31÷	A super food

C

Cabbage	★	An everyday food

CAKES

Angel food cake, plain	67▼	
Banana cake, home-made	51÷▼	
Chocolate cake, made from packet mix		
with frosting, Betty Crocker	38▼	
Cupcake with strawberry icing, Farmland	73▼	
Lamingtons, Farmland	87▼	Take it easy—indulgence foods
Pound cake, plain	54▼	
Sponge cake, plain, unfilled	46▼	
Vanilla cake, made from packet mix		
with vanilla frosting, Betty Crocker	42▼	
Calamari rings, squid, not battered or crumbed	★	Try prepared with unsaturated fats
Calci Forte, calcium-enriched soy milk, So Natural	36	A good choice
Calrose rice, white, medium-grain, boiled	83	Take care—use lower GI rice more often
Cannellini beans	31	All five-star food
Cape Seed Loaf, grainy bread, Bakers Delight	48	Delicious everyday food
Capellini pasta, white, boiled	45	Good choice; watch portion size
Capsicum	★	An everyday food
Carrot juice, freshly made	43	Go for it
Carrots, peeled, boiled	41÷	An everyday food
Cashew nuts, salted, Farmland	22	A great snack, in moderation—best unsalted
Cauliflower	★	An everyday food
Celery	★	Whenever you like

÷ average   ★ little or no carbs   ▼ high in saturated fat

FOOD   GI VALUE

Food	GI Value	Comment
Cheese	★▼	Energy dense; best in small amounts
Cheese tortellini, cooked	50▼	In moderation
Cherries, dark, raw	63	Enjoy in moderation
Chicken	★▼	Eat it lean without skin
Chicken nuggets, frozen, reheated in microwave 5 mins	46▼	Go slow
Chickpeas, canned in brine	40	A convenient and nutritious food
Chickpeas, dried, boiled	28÷	One of nature's super foods
Chillies, fresh or dried	★	An everyday food
Chives, fresh	★	An everyday food
CHOCOLATE		
Cadbury's® Milk Chocolate, plain	49▼	
Dark chocolate, plain, regular	41÷▼	
Dove®, milk chocolate	45▼	
Mars Bar®, regular	62▼	
Milk, plain, Nestlé®	42▼	Indulgence food—energy dense
Milk, plain, reduced sugar	35▼	
Milk, plain, regular	41÷▼	
Milk, plain, with fructose instead of regular sugar	20▼	
Milky Bar®, white, Nestlé®	44▼	
Snickers Bar®, regular	41▼	
Chocolate cake, made from packet mix with frosting, Betty Crocker	38▼	Special occasion food
Chocolate-coated cookie, gluten free, LEDA	35	Enjoy occasionally
Chocolate Hazelnut Smoothie drink, low fat, So Natural	34	Enjoy in moderation
Chocolate hazelnut spread, Nutella®	30	Enjoy in moderation
Chocolate Mousse, Diet, Nestlé®	37	A good choice for a snack or dessert
Chocolate pudding, instant, made from packet with whole milk	47÷▼	Go slow—use low fat milk
Coca-Cola®, soft drink	53	An occasional treat
Coco Pops®, breakfast cereal, Kellogg's®	77	An occasional treat
Coffee, black, no milk or sugar	★	Drink in moderation
Condensed milk, sweetened, full fat	61▼	Go slow
Consommé, clear, chicken or vegetable	★	A nice light entrée
Cordial, orange, reconstituted, Berri	66	Okay in moderation
Corn, sweet, honey and pearl variety, boiled (New Zealand)	37	An everyday food
Corn, sweet, on the cob, boiled 20 mins	48	A good choice—take it easy with the butter
Corn chips, plain, salted	42▼	Take care—low GI due to high fat content
Corn Flakes®, breakfast cereal, Kellogg's®	77	Now and then
Corn Flakes, Crunchy Nut, breakfast cereal, Kellogg's®	72	Use as a special treat

÷ average   ★ little or no carbs   ▼ high in saturated fat

FOOD   GI VALUE

C

Food	GI	Comment
Cornmeal (polenta), boiled	68	Enjoy in moderation
Corn pasta, gluten-free, boiled, Orgran's	78	Serve al dente for a lower GI
Corn Pops®, breakfast cereal, Kellogg's®	80	Go slow
Corn Thins, puffed corn cakes, gluten-free, Real Foods	87	Take it easy
Country Grain Loaf, bread, Bakers Delight	61	A fair choice
Country Life Country Grain and Organic Rye, bread ©	48	A good choice
Country Life Gluten-free Multigrain Bread	79	A better choice than white gluten-free bread
Country Life Rye Hi-soy and Linseed ©	42	A good choice
Couscous, boiled 5 mins	65⁑	Eat in moderation

CRACKERS AND CRISPBREADS

Food	GI	Comment
Breton wheat crackers	67▼	
Corn Thins, gluten-free, puffed corn cakes, Real Foods	87	
Jatz®, plain, salted, Arnott's™	55▼	
Kavli® Norwegian Crispbread, Player's Biscuits	71	Now and then—choose lower GI,
Puffed Crispbread, Weston's	81	lower saturated fat types
Puffed Rice Cakes, white, Ricegrowers	82	
Ryvita® crispbread	69	
Sao™, plain, Arnott's™	70▼	
Water cracker, plain	71⁑	

Food	GI	Comment
Cranberries, dried, sweetened	64	Good for cooking and occasional snacks
Cranberry Juice Cocktail, Ocean Spray	52	Enjoy in moderation
Crème Caramel, Diet, Nestlé®	33	A good choice for desert
Crispix®, breakfast cereal	87	Go slow
Croissant, plain	67▼	Indulgence food
Crumpet, white	69	Enjoy in moderation
Crunchy Nut Corn Flakes Bar, Kellogg's®	72	Indulgence food
Crunchy Nut Corn Flakes, breakfast cereal, Kellog's®	72	An occasional treat
Cucumber	★	An everyday food
Cupcake, strawberry-iced, Farmland	73▼	Go slow
Custard, home-made from milk, wheat starch and sugar	43▼	Okay occasionally—use low fat milk
Custard, Trim, vanilla, reduced fat	37	Good with fruit as a dessert
Custard apple, fresh, flesh only	54	Great anytime

D

DAIRY FARMERS™ MILKS

Food	GI	Comment
Farmer's Best Milk with omega 3	27	
Lite White, reduced fat (1.4%) milk ©	30	
Shape, calcium-enriched, low fat (0.1%) milk	34	All low GI—use lower fat varieties
Skim, low fat (0.1%) milk ©	32	
Take Care, calcium-enriched, reduced fat (1%) milk ©	23	

⁑ average   ★ little or no carbs   ▼ high in saturated fat

FOOD	GI VALUE	
Whole milk (3.6% fat)	27	All low GI—use lower fat varieties
Dark rye bread, Schinkenbrot, Riga®	86	Take it easy
Dates, Arabic, dried, vacuum-packed	39∻	High energy—enjoy a small serve now and then
Dates, dried	103	A special treat
Desiree potato, peeled, boiled 35 mins	101	Go slow
Dessert Maid figs, dried, tenderised	61	A nutritious snack now and then
Diet jelly, made from crystals with water	★	A low kilojoule alternative to regular jelly
Diet soft drinks	★	Low in kilojoules and nutrients—enjoy in moderation
Dietworks® Hazelnut and Apricot bar	42	A dietary supplement
Digestive biscuits, plain	59∻▼	Take it easy
Digestives, gluten-free, Nutricia	58▼	An occasional treat
Doongara rice, white, boiled	56∻	A clever choice
Dried apple	29	Great for snacks—in moderate amounts
Duck	★▼	Serve the meat lean without skin
Eggplant	★	An everyday food
Eggs	★▼	Nutritious; use unsaturated fat in cooking
Endive	★	An everyday food
Ensure™, vanilla drink	48	A medical nutrition product
Fanta®, orange soft drink	68	An occasional treat
Farmer's Best Milk with omega 3	27	A good choice
Fennel	★	An everyday food
Fettuccine, egg, cooked	32	The GI will increase if overcooked
Fibre Plus breakfast cereal bar, Uncle Tobys	78	Now and then
Figs, dried, tenderised, Dessert Maid	61	A nutritious snack now and then
Fish	★	A fantastic food—prepare with minimal fat
Fish fingers	38▼	Go slow—low GI due to fat content
Four bean mix, canned, drained, Edgell	37	An everyday food
French fries, frozen, reheated in microwave	75▼	Take it easy
French Vanilla ice-cream, premium, Sara Lee®	38▼	Indulgence food
Froot Loops®, breakfast cereal	69	Take it easy
Frosties®, Kellogg's®	55	An occasional treat
Frûche, low fat, Berry Compote	37	
Frûche, low fat, Duet Peach on Pineapple	34	
Frûche, low fat, Lemon Sorbetto	34	Enjoy in moderation
Frûche, low fat, Orange Sorbetto	34	
Frûche, low fat, Peach Roulade	37	

∻ average ★ little or no carbs ▼ high in saturated fat

FOOD	GI VALUE	
F Fructose, pure	19⁚	Powdered sugar that naturally occurs in fruit
Fruisana ©	19	Low GI sweeteners-- use in moderation
FRUIT, CANNED		
Apricots, in light syrup	64	
Fruit cocktail	55	
Lychees, in syrup, drained	79	
Peach, in heavy syrup	58	Enjoy the fruit, avoid the syrup (it's energy dense)
Peach, in light syrup	57⁚	
Peach, in natural juice	45	
Pear, in natural juice	44⁚	
FRUIT, DRIED		
Apple	29	
Apricots	31⁚	
Cranberries, sweetened	64	
Dates, pitted	103	Nutritious, but concentrated—enjoy in moderation
Figs, dried, tenderised, Dessert Maid	61	
Prunes, pitted	29	
Raisins	64	
Sultanas	56	
FRUIT, FRESH		
Apple	38⁚	
Apricots	57	
Banana	52⁚	
Breadfruit	68	
Cherries, dark	63	
Custard apple, fresh, flesh only	54	All fruit is rich in anti-oxidants and nutrients—
Grapefruit	25	a high GI should not deter you
Grapes	53⁚	
Kiwi fruit	53	
Mango	51⁚	
Orange	42⁚	
Paw paw	56	
Plum	39⁚	
Fruit and Spice Loaf, Buttercup	54	Now and then
Fruit cocktail, canned fruit	55	Fresh fruit salad is a better choice
Fruit Fingers, Heinz Kidz™, banana	61	Okay occasionally
FRUIT JUICE		
Apple, clear, no added sugar, Wild About Fruit® ©	44	Enjoy in small amounts–eating fresh fruit
Apple, cloudy, no added sugar, Wild About Fruit® ©	37	is much more satiating

⁚ average ★ little or no carbs ▼ high in saturated fat

FOOD   GI VALUE

F

Apple, Granny Smith, pure, Ducat's	44	
Apple, no added sugar	40÷	
Apple and Blackcurrant, pure, Berri	45	
Apple and Cherry, pure, Wild About Fruit® ©	43	
Apple and Mandarin, pure, Wild About Fruit®	53	
Apple and Mango, pure, Wild About Fruit® ©	47	Enjoy in small amounts—eating fresh fruit
Carrot, freshly made	43	is much more satiating
Cranberry Juice Cocktail, Ocean Spray	52	
Grapefruit, unsweetened	48	
Orange, unsweetened, fresh	50÷	
Orange, unsweetened, from concentrate, Quelch	53	
Pineapple, unsweetened	46	
Tomato, no added sugar, Berri	38	
Fruit Loaf, Bürgen® ©	44	A good choice
Fruit loaf, continental	47	Enjoy in moderation
Fruitful Lite, breakfast cereal, Hubbard's	61	A fair choice
Fruity-Bix bars, Fruit and Nut, Sanitarium®	56	A reasonable snack
Fruity-Bix bars, Wild Berry, Sanitarium®	51	A reasonable snack
Frutia™, low fat frozen fruit dessert, Mango	42	A good choice in moderation

G

Garlic	★	An everyday food
Gatorade® sports drink	78	A dietary supplement for serious sportspeople
Gelati, sucrose-free, chocolate, Alba	37	Low GI, low fat dessert
Gelati, sucrose-free, vanilla, Alba	39	Low GI, low fat dessert
Ginger	★	An everyday food
Glucodin™ glucose tablets	100	A dietary supplement—use with care
Gluten-free breakfast cereals, Vita Pro®	52	A good choice with low fat milk and fruit
Gluten-free corn pasta, Orgran	78	Avoid overcooking, so GI doesn't rise further
Gluten-free Multigrain Bread, Country LIfe	79	Has more fibre than white gluten-free bread
Gluten-free Muesli, Freedom Foods, with 1.5% fat milk	39	A great gluten-free breakfast choice
Gluten-free rice and maize pasta, Ris'O'Mais, Orgran	76	Look for protein-enriched varieties
Gluten-free split pea and soy pasta shells, Orgran	29	An excellent choice
Gluten-free spaghetti, canned in tomato sauce, Orgran	68	A fair choice
Glutinous rice, white, cooked in rice cooker	98	Go slow
Gnocchi, cooked, Latina®	68	A fair choice
Golden Fruit biscuits, Griffin's New Zealand	77▼	Now and then
Golden syrup	63	An occasional treat
Golden Wheats™, breakfast cereal	71	Now and then
Gradual Release breakfast cereal with reduced fat milk	68	Take it easy

÷ average   ★ little or no carbs   ▼ high in saturated fat

FOOD	GI VALUE	

G

Granny Smith apple juice, unsweetened, Ducat's	44	Enjoy in moderation—about one glass a day
Grape jelly, Chateau Barrosa ©	52	
Grape nectar, Chateau Barrosa ©	52	Low GI sweeteners—use in moderation
Grape syrup, Chateau Barrosa ©	52	
Grapefruit, fresh	25	An everyday food
Grapefruit juice, unsweetened	48	Drink in moderation
Grapes, fresh	53÷	An everyday food
Green beans	★	Any time you like
Green pea soup, canned	66	A fair choice
Guardian®, breakfast cereal	37	An excellent choice
Gummi confectionery, based on glucose syrup	94÷	Go slow—an occasional treat

H

Ham, leg or shoulder	★▼	Use lean cuts and eat in moderation
Hamburger bun, white	61	Take it easy
Haricot beans, cooked, canned	38÷	A star performer
Haricot beans, dried, boiled	33÷	A star performer
HEALTH PLUS DAIRY SNACKS, PAUL'S®		
Lemon Cream	32	
Raspberry Cream	32	A great low fat yoghurt alternative
Vanilla Cream	35	
Healthwise™ for Bowel Health, breakfast cereal	66	A fair choice
Heinz® Baked Beans in tomato sauce, canned	51	A good choice
Helga's™ Classic Seed Loaf	68	Take it easy
Helga's™ Traditional Wholemeal Bread	70	Go slow
Herbs, fresh or dried	★	An everyday food
Hi-Bran Weet-Bix®, regular, Sanitarium®	61	A lower GI version of Weet-Bix®
Hi-Bran Weet-Bix® with Soy and Linseed, Sanitarium®	57	A good choice
Highland Oatcakes, Walker's	57▼	Now and then
Highland Oatmeal biscuits, Weston's	55▼	Okay occasionally
High-Pro™ energy drink powder in reduced fat milk, Harrod Foods	36	A dietary supplement
HONEY		
Capilano, blended	64÷	
Ironbark	48	
Red Gum	53÷	Best used in moderation—the lower GI
Salvation Jane	64	types are pure floral honeys, look for them at
Stringybark	44	health food shops, markets and orchards
Yapunya	52	
Yellowbox	35	

÷ average   ★ little or no carbs   ▼ high in saturated fat

FOOD	GI VALUE	
Honey Rice Bubbles®, breakfast cereal, Kellogg's	77	Take it easy
Honey Smacks®, breakfast cereal, Kellogg's	71	Now and then
Hommous, regular	6	A great alternative to butter
Hyfibe® white sandwich bread, Tip Top®	70	Take it easy

ICE-CREAM

Bulla Light low fat ice-cream, chocolate ◎	27	
Bulla Light low fat ice-cream, English toffee ◎	27	
Bulla Light low fat ice-cream, mango ◎	30	
Bulla Light low fat ice-cream, vanilla ◎	36	Enjoy in moderation
Nestlé® Peter's® Carb Smart, vanilla	7	
Nestlé® Peter's® Carb Smart, vanilla and chocolate	32	
Nestlé® Peter's® Light and Creamy, low fat, chocolate ◎	49	
Nestlé® Peter's® Light and Creamy, low fat, raspberry ripple	55	
Nestlé® Peter's® Light and Creamy, low fat, vanilla ◎	46	
Norco Light Prestige, low fat, Golden Macadamia	37	Indulgence food—energy dense, so limit your serve size
Norco Light Prestige, low fat, Rich Vanilla	47	
Norco Light Prestige, low fat, Traditional Toffee	37	
Regular, full fat, average of several types	47÷▼	
Sara Lee®, full fat, French Vanilla	38▼	
Sara Lee®, full fat, Ultra Chocolate	37▼	
Instant mashed potato	69÷	Take it easy
Instant rice, white, cooked 6 mins	87	Go slow
Ironman PR® bar, chocolate	39	A dietary supplement for sportspeople
Isostar® sports drink	70	A special event product—not for general use
Jam, apricot fruit spread, reduced sugar	55	Enjoy in moderation
Jam, strawberry, regular	56÷	Enjoy in moderation
Jasmine rice, white, long-grain, cooked in rice cooker	109	Keep as an occasional treat
Jatz®, plain salted cracker biscuits	55▼	For special times only—high in saturated fat
Jelly, diet, made from crystals with water	★	A low kilojoule alternative to regular jelly
Jelly beans	78÷	Go slow
Jevity®, fibre-enriched drink	48	A medical nutrition product
Just Right®, breakfast cereal, Kellogg's®	60	A fair choice
Just Right® Just Grains, breakfast cereal, Kellogg's®	62	A fair choice

÷ average   ★ little or no carbs   ▼ high in saturated fat

FOOD   GI VALUE

(K)

Kaiser bread rolls, white	73	Go slow
Kavli™ Norwegian crispbread, Player's Biscuits	71	Eat in moderation
Kidney beans, red, canned, drained, Edgell	36✢	A convenient everyday food
Kidney beans, red, dried, boiled	28✢	A super food
Kidz™, Heinz®, Fruit Fingers, banana	61	Okay occasionally
Kiwi fruit, fresh	58	A good choice
Komplete®, breakfast cereal, Kellogg's®	48	Enjoy in moderation
K-Time® Just Right™ breakfast cereal bar	72	An occasional treat

(L)

Lamb	★	Keep it lean
Lamingtons, Farmland	87▼	Indulgence food
Lean Cuisine®, French-style Chicken with Rice	36	A low GI convenience meal
LEAN NUTRITION PRODUCTS		
LEAN Fibergy™ bar, Harvest Oat	45	
LEAN Life long Nutribar™, Chocolate Crunch	32	Low GI meal replacement products and snacks
LEAN Life long Nutribar™, Peanut Crunch	30	
LEAN Nutrimeal™, drink powder, Dutch Chocolate	26	
Lebanese bread, white	75	Take it easy
Leeks	★	An everyday food
Lentil soup, canned	44	A good choice
LENTILS		
Green, canned	48✢	
Green, dried, boiled	30✢	One of nature's super foods
Lentils, red, dried, boiled	26✢	
Lettuce	★	An everyday food
Licorice, soft, Farmland	78	Go slow
Life Savers®, peppermint	70	An occasional treat
LIGHT PRESTIGE ICE-CREAMS, NORCO		
Golden Macadamia	37	
Rich Vanilla	47	Enjoy in moderation
Traditional Toffee	37	
Light rye bread	68	A fair choice
Light soy milk, reduced fat, So Natural	44	A good choice
Lima beans, baby, frozen, reheated in microwave	32	An everyday food
Linguine pasta, thick, durum wheat, boiled	46✢	Serve with low fat sauces
Linguine pasta, thin, durum wheat, boiled	52✢	Don't overcook—the GI will rise
Linseed and Soy Loaf, bread, Bakers Delight	55	Good for everyday eating
Lite White, reduced fat milk, Dairy Farmers	30	A good choice
Liverwurst	★▼	High in saturated fat—use in small amounts
Lucozade®, original, sparkling glucose drink	95	A nutrition supplement—use with care

✢ average   ★ little or no carbs   ▼ high in saturated fat

FOOD GI VALUE

L

| Lungkow bean thread noodles, dried, boiled | 33÷ | A low GI noodle |
| Lychees, canned, in syrup, drained | 79 | Avoid the syrup, it's energy dense |

M

M&M's®, peanut	33▼	Go slow
Macaroni, white, plain, boiled	47÷	Serve with low fat sauces
Macaroni and cheese, made from packet mix, Kraft	64▼	Now and then
Maggi 2 Minute noodles, regular	54▼	Take it easy
Maggi 2 Minute noodles, 99% fat free	67	An occasional choice
Maltmeal Wafer Biscuits, Griffin's New Zealand	50▼	An occasional treat
Malted Milk Powder, Nestlé, in whole milk	45▼	Once in a while
Mango, fresh	51÷	Enjoy on a regular basis when in season
Mango Frutia™, low fat frozen fruit dessert, Weis	42	A good choice in moderation
Mango smoothie	32	Make with low fat dairy
Maple flavoured syrup, Cottee's®	68	Take it easy
Maple syrup, pure, Canadian	54	Use in moderation
Marmalade, orange	55÷	Enjoy in moderation
Mars Bar®, regular	62▼	Indulgence food—go slow
Marshmallows, plain, pink and white	62	Occasional treat
McDonald's Vege Burger	59	Now and then
Melba toast, plain	70	Occasional use
Milk, condensed, sweetened	61▼	Go slow

MILK, DAIRY FARMERS™

Farmer's Best Milk with omega 3	27	
Lite White, reduced fat (1.4%) milk ©	30	
Shape, calcium-enriched, low fat (0.1%) milk	34	All low GI—choose low fat varieties
Skim, low fat (0.1%) milk ©	32	
Take Care, calcium-enriched, reduced fat (1%) milk ©	23	
Whole milk (3.6 % fat)	27▼	
Milk, full fat cow's milk, fresh	31▼	Choose low fat milk for weight control
Milk, low fat, chocolate, with aspartame	24	A better choice
Milk, low fat, chocolate, with sugar, Lite White®	34	Enjoy in moderation
Milk, skim	32÷	A good choice
Milk Arrowroot biscuits	69▼	Take it easy

MILK CHOCOLATE

Cadbury's® Milk Chocolate, plain	49▼	
Dove®, milk chocolate	45▼	
Plain milk chocolate, regular	41÷▼	Indulgence food
Plain milk chocolate, reduced sugar	35÷▼	
Plain, with fructose instead of regular sugar	20▼	

÷ average ★ little or no carbs ▼ high in saturated fat

FOOD	GI VALUE	
M		
Nestlé® plain milk chocolate	42▼	Indulgence food
Milky Bar®, plain white chocolate, Nestlé®	44▼	An occasional indulgence
Millet, boiled	71	Now and then
MILO® DRINKS, NESTLÉ®		
Malt Milo® powder in full fat milk	37▼	
Malt Milo® powder in reduced fat milk	40	
Malt Milo® powder in skim milk	46	
Milo®, ready to drink, in 600 ml plastic bottle	30▼	Enjoy in moderation with low fat milk
Milo®, ready to drink, in 250 ml Tetra Pak	35▼	
Milo® powder in full fat milk	33▼	
Milo® powder in reduced fat milk ©	36÷	
Milo® powder in skim milk	39	
Milo® Bar, Nestlé®	40▼	An occasional treat
Minestrone soup, Campbell's® Country Ladle Traditional	39	A healthy convenience food
Mini Wheats®, blackcurrant breakfast cereal, Kellogg's®	72	Go slow
Mini Wheats®, whole-wheat breakfast cereal, Kellogg's®	58	A fair choice
Morning Coffee biscuits	79▼	Go slow
Mother Earth apricot-filled fruit bar with wholemeal pastry	50▼	Okay for an occasional snack
MUESLI		
Gluten-free Muesli, Freedom Foods, with 1.5% fat milk	39	
Naytura Premium, Untoasted, with Nuts	65	GI and fat content varies—choose lower saturated fat varieties
Purina Toasted Muesli	43	
Swiss Formula Muesli, Uncle Tobys	56	
Vogel's® Oven-crisp Muesli	52	
Muesli bar, crunchy with dried fruit	61	An occasional treat
Muesli bar, chewy with choc chips or fruit	54÷▼	Now and then
MUFFINS		
Apple muffin, home-made	46÷▼	
Blueberry, commercially made	59▼	
Bran, commercially made	60▼	Enjoy occasionally—choose lower fat types
Carrot, commercially made	62▼	
Oatmeal, made from packet mix	69▼	
Multigrain sandwich bread, Tip Top®	65	Take it easy
Multigrain 9 Grain bread, Tip Top® ©	43	A good choice
Mung beans	39	A five-star food
Mung bean noodles (Lungkow bean thread), dried, boiled	33÷	A good choice
Mushrooms	★	An everyday food
N		
Naytura Premium Muesli, untoasted, with nuts	65	A fair choice

÷ average   ★ little or no carbs   ▼ high in saturated fat

FOOD   GI VALUE

N

Nectar, grape, Chateau Barrosa ©	52	An alternative to honey—use in moderation
Nesquik® powder, Chocolate, in 1.5% fat milk	41	Okay now and then
Nesquik® powder, Strawberry, in 1.5% fat milk	35	Okay now and then
Nestlé® Aero Chocolate Mousse	37	Great for a snack or dessert
Nestlé® Citrus Flavour Mousse, dessert mix	47	Enjoy in moderation
Nestlé® Diet Chocolate Mousse ©	37	A good choice
Nestlé® Diet Crème Caramel	33	A good choice
Nestlé® Diet Lemon Cheesecake	31	A good choice
Nestlé® Diet Peach and Mango Yoghurt	21	A superb choice
Nestlé® Diet Strawberry Yoghurt	19	A superb choice
New potato, unpeeled and boiled 20 mins	78	Take it easy
New potato, canned, microwaved 3 mins,		
Edgell Mint Tiny Taters	65	A lower GI potato

NOODLES

Dried rice, boiled	61	
Fresh rice, boiled	40	
Instant 2 Minute Maggi, regular	51÷	
Mung bean (Lungkow bean thread), dried, boiled	33÷	Try lower GI, lower fat types for everyday
Maggi 2 Minute noodles, regular	54	eating
Maggi 2 Minute noodles, 99% fat free	67	
Soba noodles, instant, served in soup	46	
Udon, plain, Fantastic	62	

NORCO LIGHT PRESTIGE ICE-CREAMS

Golden Macadamia	37	
Rich Vanilla	47	Enjoy in moderation
Traditional Toffee	37	
Nutella®, chocolate hazelnut spread ©	33	Enjoy in moderation
Nutri-Grain®, breakfast cereal	66	Take it easy

O

Oat 'n' Honey Bake, breakfast cereal, Kellogg's®	77	Now and then
Oat bran, unprocessed	55÷	A useful source of fibre—add to porridge or cereal
Oat Bran and Honey bread, Bürgen® ©	49	An everyday food
Oats, raw, rolled, Lowan®	59	A fair choice
Okra	★	An everyday food
Onions	★	An everyday food
Orange, fresh	42÷	Great anytime
Orange cordial, reconstituted, Berri	66	Drink occasionally
Orange juice, unsweetened	50÷	Drink in moderation

÷ average   ★ little or no carbs   ▼ high in saturated fat

FOOD	GI VALUE	
Organic stoneground sourdough wholemeal bread, Bill's Bakery	59	A fair choice
ORGRAN GLUTEN-FREE PRODUCTS		
Buckwheat pancake mix, ready to eat	102	
Corn pasta, boiled	78	
Rice and maize pasta, Ris'O'Mais	76	Gluten-free alternatives for common carb-rich foods
Spaghetti, rice and split pea, canned in tomato sauce	68	
Split pea and soya pasta shells, boiled	29	
Original Soy Milk, full fat, So Natural	44	A good choice
Oven-crisp Muesli, Vogel's®	52	A good choice
Oysters, natural, plain	★	Go for it!
Pancakes, prepared from shaker mix, Green's	67▼	Enjoy as a special treat
Pancakes, buckwheat, gluten-free, made from packet mix, Orgran	102	Take it easy
Parsnips	97	Modest serves are no problem
Party pies, beef, cooked, Farmland	45▼	Go slow
PASTA		
Capellini, white, boiled	45	
Cheese tortellini, cooked	50	
Corn pasta, gluten-free, boiled, Orgran	78	
Fettuccine, egg, boiled	40÷	
Linguine, thick, durum wheat, boiled	46÷	
Linguine, thin, durum wheat, boiled	52÷	
Macaroni, white, durum wheat, boiled	47÷	
Macaroni and cheese, from packet mix, Kraft	64	
Proti pasta, protein-enriched, boiled	28	
Ravioli, meat-filled, boiled	39	
Rice and maize pasta, Ris'O'Mais, gluten-free, Orgran	76	Choose lower GI types for everday eating
Rice pasta, brown, boiled, Ricegrowers	92	
Rice vermicelli, dried, boiled, Chinese	58	
Spaghetti, gluten-free, canned in tomato sauce, Orgran	68	
Spaghetti, protein-enriched, boiled	27	
Spaghetti, white, durum wheat, boiled 10–15 mins	44÷	
Spaghetti, wholemeal, boiled	42	
Spirali, white, durum wheat, boiled, Vetta	43	
Split pea and soya pasta shells, gluten-free, Orgran, boiled	29	
Star Pastina, white, boiled 5 mins	38	

÷ average   ★ little or no carbs   ▼ high in saturated fat

FOOD   GI VALUE

Food	GI Value	Comment
Vermicelli, white, durum wheat, boiled, Vetta	35	
PAUL'S® HEALTH PLUS DAIRY SNACKS		
Paul's® Health Plus Lemon Cream dairy snack	32	Low saturated fat, calcium-rich foods— a top choice
Paul's® Health Plus Raspberry Cream dairy snack	32	
Paul's® Health Plus Vanilla Cream dairy snack	35	
Paw paw, fresh	56	A good choice
Peach, canned, in heavy syrup, Letona	58	Okay; try those in natural juice
Peach, canned, in light syrup	57÷	Okay; try those in natural juice
Peach, canned, in natural juice	45	Enjoy when fresh aren't available
Peach, fresh	42÷	Great anytime
Peach and Mango Diet Yoghurt, Nestlé®	21	A superb snack or dessert
Peanuts, roasted, salted	14÷	A great snack, in moderation
Pear, fresh	38÷	Great anytime
Pear halves, canned, in natural juice	44÷	A good choice
Pear halves, canned, in reduced-sugar syrup, SPC Lite	25	Good with cereal or low fat yoghurt
Peas, dried, boiled	22	A nutritious food—add to stews and soups
Peas, green, frozen, boiled	48÷	An everyday food
Pecan nuts, raw	10	A great snack or recipe ingredient
Pelde rice, brown, boiled	76	Now and then
PerforMAX multigrain bread ©	38	An excellent choice
Pies, party, beef, Farmland	45▼	Go slow
Pikelets, Golden	85	An occasional treat
Pineapple, fresh	59÷	A good choice
Pineapple juice, unsweetened	46	Enjoy in moderation—one glass a day
Pinto beans, canned, in brine	45	A nutritious convenience food
Pinto beans, dried, boiled	39	A star performer
Pita bread, white	57	A fair choice—try wholemeal
PIZZA		
Super Supreme, pan, Pizza Hut	36▼	Go slow—occasional indulgence
Super Supreme, thin and crispy, Pizza Hut	30▼	
Vegetarian Supreme, thin and crispy, Pizza Hut	49▼	
Plum, raw	39÷	An everyday food
Polenta, boiled	68	Enjoy occasionally
Pontiac potato, peeled, boiled whole 30–35 mins	72÷	Take it easy
Pontiac potato, peeled, cubed, boiled 15 mins, mashed	91	Take it easy
Pontiac potato, peeled, microwaved 7 mins	79	Take it easy
Popcorn, plain, cooked in microwave	72÷	Skip the butter and make it a high fibre snack
Pop-Tarts™, Double Chocolate	70	Indulgence food
Pork	★▼	Eat it lean

÷ average   ★ little or no carbs   ▼ high in saturated fat

FOOD	GI VALUE	

P

Porridge, instant, made with water, Uncle Tobys	82	Go slow—use traditional oats instead
Porridge, made from steel-cut oats with water	52	Look for these at a health food shop
Porridge, multigrain, made with water, Monster Muesli	55	A good choice—serve with lower fat milk
Potato chips, plain, salted	54÷▼	Indulgence food

POTATOES

Desiree, peeled, boiled 35 mins	101	
Instant mashed potato, Edgell	86	
Nardine, peeled, boiled	70	
New, canned, microwaved 3 mins	65	
New, unpeeled, boiled 20 mins	78	All potatoes tend to be high GI—sweet potato
Pontiac, peeled, boiled 15 mins, mashed	91	can be substituted
Pontiac, peeled, boiled whole 30–35 mins	72÷	
Pontiac, peeled, microwaved 7 mins	79	
Sebago, peeled, boiled 35 mins	87	
Sweet potato, baked	46÷	

Pound cake®, plain	54▼	Indulgence food
Power Bar®, chocolate	56÷	A nutrition supplement for serious sportspeople
Pretzels, oven-baked, traditional wheat flavour	83	Take it easy; energy dense
Proti pasta, protein-enriched, boiled	28	An excellent choice with low fat sauce
Prunes, pitted, Sunsweet	29	A handful makes a great snack
Pudding, chocolate, instant, made from packet with whole milk	47÷▼	Okay occasionally—use low fat milk
Pudding, vanilla, instant, made from packet mix and whole milk	40▼	Okay occasionally—use low fat milk
Pudding, Sustagen®, instant vanilla, made from powdered mix	27	A dietary supplement
Puffed buckwheat cereal	65	Puffing grains increases their GI
Puffed crispbread, white	81	Go slow
Puffed rice cakes, white	82	An occasional snack
Puffed Wheat, breakfast cereal, Sanitarium®	80	Take it easy
Pumpernickel bread	50÷	An excellent choice
Pumpkin	75	Eat freely; low in carbs
Pure Canadian maple syrup	54	Use in moderation

Q

| Quinoa, organic, boiled | 53 | An excellent grain food |

R

Radishes	★	An everyday food
Raisins	64	Enjoy in moderation
Ravioli, durum wheat flour, meat-filled, boiled	39▼	A good choice with a tomato-based sauce

÷ average   ★ little or no carbs   ▼ high in saturated fat

FOOD GI VALUE

R

Food	GI Value	Note
Real Fruit bar, strawberry, Uncle Tobys	90	An occasional treat
RICE		
Arborio risotto rice, white, boiled, SunRice®	69	
Basmati rice, white, boiled, Mahatma	58	
Broken rice, Thai, white, cooked in rice cooker	86	
Brown Pelde rice, boiled	76	
Calrose rice, brown, medium-grain, boiled	87	
Calrose rice, white, medium-grain, boiled	83	
Doongara rice, brown, Ricegrowers	66	
Doongara rice, white, boiled, Ricegrowers	56	Choose lower GI varieties for everyday eating
Glutinous rice, white, cooked in rice cooker	98	
Instant rice, white, cooked 6 mins with water	87	
Jasmine rice, white, long-grain, cooked in rice cooker	109	
Long-grain rice, white, boiled 15 mins, Mahatma	50	
Pelde parboiled rice, Sungold	87	
Sunbrown Quick® rice, Ricegrowers	80	
Wild rice, boiled	57	
Rice Bran, extruded, Ricegrowers	19	A good source of fibre to add to cereal
Rice Bubbles®, breakfast cereal	87	Go slow
Rice Bubble Treat™ bar, Kellogg's®	63	An occasional treat
Rice cakes, puffed, white	82	Go slow
Rice drink, natural, low fat, Australia's Own	92	Go slow
Rice Krispies®, breakfast cereal, Kellogg's®	82	Now and then
Rice noodles, dried, boiled	61	Take it easy
Rice noodles, freshly made, boiled	40	A smart choice
Rice pasta, brown, gluten-free, boiled	92	Go slow
Rice vermicelli, dried, boiled	58	A fair choice
Rich Tea® biscuits	55▼	Limit your intake
Ricies™, breakfast cereal, Sanitarium®	95	Go slow
Ris'O'Mais pasta, gluten-free, Orgran	76	Take it easy
Risotto rice, Arborio, boiled, Sun Rice®	69	Enjoy in moderation
Rocket	★	Any time you like—great in salads and sandwiches
Rockmelon, fresh	67✧	Eat in moderation
Roll (bread), Kaiser, white	73	Go slow
Roll-Ups®, processed fruit snack	99	An occasional treat—fresh fruit is best
Romano beans	46	An everyday food
RUSH™, LOW FAT FLAVOURED MILK, PAUL'S®		
Rush™ Absolute Caramel	42	Enjoy in moderation
Rush™ Heavenly Vanilla Malt	42	

✧ average ★ little or no carbs ▼ high in saturated fat

FOOD	GI VALUE	

R

Rush™ Ultimate Chocolate	38	⎫
Rush™ Wicked Latte	38	⎬ Enjoy in moderation
Rush™ Wild Strawberry	38	⎭
Rye	34	An excellent choice
Rye bread, Bürgen® Ⓖ	51	An everyday food
Rye bread, wholemeal	58	A fair choice
Ryvita® crispbread	69	Take it easy
Ryvita ® Currant Breaks crispbread	66	Enjoy occasionally

S

Salami	★▼	Go slow—high in fat
Salmon	★	A fantastic food
Santal Active Energising Exotic Fruit drink, Paul's®	52	Enjoy in moderation
Santal Active Revitalising Red Fruit drink, Paul's®	55	Enjoy in moderation
Sao™, plain crackers	70▼	Go slow
Sardines	★	A good choice, fresh or canned in brine or water
Sausages, fried	28▼	Go slow—choose lean varieties
Scallops, natural, plain	★	Eat in moderation, avoid saturated fat in cooking
Scones, plain, made from packet mix	92	Special occasion food
Sebago potato, peeled, boiled 35 mins	87	Avoid overcooking or mashing
Semolina, cooked	55✛	Good alternative to instant oatmeal porridge
Sesame seeds	★	Nutritious but high in fat—use in moderation
Shallots	★	An everyday food
Shape, calcium-enriched, low fat (0.1%) milk, Dairy Farmers™	34	An excellent choice
Shellfish (prawns, crab, lobster, etc.)	★	Fantastic food
Shortbread biscuits, Arnott's™	64▼	Indulgence food—high in saturated fat
Shredded Wheat breakfast cereal	75✛	Go slow
Shredded Wheatmeal biscuits, Arnott's™	62▼	Take it easy
Silverbeet	★	An everyday food
Ski™ no fat yoghurts, all flavours, with sugar	40✛	A good choice
Skim, low fat (0.1%), milk, Dairy Farmers™ Ⓖ	32✛	An everyday food
Skippy cornflakes™, Sanitarium®	93	Go slow
Skittles®	70▼	A special treat
Slim-Fast® Drink, can, vanilla or chocolate	39✛	A meal replacement drink
Slim-Fast® Drink powder, all flavours, made with skim milk	35✛	A meal replacement drink

SNACK RIGHT FRUIT BARS, ARNOTT'S™

Apple and Blackberry	43	⎫
Apricot and Raisin	46	⎬ Enjoy in moderation
Wild Berry	55	⎭

✛ average   ★ little or no carbs   ▼ high in saturated fat

FOOD GI VALUE

S

SNACK RIGHT FRUIT BITES, ARNOTT'S™

Apple and Sultana	45	} Enjoy in moderation
Wild Berry	52	

SNACK RIGHT FRUIT ROLL BISCUITS, ARNOTT'S™

Apple and Blackberry	43	} Enjoy in moderation
Spicy Apple and Sultana	45	

SNACK RIGHT FRUIT SLICE BISCUITS, ARNOTT'S™

Mango and Passionfruit	49	
Mixed Berry	50	
Spicy Apple and Sultana	45	} Enjoy in moderation
Sultana	48	
Sultana with a Touch of Chocolate	45	

Snake beans	★	An everyday food
Snickers Bar®, regular	41▼	Indulgence food
Snowpea sprouts	★	An everyday food

SO NATURAL SOY PRODUCTS

Calciforte soy milk, full fat (3%), calcium-enriched	36	
Light soy milk, reduced fat (1.5%), calcium-fortified	44	
Original soy milk, full fat (3%)	44	} Use in moderation
Smoothie Drink, Banana, low fat	30	
Smoothie Drink, Chocolate Hazelnut, low fat	34	
Soy yoghurt, Peach and Mango, 2% fat	50	

Soba noodles, instant, served in soup	46	A good choice

SOFT DRINKS

Coca-Cola®	53	
Diet varieties	★	} Save for special occasions
Fanta®, orange soft drink	68	
Solo®, lemon squash soft drink	58	

SOUP

Black bean, canned	64	
Clear consommé, chicken or vegetable	★	
Green pea, canned	66	
Lentil, canned	44	} Choose lower GI, low fat varieties
Split pea, canned	60	
Tomato, canned	45÷	
Traditional Minestrone, Campbell's® Country Ladle	39	

Sourdough bread, stoneground, wholemeal, Bill's Bakery	59	A fair choice
Sourdough rye bread	48	An everyday food
Sourdough wheat bread	54	A good choice

÷ average   ★ little or no carbs   ▼ high in saturated fat

FOOD	GI VALUE	

S SOY MILK

So Natural Calci Forte, calcium-enriched, full fat	36	⎫
So Natural Light, calcium-fortified, reduced fat	44	⎬ Choose lower fat types to limit your fat intake
So Natural Original, full fat (3%)	44	⎭
Soy Smoothie Drink, Banana, So Natural	30	Enjoy in moderation
Soy Smoothie Drink, Chocolate Hazelnut, So Natural	34	Now and then
Soy yoghurt, Peach and Mango, So Natural	50	Eat in moderation
Soybeans, canned	14	An excellent choice
Soybeans, dried, boiled	18÷	A five-star food
Soy-Lin, soy and linseed bread, Bürgen® ©	36	An everyday food
Soytana®, breakfast cereal, Vogel's®	58	A good choice
Spaghetti, gluten-free, canned in tomato sauce, Orgran	68	Lower GI than other gluten-free pastas
Spaghetti, white, durum wheat, boiled 10–15 mins	44÷	Serve with non-creamy sauces
Spaghetti, wholemeal, boiled	42	An everyday food
Special K®, regular, breakfast cereal, Kellogg's®	56÷	A fair choice
Spelt multigrain bread, Pav's Allergy Bakery	54	An everyday food
Spinach	★	An everyday food
Spirali pasta, white, durum wheat, boiled, Vetta	43	An everyday food
Split pea and soy pasta shells, gluten-free, Orgran	29	An excellent product
Split pea soup	60	A fair choice
Split peas, yellow, boiled 20 mins	32	Excellent—nutritious and versatile
Sponge cake, plain	46	An occasional treat
Spring onions	★	An everyday food
Squash, yellow	★	An everyday food
Squid or calamari, not battered or crumbed	★	Enjoy prepared in low fat ways
Steak, any cut	★▼	Buy lean steak; grill or barbecue
Stoned Wheat Thins, crackers	67	For special occasions
Strawberry jam, regular	54÷	Enjoy in moderation
Strawberries, fresh	40	Any time you like
Stuffing, bread	74	Go slow
Sugar	68÷	Sugar can be a source of excess calories— go slow
Sultana Bran, breakfast cereal, Kellogg's®	73	Take it easy
Sultanas	56	Enjoy in moderation
Sunblest white bread, Tip Top®	71	Use lower GI bread for everyday eating
Sunbrown Quick® rice, boiled	80	Add some barley to lower the GI
Sunflower and Barley bread, Riga®	57	A fair choice
Sunripe School Straps, dried fruit snack ©	40	Lower GI than other dried fruit snacks
Sunsweet pitted prunes	29	Great for snacks or with breakfast cereal

÷ average   ★ little or no carbs   ▼ high in saturated fat

FOOD   GI VALUE

S

Super Supreme pizza, pan, Pizza Hut	36▼	Low GI but high saturated fat content—go slow
Super Supreme pizza, thin and crispy, Pizza Hut	30▼	Indulgence food
Sushi, salmon	48	A good choice
Sustagen® drink, Dutch Chocolate	31	Nutrition supplement
Sustagen® pudding, instant vanilla, made from powdered mix	27	A dietary supplement
Sustagen Sport®, milk-based drink	43	Nutrition supplement
Sustain®, breakfast cereal	68	A fair choice
Sustain® Breakfast Cereal Bar	57	An occasional treat
Swede, cooked	72	Now and then
Sweet corn, whole kernel, canned, drained	46	An everyday food
Sweet corn, on the cob, boiled	48	An everyday food
Sweet potato, baked	46⬧	A low GI substitute for regular potato
Sweetened condensed whole milk	61▼	Go slow
Sweetened dried cranberries	64	Eat in moderation
Syrup, golden	63	Enjoy in sensible amounts—occasionally
Syrup, Maple, pure Canadian	54	Use in moderation
Syrup, Maple flavoured, Cottee's®	68	Take it easy

T

Taco shells, cornmeal-based, baked	68	Serve with filling made from lean mince
Tahini, pure	★	High in fat—use in small amounts
Take Care, calcium-enriched, reduced fat milk	23	An excellent choice
Tapioca, boiled, with milk	81	Go slow
Taro	54	A low GI substitute for potato
Tea, black or green, no milk or sugar	★	Any time you like
Tiger Loaf, white bread, Bakers Delight	71	Now and then
Tofu (bean curd), plain, unsweetened	★	Use low fat cooking methods
Tomato juice, no added sugar, Berri	38	Drink in moderation
Tomato soup, canned	45⬧	A good choice—serve with low GI bread
Tooheys® New Draught Beer (4.6% alcohol)	66	Take it easy—drink in moderation
Tortellini, cheese, boiled	50▼	In moderation
Trim custard, vanilla, reduced fat, Paul's®	37	Good with fruit as a dessert
Trout, fresh or frozen	★	Fantastic food
Tuna, fresh or canned in water or brine	★	Fantastic food
Turkey	★▼	Serve it lean without the skin
Twisties®, cheese-flavoured snack	74▼	Indulgence food
Twix® bar	44▼	Indulgence food
2 Minute noodles, 99% fat free, Maggi	67	An occasional choice
2 Minute noodles, regular, Maggi	51⬧▼	Take it easy

⬧ average   ★ little or no carbs   ▼ high in saturated fat

FOOD	GI VALUE	
U		
Udon noodles, plain, Fantastic	62	Now and then
Ultra Bran Soy and Linseed, breakfast cereal, Vogel's®	41	An excellent choice
Ultra Chocolate ice-cream, premium, Sara Lee®	37▼	Indulgence food
Up & Go, drink, cocoa malt, Sanitarium®	43	A liquid meal product
Up & Go, drink, original malt, Sanitarium®	46	Good for a light meal or snack
V		
VAALIA® LOW FAT YOGHURT		
Apricot, Mango and Peach	26	
French Vanilla	26	
Lemon Creme	43	
Luscious Berries	28	Good for a snack or dessert
Passionfruit	32	
Tempting Strawberry	28	
VAALIA® NO FAT YOGHURT		
French Vanilla	40	
Mango	39	
Tempting Strawberry	38	Makes a good snack or dessert
Wild Berries	38	
Vanilla cake made from packet mix with vanilla frosting, Betty Crocker	42▼	Indulgence food
Vanilla custard, Trim, reduced fat, Paul's®	37	Good with fruit as a dessert
Vanilla pudding, instant, made from packet mix and whole milk	40▼	Now and then
Vanilla wafer biscuits	77▼	Special treat
Veal	★	A nutritious food—eat it lean
Vege Burger, McDonald's	59	Go slow
Vegetarian Supreme Pizza, thin and crispy, Pizza Hut	49▼	Indulgence food
Vermicelli, white, durum wheat, boiled, Vetta	35	An everyday food
Vinegar	★	Everyday food—great as a salad dressing
Vita-Brits®, breakfast cereal, Uncle Tobys	68	Eat in moderation
Vita-Pro®, gluten-free breakfast cereal, Vogel's®	52	A good choice
Vitari, Wild Berry, non-dairy, frozen fruit dessert	59	Okay in moderation
Vitasoy® calcium-enriched rice milk	79	Take care
VOGEL'S® BREAKFAST CEREALS		
Oven-crisp Muesli	52	
Soytana®	58	A good choice with low fat milk and fruit
Ultra Bran Soy and Linseed cereal	41	
Vita-Pro® gluten-free breakfast cereal	52	

❖ average ★ little or no carbs ▼ high in saturated fat

FOOD   GI VALUE

W

Food	GI Value	
Wafer biscuits, vanilla, plain	77▼	Now and then
Waffles, plain	76▼	An occasional treat
Water crackers, plain	78	Special occasion food
Watercress	★	An everyday food
Watermelon, raw	76÷	No problem in moderation; low in carbs
Weis Mango Frutia™, low fat frozen fruit dessert	42	A good choice in moderation
Wheat, cracked, bulgur, ready to eat	48÷	Excellent in salads such as tabbouli

WHEAT BISCUITS BREAKFAST CEREAL

Goldies, Sultana, Kellogg's®	65	
Goldies, Whole Wheat, Kellogg's®	70	
Good Start, muesli wheat biscuits, Sanitarium®	68	
Hi-Bran Weet-Bix® with Soy and Linseed, Sanitarium®	57	Choose lower GI types for everyday eating
Lite-Bix, Sanitarium®	70	
Oat Bran Weet-Bix®, Sanitarium®	57	
Weet-Bix®, plain, Sanitarium®	69÷	
Vita-Brits®, Uncle Tobys	68	
Wheat-bites™, breakfast cereal, Uncle Tobys	72	Go slow

WHITE BREAD

Hyfibe® sandwich bread, Tip Top®	70	
Kaiser rolls	73	
Lebanese bread, white, Seda Bakery	75	
Pita bread, white	57	
Regular, sliced white bread	71÷	Take it easy
Sunblest, Tip Top®	71	
Tiger Loaf, Bakers Delight	71	
Wonder White®, white bread, Buttercup	80	

WHOLEMEAL BREAD

Wholemeal Block Loaf, Bakers Delight	71	
Wholemeal bread, plain, sliced	71÷	Take it easy
Wholemeal Sandwich Bread, Tip Top®	65	
Whole-wheat kernels	41	An excellent choice

WILD ABOUT FRUIT® PURE APPLE JUICES

Apple and Cherry juice ◎	43	
Apple and Mandarin juice	53	
Apple and Mango juice ◎	47	Enjoy in moderation—about one glass a day
Clear Apple juice, filtered ◎	44	
Cloudy Apple juice ◎	37	
Wild rice, boiled	57	
Wonder White®, white bread, Buttercup	80	Go slow

÷ average   ★ little or no carbs   ▼ high in saturated fat

FOOD	GI VALUE	
Y		
Yam, peeled, boiled	37✢	A five-star food
Yakult™, fermented probiotic milk drink	46	} A dietary supplement
Yakult™ LIGHT, fermented probiotic milk drink	36	
YOGHURT		
Diet, low fat, no added sugar, vanilla or fruit	20✢	
Nestlé® All Natural Light Apricot ☺	49	
Nestlé® All Natural Light Banana ☺	38	
Nestlé® All Natural Light Forest Berry ☺	37	
Nestlé® All Natural Light Mango ☺	55	A great dessert or snack
Nestlé® All Natural Light Passionfruit ☺	47	
Nestlé® All Natural Light Strawberry ☺	37	
Nestlé® All Natural Light Tropical Fruit Salad ☺	38	
Nestlé® All Natural Light Vanilla ☺	37	
Jalna Bio Dynamic, Bush Honey	26	
Jalna Fat Free Natural	19	
Jalna Fat Free, Passionfruit	27	
Jalna Leben European-style	11	
Jalna Premium Blend, Creamy Vanilla	18	Low GI—choose lower fat varieties
Jalna Premium Blend, Greek-style	12	
Jalna Vitalise Multivitamin Cultured Milk Fruit Drink	24	
Jalna Wildberry Yoghurt on the Go	19	
Nestlé® diet, low fat, Peach and Mango	21	
Nestlé® diet, low fat, Strawberry	19	
Ski™, low fat, with sugar, Strawberry	33	
Ski d'Lite™, low fat, with sugar, Honey Buzz	47	
Ski d'Lite™, low fat, with sugar, Vanilla Crème	46	
Ski™, no fat, with sugar, all flavours	40✢	
Ski d'Lite™, low fat, with sugar, Wild Strawberry	31	
So Natural, soy yoghurt, Peach and Mango, with sugar	50	
Vaalia®, low fat with sugar, Apricot, Mango and Peach	26	Choose lower fat types for everyday eating
Vaalia®, low fat with sugar, French Vanilla	26	
Vaalia®, low fat with sugar, Lemon Creme	43	
Vaalia®, low fat with sugar, Luscious Berries	28	
Vaalia®, low fat with sugar, Passionfruit	32	
Vaalia®, low fat with sugar, Tempting Strawberry	28	
Vaalia®, no fat with sugar, French Vanilla	40	
Vaalia®, no fat with sugar, Mango	39	
Vaalia®, no fat with sugar, Tempting Strawberry	38	
Vaalia®, no fat with sugar, Wild Berries	38	
Z Zucchini	★	An everyday food

✢ average   ★ little or no carbs   ▼ high in saturated fat

Daily food, television and activity diary

Make three photocopies of this page and complete a three-day diary at frequent intervals (once a month to start with, then every three months in the first 12 months) to help you focus on your strengths and weaknesses.

Date _____

Meal	Time	Foods and drinks consumed *(indicate item and amount)*	Did you include (tick):			Situation How did you feel? (e.g. happy, sad, angry)
			Low GI carbs?	Protein?	Good fats?	

TV duration *(circle):*   0   30   60   90   120   150   180   or more ___ minutes

Exercise type *(tick):*   ☐ Aerobic   ☐ Resistance

Exercise duration *(circle):*   0   5   10   15   20   30   45   60   or more ___ minutes

Rate of perceived exertion *(circle):*   1   2   3   4   5   6   7   8   9   10

Low GI foods and weight:
a summary of the scientific evidence

Country	Subjects	Study design	Findings	Reference details
Australia	Overweight young adults	89 subjects followed 1 of 4 diets for 12 weeks: 1) standard low fat; 2) low GI; 3) higher protein; 4) low GI and protein	Compared with the standard low fat diet, all 3 modified diets produced around 50% more fat loss. Risk factors for heart disease improved more on the low GI diet	McMillan-Price et al, unpublished findings, 2004.
USA	Overweight young adults	39 subjects consumed a low GI or low fat diet to achieve a 10% weight loss in both groups	Resting metabolic rate declined less in the low GI group (–6%) than the low fat group (–11%). Risk factors for heart disease improved more on the low GI diet	Pereira et al, in press
USA	Overweight adolescents	16 subjects followed a low fat diet or a low glycemic load diet for 12 months	Those who followed the low GL diet lost more body fat and kept it off. The low fat group gained body fat during the second 6 months	Ebbeling et al, *Archives of Pediatric and Adolescent Medicine*, 2003
UK	Overweight men	17 men consumed 1 of 4 diets for 24 days	Despite efforts to maintain identical energy intake, men on the low GI diet lost weight compared with those on the high GI, high fat and high sugar diets	Byrnes et al, *British Journal of Nutrition*, 2003

France |

Country	Subjects	Study design	Findings	Reference details
	Overweight men	11 subjects followed high or low GI diets for 5 weeks each without aiming to lose weight	During the low GI period, the men lost 500 g of body fat from around the waist	Bouche et al, *Diabetes Care*, 2003
USA	Overweight children	109 children consumed either a low GI or a conventional low fat diet for 4 months	17% of the children in the low GI group achieved a 3-unit decrease in body mass index, compared with only 2% in the low fat group	Spieth et al, *Archives of Pediatric and Adolescent Medicine*, 2000
Germany	Adults with type 1 diabetes	Cross-sectional study with 1500 adults in 31 clinics across Europe	The GI of the diet correlated positively with waist circumference in men	Buyken et al, *International Journal of Obesity*, 2001
USA	Pregnant women	12 women ate a high or low GI diet during pregnancy	Those on the low GI diet gained 12 kg compared with 20 kg in women on the high GI diet	Clapp J, *Archives of Gynaecology and Obstetrics*, 1997
South Africa	Overweight women	30 women consumed a high or low GI diets for two 12-week periods	Those on the low GI diet lost 2 kg more in the first 12 weeks and then 3 kg more in the second 12 weeks	Slabber et al, *American Journal of Clinical Nutrition*, 1994

N.B. Animal studies, both long and short term, also indicate that conventional low fat diets increase body fat over time (for review, see Brand-Miller et al, *American Journal of Clinical Nutrition*, 2002).

Acknowledgments

The extract on page iv is from *Diary of a Fat Man*, by Paul Jeffreys 2003, Penguin, Auckland.

The diagram on page 7 is redrawn from *Pocket Picture Guide to Obesity* by Caterson ID and Broom J, 1997, Excerpta Medica, London.

The diagram on page 25 is redrawn from Holt SHA, Brand-Miller JC and Petocz P (1997), 'An insulin index of foods: Insulin demand generated by 1000 kJ portions of common foods', *American Journal of Clinical Nutrition*, 66; 1264–76.

The diagram on page 34 is redrawn from Ludwig DS, Majzoub JA, Al-Zahrani A, Dallal GE, Blanco I and Roberts SB (1999), 'High glycemic index foods, overeating, and obesity', *Pediatrics*, 103 (3).

The diagram on page 37 (top) is redrawn from Ebbeling CB, Leidig MM, Sinclair KB, Hangen JP and Ebbeling DS (2003), *Archives of Pediatric and Adolescent Medicine*, 157: 725–727.

The extract on page 68 is from 'The deadliest sin' by Jonathan Shaw © 2004 *Harvard Magazine* Inc. All rights reserved. Reprinted with permission; from the March–April 2004 issue.

The information on stages of change on pages 101–3 is copyright © 1992 by the American Psychological Association. Reprinted with permission.

The exercise selector on pages 249–54 is adapted from the 3rd edition of *The Fitness Leader's Handbook* by Garry Egger and Nigel Champion, 1988, Kangaroo Press, Sydney.

A book like this doesn't happen without a great deal of help. We would particularly like to acknowledge and thank Fiona Atkinson and the dedicated GI testing team—Anna, Marian and Kai Lyn and all our cheerful, well-fed volunteers. We would also like to thank Associate Professor Gareth Dwyer for his invaluable help with the database. Everyone at Hachette Livre Australia deserves a medal for professionalism, but we want to single out our editor Siobhan Gooley, who gave it everything she had, and Lisa Highton, ever active and committed on our behalf, making the vital strategic decisions that have made the *New Glucose Revolution* series the success it is. We would be nowhere without our literary agent, Philippa Sandall, who shepherded us from start to finish and literally pulled us across the finishing line. Matthew Lore, our New York editor, inspired us and made sure we didn't forget the stress eaters and night-time diners. We picked the brain of Professor Ian Caterson to distill the most up-to-date knowledge on the causes and treatment of obesity. Likewise, Professor Garry Egger (Professor Trim!) gave us his expertise on the role of exercise in weight loss management. We thank Associate Professor David Ludwig at Boston Children's Hospital for his wise counsel and research on the GI and obesity. Thank you also to Linda Cumines, Sangita Nayak and Johanna Burani for providing additional recipes. We are grateful to all the subjects who took part in our recent weight loss trials—their efforts have strengthened our story and provided objective evidence of the benefits of following a low GI diet. We would also like to thank Isa Hopwood who 'road-tested' the Action Plan. Finally, a big thank you to all our readers, colleagues, acquaintances and clients for their inspiring feedback on how the GI has worked wonders for them. And of course we wouldn't have made it through so many late nights and working weekends without the loving support of our husbands, John Miller, Jonathan Powell and Michael Price: a big hug and thank you.

About the authors

Professor Jennie Brand-Miller is Professor of Human Nutrition in the Human Nutrition Unit at the University of Sydney. She is the current president of the Nutrition Society of Australia and the director of the University of Sydney's commercial GI testing service (www. glycemicindex.com). Together with Diabetes Australia and the Juvenile Diabetes Research Foundation, she manages a GI food labelling program in Australia (www.gisymbol.com.au), which ensures that claims about the GI are scientifically correct and applied only to nutritious foods. She was recently honoured with a Clunies Ross National Science and Technology Award 'for those who have persevered against the odds to the point where they have made a difference'.

Kaye Foster-Powell is a graduate of the University of Sydney and holds a BSc (Hons) in Biochemistry and a Master of Nutrition and Dietetics. She is the senior dietitian at the Wentworth Area Diabetes Service, where she conducts education and weight loss programs, and counsels hundreds of people each year on how to improve their health and wellbeing and reduce their risk of diabetic complications through a low GI diet. Her most recent nutritional interest has been the development of children's eating habits and food preferences.

Joanna McMillan-Price holds a BSc (Hons) in Nutrition and Dietetics and is currently writing her PhD in the area of weight loss and the glycemic load. She is also a certified fitness leader and continues to teach group exercise classes in a Sydney health club. Originally from Scotland, Joanna emigrated to Australia in 1999, where she met Jennie Brand-Miller, later joining her GI research group. She has also written *Reality Food: Healthy Eating in the Real World*.

Index

Recipe index

A Hodder Book

Published in Australia and New Zealand in 2004
by Hodder Australia
(An imprint of Hachette Livre Australia Pty Ltd)
Level 17, 207 Kent St, Sydney NSW 2000
Website: www.hachette.com.au

Reprinted in 2004 (twice)
This revised and updated edition published in 2006

National Library of Australia
Cataloguing-in-Publication data

Brand-Miller, Jennie, 1952– .
The low GI diet: 12-week action plan.

ISBN 0 7336 2053 1.

1. Reducing diets. 2. Glycemic index. 3. Diet therapy.
4. Food — Carbohydrate content. 5. Dietetics.
I. Foster-Powell, Kaye. II. McMillan-Price, Joanna.
III. Title.

641.5638

Author photos by Joy Lai
Cover photography by Ian Hofstetter
Cover and text design by Ellie Exarchos
Typesetting by Egan-Reid Ltd, Auckland
Printed in Australia by Griffin Press, Adelaide